Creating the Nonsexist Classroom

A MULTICULTURAL APPROACH

Creating the Nonsexist Classroom

A Multicultural Approach

Theresa Mickey McCormick

Foreword by Nel Noddings

Teachers College, Columbia University
New York and London

All photographs in the chapter openers are provided by the author.

Permission has been granted by Sheryl Barta to use the mathematics, science, and social studies curiculum ideas that appear in Chapter Four.

Permission to use the logo that appears as Figure 5.3 in Chapter Five has been granted by Esteem International, Inc.

Published by Teachers College Press, 1234 Amsterdam Avenue
New York, NY 10027

Library of Congress Cataloging-in-Publication Data

McCormick, Theresa Mickey.
    Creating the nonsexist classroom : a multicultural approach / Theresa Mickey McCormick ; foreword by Nel Noddings.
       p. cm.
    Includes bibliographical references and index.
    ISBN 0-8077-3348-2.—ISBN 0-8077-3347-4 (pbk.)
    1. Sexism in education—United States. 2. Sex discrimination in education—United States. 3. Multicultural education—United States. 4. Educational equalization—United States. I. Title.
LC212.82.M33   1994
370.19'345—dc20   94-9674

ISBN 0-8077-3348-2
ISBN 0-8077-3347-4 (pbk.)

Printed on acid-free paper
Manufactured in the United States of America
98 97 96 95 94 8 7 6 5 4 3 2 1

Dedicated lovingly to
my children,
Michelle McCormick-Mohr and Bailie Grant McCormick

Contents

Foreword

Theresa McCormick has written a book that should be used widely in teacher education. Readers who have little knowledge of sexism and its history will be sensitized to the issues, and even those who are convinced that sexism presents problems on the contemporary scene will find help to avoid unintentionally sexist acts. Teachers at all levels should read this book.

McCormick's work does not stop with a call for equality and strategies to reach it. Her recommendations do not entail the complete assimilation of females to the work world as it has been defined by males. Rather, in *Creating the Nonsexist Classroom*, she explores the rich possibilities of a gender-sensitive curriculum, one that celebrates women's lives, tasks, contributions, and values. Just as various racial and ethnic groups want to share in our society's opportunities without losing their identities, so women now aspire to be full participants without losing their identity as women. Further, women's traditions should influence the curriculum for all students. Boys should learn many of the things that have routinely been taught to girls, just as girls should have far greater exposure to mathematics and science.

Ambiguities and uncertainties are treated honestly and reflectively in this text. For example, readers may be astonished to learn that the government's attempt (through Title IX) to equalize expenditures for men's and women's athletics actually contributed to the loss of many positions for female coaches. When more teams became co-ed, a coach of either sex was acceptable, and, because men generally had more years of experience, they were more often chosen for these new positions. Thus what women gained in one area, they lost in another. (Expenditures, by the way, are still not equal, although the disparity has been considerably reduced.)

In offering strategies for nonsexist education, McCormick makes a host of connections to other promising educational movements. She includes fine discussions of learning styles, cooperative learning, and the uses of intuition. Many of the methods she discusses have been identified as especially attractive to females, but McCormick makes a convincing plea for their incorporation in the standard curriculum.

Instructors will find lots of practical help here. The text includes "research exercises" and "reflective exercises" that engage students in empirical investigation and analytical thinking. These exercises also furnish a host of ready-made assignments that offer students some choice.

Finally, although the text concentrates on gender issues, it embeds these issues in a multicultural context. McCormick does not make the mistake of supposing that questions of gender are uncomplicated by race, ethnicity, and class. Students may well be somewhat discouraged and even resistant as they learn about the role education has played in supporting sexism, racism, and classism. But with sensitive teaching and discussion, what they learn from this text should help them to make future education more equitable.

Nel Noddings
Lee L. Jacks Professor of Child Education
Stanford University

Acknowledgments

I greatly appreciate the help and encouragement from many friends, my daughter and son, and colleagues to undertake and complete this book. Numerous helpful people come to mind, but I would particularly like to thank these colleagues from Iowa State University: Brenda O. Daly and Kathleen Stinehart for critiquing my ideas and writing; Carlie Tartakov, who lent moral support by listening and encouraging me throughout this project; Bonney Rega, who inspires me with her joy for life and creativity; and Ann Thompson, chair of my department, who provided support for finishing the project. My appreciation goes to Iowa State University for granting me a semester of faculty released time to conduct research for the book. I also wish to thank these I.S.U. students: Kim Kasperbauer and Susie Swalla, for their research assistance, and Jing Fong Hsu and Mary Herring, for their technical help. To the beautiful children smiling at you in the photographs that grace the pages of this book, I say: "You're our future. You're what this book is all about. Thanks for being here!" I give a special thanks to my editors at Teachers College Press, Carol Collins and Sarah Biondello, for their extraordinary help and patience.

During my semester of released time, I searched for primary source materials at the Northwestern University Library Special Collections Department, Evanston, Illinois, and greatly appreciate the patience and persistence of the librarians who led me to "treasures" of information in the Women's Ephemera Files (WEF).

Special thanks go to the faculty members and staff at the Southwest Institute for Research on Women (SIROW), University of Arizona, Tucson, for their hospitality and assistance while I conducted research there. I would like to thank my son, Grant McCormick, for his encouragement and hospitality while I was conducting research in Tucson and for pointing me toward Antigone Books, a shop specializing in books by and about women.

Also, while I was in Tucson, I was very fortunate to be able to interview Nancy Mairs, who had worked at SIROW years ago. Several months before my stay in Tucson, I was visiting my daughter, Michelle McCormick-Mohr, in

Vashon Island, Washington. Nancy's spirit, as manifested in *Plaintext—Deciphering a Woman's Life*, first came to me in a used bookstore that Michelle, her husband Bob, and I were browsing in. The effect of that book led me to search her out later when I was in Tucson. She was excited about the publication of her newest book of essays, *Carnal Knowledge*, when I arrived at her home. I was honored to experience face to face the wit, honesty, and eloquence that had so moved me in her writing. Nancy's life and her writing are powerful and inspiring because they express her strength and determination to enjoy the "gift" of a difficult life, beset by multiple sclerosis. After the interview, I felt strong and inspired to continue the research and complete this book. Thank you, Nancy.

Introduction

WHAT IS MEANT BY NONSEXIST EDUCATION?

Nonsexist approaches to educational programs attempt to ensure fairness and equity to all students regardless of gender and to foster knowledge, respect, and appreciation for the contemporary and historical contributions of *both* sexes to society. Nonsexist programs provide equal educational opportunity (e.g., equal access to and participation in courses and programs) to both female and male students and reflect the wide variety of roles open to both women and men through the instructional materials presented to students. The study of nonsexist education encompasses a wide variety of sociocultural conditions and equity issues that are relevant to educators and young people in schools. The issues and concepts of nonsexist education apply to all levels of education (from preschool to graduate school), to all curriculum content areas, and to the education of males as well as females. Overarching goals of nonsexist education are to help all students, regardless of gender, develop their full potential for academic, social, and vocational success and to help them overcome the negative effects of sexism, racism, and classism.

WHO IS INCLUDED IN NONSEXIST EDUCATION?

My assumption is that nonsexist education is for everyone, regardless of sex, sexual orientation, race, ethnicity, social class, religion, ability/disability, or language. Since sex equity is frequently misperceived as a women's issue, it is necessary to reiterate that nonsexist education applies to males also. We live in a multicultural society of people of different backgrounds and natural differences. It is as varied and rich as an Oriental tapestry. Sex and gender issues are just one of the patterns that add to the complexity of this tapestry.

Many people feel threatened and fearful of the diversity in our society and see it as divisive. Thus they reject, exclude, or strike out against those perceived to be different. Their attitudes have been formed by a barrage of distorted messages, misconceptions, and stereotypes about those who are different from themselves. Thus a powerful antidote is needed to counteract the sexist, racist, and homophobic messages that society gives youth today. Although some strides have been made in raising awareness about sexism and racism during the last 20 years, the eradication of these and other forms of oppression is far from accomplished in society and schools.

PURPOSE OF THE BOOK

Few comprehensive texts have been published in recent years that specifically assist preservice and in-service teachers in developing nonsexist education approaches for application across the curriculum. Usually, when sex and gender issues are incorporated in texts, they are included under the umbrella of multicultural education or human relations studies and, in my view, receive inadequate attention. Most multicultural education texts focus mainly on race, ethnic group, social class, and language differences. In this book, the primary focus is on sex/gender issues in education, which are placed firmly within a multicultural context—that is, examples, illustrations, photographs, stories, reading selections, contributions and authors cited, and perspectives on problems and issues are multicultural.

I wrote this book to fill a need that I have identified through my years of teaching in public schools and then teaching undergraduate and graduate courses on multicultural nonsexist education. These teaching experiences as well as experience directing programs (from preschool to graduate school) and conducting research have clearly demonstrated the need for more specific and discrete attention to sex and gender issues both in the day-to-day implementation of the school curriculum and in teacher-preparation courses. I have seen blatant sex-role stereotyping and polarizing of boys and girls in schools, along with differential treatment and expectations of them. I have worked with teachers (mostly women) who loved children but felt largely powerless to make significant change in the schools. The need for more attention to sex and gender issues in schools is particularly glaring since the teaching force is still predominantly female and the administration, predominantly male. It is critical that teachers recognize the sexist structure of the field of teacher education and public school education so that they can be agents of change rather than tools for reproducing the same system generation after generation. I wrote this book with the hope that its ideas could lay the foundation for cultural and curricular transformations that point the way to a more equitable society in the twenty-first century.

Creating the Nonsexist Classroom: A Multicultural Approach is intended for teacher educators to use in their undergraduate and graduate classes. It is designed to help their students, present and future teachers, to acquire the concepts, content, strategies, and resources to teach in a nonsexist, culturally inclusive manner and to learn how to infuse such concepts and content into the total school curriculum. It offers both theoretical and practical guidelines for developing and implementing such a curriculum. Put another way, the book has a dual purpose: To inform (by providing historical, theoretical, and research bases for nonsexist education) and to provide practical applications for the classroom. In my undergraduate and graduate courses, I find that student learning is enhanced if I first create a theoretical and historical framework to support our inquiry. Taking the time to contextualize the subject matter pays off in enhanced student understanding, more participation, and greater readiness to apply the concepts of nonsexist, culturally inclusive education. This book is organized with the same model in mind: It begins with a history of the women's movement in order to provide a social and historical context for understanding sex and gender issues today; continues with the development of a theoretical, research-based framework for understanding sexism; and concludes with curriculum and instruction applications for the teacher. Other professionals in the social services will find the book useful in understanding the complexity of sex and gender issues and their interrelation with race, ethnicity, social class, and age.

It must be noted that there is an ongoing debate among feminist theorists, critical theorists, and nonsexist educators about the premise of integration of gender with the other concepts (see, for instance, Katrina Irving's [1989] excellent analysis of the different camps of feminist thought). I integrate gender with the other concepts because of the complex interrelation it has with other defining attributes, such as race, social class, and age (described as the "multiple statuses" of women by Diane Pollard [1992, p. 1]), and because of the overriding issues of power and oppression that link women together. I believe this approach helps overcome a problem—assuming that all women are white—that too much of previous work and some current work is guilty of (see Butler [1993] for a rationale supporting this position on gender and the related "isms").

A major theme of *Creating the Nonsexist Classroom: A Multicultural Approach* is that contemporary education functions to maintain a system that supports and perpetuates sexism (as well as racism). The main concern of the book is how to educate preservice and in-service teachers to be aware of, sensitive to, and informed about sex and gender issues and how to help them transmit this new gender consciousness to their students (preschool through twelfth grade). The book elaborates on ways that the culture in most schools helps reproduce sexism and racism, and it provides educators with strategies for creating a more equitable school culture and practice. It reflects the philosophy that educational excellence cannot be attained in the absence of educational equity for all.

Creating the Nonsexist Classroom: A Multicultural Approach is based on the premise that nonsexist education is a *process* that involves a body of knowledge and sets of attitudes and skills that enable students to reach their potential and to function effectively with others who are different from themselves. Nonsexist education concepts and strategies are infused throughout the curriculum and in all aspects of school life.

ORGANIZATION OF THE BOOK

Chapter 1 provides a historical and theoretical framework for the book. It focuses on the women's movement of the 1960s and 1970s, but traces the origin of that movement to previous movements for women's equality. Implications of these movements for women of the 1990s are discussed. Feminist research is explored as a potential tool for transforming schools according to a nonsexist, culturally inclusive model.

Chapter 2 provides an overview of the historical and current problems of sexism and sex discrimination in society and in schools. It examines theories and research on socialization and gender identity; sex-role development, sex-typing, and stereotyping. The effects of sexism and sex-role stereotypes on the self-concept and achievement of male and female students are woven throughout the chapter. Implications for educators and school programs and a rationale for nonsexist education round out the chapter.

Chapters 3 and 4 integrate the conceptual framework established in the first two chapters with practical applications of concepts, content, strategies, and resources for teachers to use in nonsexist, culturally inclusive classrooms. Specifically, Chapter 3 discusses the nonsexist delivery of instruction, while Chapter 4 emphasizes how to transmit components of nonsexist education to students through the formal curriculum. It reviews three curriculum models (the male-as-norm model, the equal educational opportunity model, and the emerging nonsexist, culturally inclusive model).

The first part of Chapter 5 deals with factors *inside* the school (such as program evaluation) that affect equity in the school environment and explores how support services (e.g., counseling), staff and administrative practices and policies, and staff development are involved. The second part of Chapter 5 discusses influences *outside* the school (such as media) that have an impact on equity. The last section discusses some linkages with other movements (such as environmental education and peace education) that overlap with feminism and the move toward a nonsexist, culturally inclusive education system. It concludes with a discussion of some alternative paradigms of human relations and power and some considerations of the future.

Pedagogical Features

Since the book is designed for use with undergraduate prospective teachers, with graduate students in education, with practitioners, and with other social service professionals, several features have been included to enhance the book's use as an instructional tool.

An overview and a summary. Each chapter gives the student a brief overview of the chapter and then a summary. Reading these sections first, in all five chapters, will help the student get "the big picture" before reading the entire book. In fact, after getting "the big picture," students may want to choose the order in which the chapters are read. Similarly, depending upon the course being taught, instructors may find it useful to vary the order in which different chapters are assigned.

Review questions. These questions at the end of each chapter should help the student study, review, remember, and, in some cases, apply the material covered in the chapter. The instructor may find some review questions useful for stimulating class discussion or generating ideas for further classroom application.

Research activities and reflective exercises. These are interspersed within Chapters 2 through 5 to help make the material more concrete and personally meaningful to preservice and in-service teachers. Hopefully they will be a catalyst for the development of more research activities and reflective exercises by the instructor and the students using this book.

Classroom activities. Chapter 3 includes a number of classroom activities designed to develop cultural and gender literacy and awareness that are appropriate for in-service teachers to use with students in upper elementary grades (grades 4–6), middle school (grades 7–9), and high school. The activities are also appropriate for teacher educators (or other college instructors) to use with college students.

Resources and readings. Appendix A is a list of resources that will help teachers locate materials, services, people, and organizations related to sex equity. In Chapter 4, additional resources such as books, magazines, and games are identified for six different subject areas, as part of the Curriculum Guidelines.

Books and articles that are not cited in the chapters (and thus not included in the References) but are related to the topics are included in

Appendix B. These readings should add depth to students' understanding of the issues and will be useful "leads" in pursuing further study and reflection on sex and gender topics.

Language usage. A note concerning the use of language in the text is in order. Masculine pronouns are not used to refer to both sexes and, in general, use of masculine *or* feminine pronouns is avoided as much as possible, as is the "his/her" construction. Alternate constructions, such as the use of a plural rather than a singular subject, usually solve the problem (e.g., The *teachers* involved *their* students in cooperative games rather than The *teacher* involved *her* students in cooperative games).

I use the phrase *women of color*, instead of *minority women*, since *women of color* suggests differences of both race and culture and clarifies that I am referring to Hispanic-American, Asian-American, and Native American as well as African-American women. My use of the phrase is in accord with Johnella Butler's statement (1993), "Selecting the phrase *women of color* by many women of U.S. ethnic groups of color is part of their struggle to be recognized with dignity for their humanity, racial heritage, and cultural heritage as they work within the women's movement of the United States" (p. 150). Also, I avoid using *American* to refer to the U.S. population because of its ethnocentric connotation.

CHAPTER 1

The Social Movement for Women's Rights and Liberation

The question of Women's Rights is a practical one. The notion has pre-vailed that it was only an ephemeral idea; that it was but women claiming the right to smoke cigars in the streets, and to frequent bar-rooms. Others have supposed it a question of comparative sphere. Too much has already been said and written about woman's sphere. Trace all the doctrines to their source and they will be found to have no basis except in the usages and prejudices of the age.

(Lucy Stone, 1855, cited in Schneir, 1972, p. 107)

Keeping up the momentum for erasing centuries-old sex biases is as important in the 1990s as it was in the 1800s. Passing the torch for women's rights and liberation from one generation to the next has always been of concern to feminists of different eras. While the "texture" of sex discrimination is different now than in the nineteenth century, it is cut out of the same cloth, woven of stereotypes, rigid sex roles, and prejudice.

In order to establish a framework for discussing current sex and gender issues in education, I begin with a historical background of the women's move-ment of the 1960s and 1970s and trace the roots of that movement to earlier movements for women's equality. Establishing a theoretical and historical foundation for our inquiry hopefully will provide a greater understanding of the social, political, and economic context of sex and gender issues today. I believe that having a firm grasp on the history of the social movement for women's rights will help today's teachers apply the concepts of nonsexist education with more meaning and conviction in their classrooms.

OVERVIEW

This chapter examines the contemporary women's movement, which started in the mid-1960s. A brief history of this social movement is presented, including its goals, activities, and legal (and other) accomplishments. But first, the chapter traces the contemporary movement to its roots in the nineteenth-century social movement for women's rights and suffrage. Then a delineation of the years from enfranchisement (1920) to the mid-1960s shows how the women's movement, even though it was "put on hold" for 40 years, managed to survive even in a hostile social and political environment. Key leaders of these eras are highlighted. The current status and agendas of feminism and the women's movement are summarized. Finally, the implications of feminist scholarship and research for education are discussed and review questions are provided for use in teacher education classes.

NINETEENTH-CENTURY FEMINISM AND SUFFRAGE

Early efforts for women's emancipation, dating back to the 1830s, were shrouded in the activities of women involved in the antislavery movement. It was in London at the World Anti-Slavery Convention in 1840 that the U.S.A. suffragists, Elizabeth Cady Stanton and Lucretia Mott, met for the first time. They and the other female delegates were excluded from the convention. This discrimination prompted Stanton and Mott to make a mutual promise—which each kept—to work on improving conditions for women, and it also prompted William Lloyd Garrison, the most noted abolitionist from the United States, to refuse to participate in the convention. He, along with Frederick Douglass and a handful of other male abolitionists, was supportive of the feminist cause. Thus, as Schneir (1972) notes, "the anti-slavery movement provided a base of male support for the fledgling woman's rights movement as well as a training ground for the female leadership" (p. 86).

From 1847 to 1857, Lucy Stone spoke on behalf of the Anti-Slavery Societies in different parts of the country. Although speaking under the auspices of these societies, she admitted that, "I was so possessed by the woman's rights idea that I scattered it in every speech" (quoted in Schneir, 1972, p. 103).

The most pivotal event in the nineteenth-century women's movement in the United States was a meeting in Seneca Falls, New York, on July 19, 1848, that resulted in the adoption of the Seneca Falls Declaration of Sentiments and Resolutions. Organized by Elizabeth Cady Stanton, this women's rights meeting featured Lucretia Mott, a speaker who was a Quaker "minister" and well known for her antislavery speeches. Mott's husband, James, chaired the meeting, which was attended by about 300 people. The declaration, modeled on the Declaration of Independence, included twelve resolutions. Eleven were adopted unanimously, but the twelfth, which pertained to giving women the right to vote, barely passed "only after Frederick Douglass stoutly defended it from the floor" (Schneir, 1972, pp. 76–77).

By the 1890s, three of the major demands of the Seneca Falls Declaration (access to education, participation in the professions, and property rights) were fairly well established. However, two other important goals had not been secured: the right to vote "and the end to the double standard of morality, whereby male sexual indiscretions were tolerated and female indiscretions were prohibited" (Banner, 1974, p. 41). In the following years, both became major goals of the women's movement that proved difficult to achieve.

To grasp the historic significance of the woman suffrage movement, one must realize the high expectations that suffragists attached to getting the vote. They expected it to have the power to change their lives and men's attitudes toward women. They realized that voting was directly linked to social power and believed that it would be a sure way to achieve equality with men (DuBois, 1978).

After the Civil War, in 1866, Elizabeth Cady Stanton and other leaders of the women's movement, who had argued long and hard for equal rights for all, were disappointed that the Fourteenth Amendment, which gave black men the right to vote, did not do the same for women. In 1867, the African American feminist, Sojourner Truth, said,

> There is a great stir about colored men getting their rights, but not a word about the colored women; and if colored men get their rights, and not colored women theirs, you see the colored men will be masters over the women, and it will be just as bad as it was before. So I am for keeping the thing going while things are stirring. . . . I want women to have their rights. In the courts women have no right, no voice; nobody speaks for them. (quoted in Schneir, 1972, pp. 129–130)

"Keeping the Thing Going While Things are Stirring"

Resistance to granting women equal rights stemmed from many sources (see "Historical Roots of Sexism" in Chapter 2), but this resistance did not keep women from "keeping the thing going" for equality. Antisuffragists appealed for the upholding of traditional values by tapping into many common fears:

> If women voted, they would hold office; if women held office they would leave the home, break up the family, and take power away from men. . . . Suffrage, according to the more hysterical antisuffragists, was a revolt against "nature." Pregnant women might lose their babies, nursing mothers their milk, and women in general might grow beards or else be raped at the polls. (Banner, 1974, pp. 89–90)

Banner notes that one reason for the latter fear was that polls were typically set up in saloons and barber shops; however, after 1920, when women gained the right to vote, they were set up in churches, schools, or firehouses.

Resistance to women's equality was primarily grounded in tired old notions that "woman's place is in the home," that to be true to her "nature," a woman's activities must be confined to the private sphere while a man's true "nature" fitted him for the public sphere. Historian Sara Evans (1990), in tracing women's history back to the American Revolution, indicates that engaging in public life was equated with happiness in those times—but women could not participate. Thus their position relative to the state (i.e., their citizenship) was problematic. During the 1800s, there was a great fear among men of women in public life. "All men are created equal" was meant literally. Women, children, and slaves were lumped together. The only way for women to be good citizens was to be good republican mothers, that is, raise good citizens (i.e., sons).

Evans convincingly argues that out of the sanctioned private activity of motherhood, nineteenth-century women created a quasi-public sphere of activity in the civil and public arena through their efforts for social reform, peace, temperance, and the abolition of slavery. While women could neither vote nor speak in public, they could petition, march, and pray. From these activities, many other organizations and social services (such as settlement houses) evolved that served the public good. In these quasi-public activities, women developed leadership skills and a sense of their strength and their need for equal rights, according to Evans (1990). These activities also nurtured a budding sense of sisterhood and an awareness of the value of solidarity for achieving common goals.

During the late nineteenth century and up to 1920, when the Nineteenth Amendment was ratified, feminists took many different approaches to women's equality. Suffrage was only one among many causes that organized women supported during those years. Banner (1974) indicates that this period saw a proliferation of women's organizations and publication of new feminist studies, as well as an awareness of a wide gamut of problems that women faced in the United States and the use of varied ways of confronting them. She writes:

> Not until the 1960s was feminism again so vigorous. Most organized women were social feminists. But there were radical women, too. Some were involved with political causes; some concentrated their efforts on women's causes. By 1914 all the segments of the women's movement had come together around a commitment to suffrage as their main goal. (p. 87)

Before 1914, women's efforts for equality took varied and interesting routes, as the following biographies illustrate.

After the Civil War, African-American women took many steps to gain civil rights both for themselves as women and for their people as a whole.

For example, Ida B. Wells-Barnett, Frances Watkins Harper, Josephine St. Pierre Ruffin, Mary Church Terrel, Mary Talbert, and Jessie Daniel Ames formed the vanguard of resistance to the Ku Klux Klan (Gozemba & Humphries, 1989). Ida B. Wells-Barnett, a suffragist, organized and led women in the fight against lynching. Born to slave parents, she became a teacher, then a lecturer and journalist. In 1895, she published *A Red Record*, the story of three years of lynchings in the South. Also, she established what was thought to be the first Negro woman suffrage organization, the Alpha Suffrage Club of Chicago. Although she is considered to have played an important role in founding the National Association for the Advancement of Colored People (NAACP) in 1910, she withdrew from the group after its formation because she felt that it was not "sufficiently outspoken" (Bigby, 1990, p. 24). Josephine St. Pierre Ruffin organized the first National Conference of Colored Women in 1895 and established a monthly black women's magazine, *Women's Era* (Jenkins, 1988).

Across the country, in the Pacific Northwest, a very different type of feminism with a different focus was being espoused by the "rebel for rights," Abigail Scott Duniway, who lived in Oregon. According to Ann Gordon (1988–89), Duniway "had nothing to do with the northeastern reformers' culture that turned out the pioneers of woman's rights. . . . However, Yankees had provided her with a vision about changing women's lives" (p. 231). Duniway's frontier style earned her a reputation as a difficult person who tried the patience of such national leaders as Susan B. Anthony and Carrie Chapman Catt. Her strength and the focus of her efforts lay in the political arena, where her skills at bargaining, making deals, and developing a constituency flourished. Her many activities included the establishment of a State Equal Suffrage Association, which she represented at a suffrage meeting in San Francisco. In 1871, she began to publish her own newspaper, the *New Northwest*. Although Duniway was the chief breadwinner for her family, she could not buy property, according to the law, without the signature of her husband, who refused to comply (Gordon, 1988–89).

Carrie Chapman Catt, with roots in the Midwest, was an educator and newspaperwoman and a late nineteenth- and early twentieth-century activist in the woman suffrage movement. She graduated from Iowa State University in 1878, at a time when few females acquired a higher education. Her strength as an activist lay in her skills as a political organizer, skills she used as president of the National Woman Suffrage Association (NWSA) from 1900 to 1904 and again from 1915 to 1920. This organization later became the League of Women Voters. Between her two terms as president of NWSA, Catt set up an International Woman Suffrage Alliance (Schneir, 1972). She also established the National Conference on the Cause and Cure for War (Banner, 1974).

Honored by her home state in 1992, Catt was the recipient of the Iowa Award, which recognizes Iowans who make a significant nationwide contribution, and then Iowa State University, her alma mater, honored her by establishing the Carrie Chapman Catt Center for Women in Politics. During the last few years of long-overdue recognition of Catt in Iowa, there has also occurred a reexamination of her life and work relative to people of color. This tough-minded, well-educated woman, who led the U.S. woman's suffrage movement to victory in 1920, had a number of "blind" spots. For example, she believed that having the vote would lead to equality with men (it has been more than 70 years since women have had the vote, and we still do not have an Equal Rights Amendment to the Constitution). Secondly, she and other suffragists were enmeshed in the rampant racism and fear of immigrants that ran rife in the late 1800s and early 1900s.

Louise Noun (1969, 1993), historian of the Iowa woman's suffrage movement, has written extensively about Carrie Chapman Catt. Upon hearing the charge recently that Catt was a bigot, Noun decided to take another look at her life. Her research revealed that Catt and other suffragists compromised their principles (e.g., all men and women are created equal) as the possibility of winning the vote increased. This compromise was made as a matter of political expediency to win allies and eliminate perceived opponents to their cause. Noun (1993) asserts that in Catt's first public lectures in 1887, she voiced "a xenophobic fear of the influence of undesirable immigrants" (p. 1-C). During this time in the United States, powerful nativistic influences engendered fear of anyone who was not a "native" (defined as a middle-class, white Anglo-Saxon Protestant). Catt's fear of immigrants ran deep in her warning in 1894 about the "danger that lies in the votes of uneducated foreign males in the slums of our cities . . . she went so far as to advocate depriving all slum residents of the vote" (p. 1-C).

According to Noun (1993), Catt's record is not so blatantly racist concerning African-Americans. She was friends with many African-Americans and, specifically, she was warmly regarded by Mary Church Terrell, president of the National Association of Colored Women, who described Catt as "completely free from racial prejudice" (p. 1-C). However, Noun (1993) maintains that "there is no question that Chapman Catt, along with the suffrage movement as a whole, was willing to ignore efforts to disfranchise [*sic*] African-Americans in the South in order to win white Southern support for women's suffrage" (p. 1-C).

WOMEN'S EMANCIPATION AS A SOCIAL MOVEMENT

The suffrage movement was not an isolated institutional reform, as it has too frequently been described by historians. "Its character as a social movement, reflecting women's aspiration for progress toward radical change in their lives, has been overlooked," according to DuBois (1978, p. 17). Just because the vote did not solve the problems of sex inequality, the suffrage movement should not be discounted nor its value to contemporary women underestimated.

DuBois (1978) argues that when the woman suffrage movement is viewed as a social movement, its relevance to women today is enormous. As such, DuBois says:

> It was the first independent movement of women for their *own* liberation. Its growth—the mobilization of women around the demand for the vote, their collective activity, their commitment to gaining increased power over their own lives—was itself a major change in the condition of those lives. . . .
>
> The word "movement" should . . . be taken seriously as a description of the emergence of suffragism and similar historical processes. It suggests an accelerating transformation of consciousness among a group of oppressed people and a growing sense of collective power. (p. 18; emphasis added)

That woman suffrage became an independent feminist movement is significant today for it demonstrates that women cannot depend on other reform movements (e.g., abolition or labor movements) to make changes that benefit women. Secondly, it shows that women have to look "to *women themselves* not only to articulate the problem, but to provide the solution to women's oppression . . ." (DuBois, 1978, pp. 201–202; emphasis added). DuBois concludes that it was women's actual involvement in the movement, far more than winning the vote, that laid the foundation for new social relations between males and females; thus "activity in the woman suffrage movement itself did precisely what Stanton and others had expected possession of the francise [*sic*] to do—it demonstrated that self-government and democratic participation in the life of the society was the key to women's emancipation. Therein lay its feminist power and historical significance" (pp. 201–202).

While most challenges to established authority eventually wither and die, scholars such as DuBois show that nineteenth-century feminism and the woman suffrage movement converged into a single social movement that persisted into the twentieth century and affected U.S. history as much as abolition. This social movement for women's rights and liberation continued after enfranchisement, albeit in abeyance until the contemporary women's movement began in the mid–1960s. Although it is today in another lull, the women's movement is still viable in the 1990s.

Enfranchisement in the 1960s

Traditional historians have held that the U.S. women's movement died after enfranchisement in 1920 and then suddenly came alive again in the 1960s.

These writers fail to see suffrage and feminism as parts of a larger independent social movement for women's liberation. DuBois (1978), Carden (1974),
Marilley (1989), Banner (1974), and Taylor (1989) are among the researchers who have examined continuities among the various efforts for women's
rights and liberation over different time periods and who look at these efforts
within the framework of an independent social movement.

Postsuffrage to World War II—1920–1945. The years from 1920 to
1945 were a time of transition and transformation for feminism and the
women's movement in the United States. What happened to the women (and
their networks and organizations) who spearheaded the woman suffrage
movement after the vote was won? These were times of factionalism, with the
women's movement splitting into different groups having different concerns
(e.g., women's employment, pacifism). Some of the old organizations were
maintained, but several new ones emerged. The mainstream organization of
the movement, the National American Woman Suffrage Association, dis-
banded and formed the League of Women Voters. It was opposed to the more
militant group, the National Woman's Party (NWP), that had been started by
Alice Paul in 1916.

Under Paul's leadership, the NWP launched an intense campaign to pass
an Equal Rights Amendment (ERA) to the Constitution. She had hoped to gain
the support of former suffragists, but her abrasive leadership style and the
decision to exclusively emphasize the ERA alienated them. Most "suffragists
feared that the ERA would eliminate the protective labor legislation that women
reformers had earlier struggled to achieve" (Balser, 1987, cited in Taylor, 1989,
p. 763).

The ERA was first introduced into the U.S. Congress in 1923. Gradually,
it gained support from other women's organizations, such as the National Federation of Business and Professional Women's Clubs, which endorsed it in
the late 1920s, and the General Federation of Women's Clubs, which endorsed
it in 1943. The Republican party included the ERA in its platform in 1940, and
the Democratic party followed suit in 1944 (Banner, 1974). Every year since
1923, the Equal Rights Amendment has been introduced in Congress, but it
was not until 1953 that a woman Representative, Katharine St. George, did
so (Rawalt, 1983).

The 1920s through 1945 were years when the solidarity of the women's
movement was dissipated. Since enfranchisement had been won, there was
no single unifying goal to hold the mass base of the movement together. Taylor
(1989) says: "Ironically, the role expansion for which the movement had
fought fractured the bonds on which the solidarity of the movement had been
built. As women's lives grew increasingly diverse, the definition of what would

benefit women grew less clear" (p. 764). In spite of the lack of a clear-cut goal and conflicts among leaders and among women's organizations, "feminist activism continued throughout the 1920s and 1930s," according to Taylor (1989, p. 763). Women were active in many groups to promote peace, social-welfare programs, and legislation for women and children, as well as to improve education, health care, and employment for women. If any common purpose unified women in these endeavors, it could best be characterized as social feminism, with Eleanor Roosevelt being its exemplar (Banner, 1974).

The women's movement on hold—1945 to the mid-1960s. Women's rights activists encountered a chilly political and social environment from 1945 to the 1960s. They had limited outlets for their activism and increasingly found themselves isolated from the majority of women relative to issues of equality. Advocates for women's rights had neither access to nor support from the existing political system (Taylor, 1989). Also, there was a resurgence of "the feminine mystique" following World War II. Emphasis was placed on domesticity and femininity as proper attributes for women, but a divergent trend was women's increasing participation in the world of work outside the home and in higher education (Banner, 1974; Taylor, 1989).

Banner (1974) indicates that there was also a virulent barrage of antifeminist rhetoric that blamed women for all of society's ills because they went to work during and after the war. She says that this antifeminist attack was greater than any that had occurred during the 1920s and 1930s and rivaled that of the antisuffrage rhetoric in the early 1900s. This bitter antifeminism, which "echoed throughout the 1950s," was based on Freudian ideas that influenced scores of sociologists, educators, law officers, welfare workers, and others to blame working mothers for the problems of youth.

Another factor that put the women's movement in abeyance during the postwar years was that it had further splintered into three overlapping interest groups with different agendas (Harrison, 1988). One was a group of women's organizations linked with the Women's Bureau of the Department of Labor whose goals were to improve working conditions for women and to defeat the ERA. The second group was a network of women active in Democratic and Republican party politics who worked for election and appointment of women to policy-making positions, usually without consideration of their stance on women's issues. The NWP, the third group, was furthest from "the established political order" in that it doggedly continued the campaign for the ERA. Taylor (1989) says:

> None of these three groups made much progress in attaining their goals in the 1940s and 1950s. Although women's organizations succeeded in having 236 bills

pertaining to women's rights introduced into Congress in the 1950s, only 14 passed. . . . This reflected not only organized women's lack of political access and their conflicts, but also the exaggerated emphasis on sex roles that emerged on the heels of the Second World War. (p. 764)

In the 1950s, women who did not conform to "the feminine mystique," which was promulgated as the cultural ideal by the new medium of television and by other popular media, were denounced. As a result of the attacks on feminism mentioned earlier, only the National Woman's Party maintained its connection with the idea of feminism. Over half of the core leaders of the NWP had been active 40 years earlier in the suffrage movement. This involvement "had a powerful and enduring effect . . . so much so that they continued even into the 1950s to promote women's rights in a society antagonistic to the idea" (Taylor, 1989, p. 766). These women, who were usually well educated, white, and of the middle or upper class,

> . . . paid for their lifelong commitment with a degree of alienation, marginality, and isolation. Nevertheless, the NWP provided a structure and status capable of absorbing these intensely committed feminists and thus functioned as an abeyance organization. (p. 765)

Taylor's research focuses on the U.S. Women's Movement from 1945 to the mid-1960s, and she uses the case of the National Woman's Party to highlight the processes by which social movements maintain continuity during dormant periods between cycles of peak activity.

Commenting on the social movements of the 1960s, Taylor (1989) says that most scholars have viewed their origins as "immaculate conceptions." From their perspective, those "'new social movements' . . . seemingly emerged out of nowhere and represented a sudden shift from the quiescent 1940s and 1950s" (p. 761). Taylor argues that recent empirical work contests this and suggests that the "break between the sixties movements and earlier waves of political activism was not as sharp as previously assumed" (p. 761). For various reasons students of the social movements of the 1960s have been blinded to the "carry-overs and carry-ons" between movements. Taylor believes that "what scholars have taken for 'births' were in fact breakthroughs or turning points in movement mobilization" (p. 761). She says that most writers trace the origins of the contemporary women's movement to the civil rights movement; but she argues that it "can also be viewed as a resurgent challenge with roots in an earlier cycle of feminist activism that presumably ended when suffrage was won" (p. 761).

RESURGENCE OF FEMINISM:
THE CONTEMPORARY WOMEN'S MOVEMENT

Feminist activity reemerged in the mid-1960s with renewed vigor and solidarity. The contemporary women's movement (variously called the new feminist movement or the women's liberation movement) once again challenged U.S. society to grant women full equality. Once again, we see the cyclical nature of the social movement for women's rights and liberation.

Harbingers of Change

Several significant pieces of literature paved the way for the resurgence of the women's movement in the mid-1960s. Simone de Beauvoir's *The Second Sex*, first published in France, appeared in the United States in 1953. Being the first modern feminist book, it was described as the classic manifesto of the liberated woman. In retrospect, U.S. feminists found it to be instructive as they struggled to redefine and solve the problems of sex inequality.

The first and most influential modern feminist book by a U.S. writer was *The Feminine Mystique* by Betty Friedan (1963). Militant in tone, the book attacked the Freudian ideas that had been so harmful to women's development. For example, Freud's concept of penis envy, which was used to describe a phenomenon he noticed in middle-class Victorian women patients in Vienna,

> . . . was seized in this country in the 1940's as the literal explanation of all that was wrong with American women. Many who preached the doctrine of endangered femininity, reversing the movement of American women toward independence and identity, never knew its Freudian origin. (pp. 96–97)

Despite its militancy, *The Feminine Mystique* had mass appeal and was instrumental in initiating a reevaluation of women's traditional role. Banner (1974) notes that Friedan's book was in tune with the tenor of the reform climate that was sweeping the U.S. in the early 1960s. Her message rang true to millions of housewives, mothers, and other women, such as myself, and served as a catalyst for change in many of our lives.

A third literary precursor to the resurgent women's movement was a paper, "Equality Between the Sexes: An Immodest Proposal," presented by Alice Rossi (1964) in October 1963 at a conference convened by the American Academy of Arts and Sciences and *Daedalus*, its journal. Rossi, a feminist and sociologist, offered some practical steps that could be taken to implement equality as a social goal. She focused on child care and the establishment of a network of child-care centers; residence (the restrictions of suburban living had to change so that women would have access to industry and schools); and education for women. These three issues have continued to be emphasized in the ideology of the women's movement over the years since Rossi first presented them. In addition to these pragmatic measures for change, Rossi described a sort of utopian state where sex equality would exist between men and women and created a hypothetical case of an ordinary woman living her life in a society in which new social conditions prevailed between the sexes. Rossi's writing went beyond "dissent to one of conversion aimed at transformation," according to Borzak (1971, p. 12).

Other occurrences in the early 1960s that facilitated the emergence of the new women's movement included several key federal and state executive actions and the passage of new federal laws that supported sex equity. In December 1961, President John F. Kennedy issued Executive Order 10980, which called for the establishment of The President's Commission on the Status of Women (PCSW). Chaired by Eleanor Roosevelt, its charge was to study the following areas: education, private and federal employment, social insurance and tax laws, protective labor laws, civil and political rights and family law, and home and community. The director of the Women's Bureau U.S. Department of Labor, Esther Peterson, was the key organizer of the commission. The discussion of discrimination against women was made respectable by the commission's activities, and this was a major point of advancement in those years (East, 1975). By 1967, commissions on women were functioning in every state (Hole & Levine, 1971).

In July 1962, President Kennedy, acting on a recommendation of the PCSW, issued an order requiring federal employees to be hired and promoted without regard to sex. Before this order, federal managers could restrict job considerations to men or women. The Equal Pay Act [29 U.S.C. 206(d)] was passed in June 1963 by the U.S. Congress after the formation of a coalition of women's organizations and unions to support it. It prohibited discrimination on the basis of sex in wages and fringe benefits by any employer in the United States (East, 1975). During the 1950s, Katharine St. George and other Congresswomen (Edna Kelly, Leonor Sullivan, and Edith Green) had introduced equal pay legislation. Green, who was on the House Education and Labor Committee, was particularly active in securing the final passage of the Equal Pay Act (Ingersoll, 1983).

Finally, two more significant things occurred that presaged the resurgent Women's Movement. First, Title VII of the Civil Rights Act of 1964 was enacted by the U.S. Congress in July 1964. It prohibited discrimination in employment because of sex, race, color, religion, or national origin. Second, in June 1965, the U.S. Supreme Court ruled in *Griswold* v. *State of Connecti-*

cut [381 U.S.C. 479] that a Connecticut law that banned contraceptives was unconstitutional because it violated the right to privacy (East, 1975).

Returning to the theme of continuities among different eras of women's activism, it is useful to summarize some key points made by Taylor (1989). She writes:

> My analysis suggests three ways in which the activism of the NWP shaped the feminist challenge that followed. It provided preexisting *activist networks,* an existing repertoire of *goals and tactics,* and a *collective identity* that justified feminist opposition. (p. 770)

Specifically, Taylor notes that the resurgent movement of the 1960s was affected by the NWP network of the 1940s and 1950s in these ways: NWP members played a critical role in the establishment of the President's Commission on the Status of Women, in securing the inclusion of sex in Title VII of the Civil Rights Act of 1964, and in the founding in 1966 of the National Organization of Women (NOW)—generally conceded to be a signpost of the beginning of the contemporary women's movement.

The "Official" Beginning of the Contemporary Women's Movement

In June 1966, at the Third National Conference of Governor's Commissions on the Status of Women, participants were concerned about inadequate enforcement of Title VII of the 1964 Civil Rights Act, relative to sex-fair employment, but a proposed resolution that called for its enforcement was not passed by the conferees. Disturbed by this, as well as by government inaction on the recommendations of various commissions on women and by the lack of enforcement of other existing laws, a group of conference participants met with Betty Friedan and decided there was a need for a national organization that would press the government for women's rights, just as civil rights organizations did for African-Americans (Banner, 1974; East, 1975). NOW evolved from this meeting, being officially formed by a group of women and men who met in Washington, D.C., on October 29–30, 1966; they elected Betty Friedan as the first president.

NOW membership consisted of old-line feminist activists, professors, business executives, government officials and employees, and labor union activists. The organization assumed leadership of the liberal wing of the women's movement (J. Freeman, 1975, cited in Taylor, 1989, p. 770). NOW had a formal structure with a board of directors, bylaws, and a statement of purpose, which was to "take action to bring women into full participation in the mainstream of American society NOW" (Carden, 1974, p. 104). It focused mostly on using legal means to advance women's rights.

The other wing of the resurgent women's movement, which was more militant, radical, and loosely organized than NOW, was made up of younger women who had been involved in New Left organizations (e.g., student and black civil rights groups) and had become disenchanted with their experiences in these groups. Banner (1974) says: "Like many nineteenth-century feminists who turned from reform to feminism, they began to identify with the disadvantaged and to ask if they, too, were not objects of discrimination" (p. 233). The focus of most women's liberation groups was on "analyzing the origins, nature, and extent of women's subservient role in society" (East, 1975, p. 4).

Consciousness-Raising Groups and Other Activities

In the late 1960s, feminist groups began to use the technique of consciousness raising to help women in small, supportive groups explore their identity, their common problems (e.g., living in an oppressive patriarchal society), and ways to take individual and collective action to challenge the oppressive conditions and ultimately to change their lives. Redstockings, a militant feminist group, was one of the first organizations to employ the concept of consciousness raising. Shulamith Firestone and Ellen Willis, who developed the idea of "the personal as political," are credited with initiating consciousness-raising groups with the Redstockings. Their thesis that men are the ones who need to change, however, never gained acceptance as a major theme in the women's movement. However, consciousness-raising groups appealed to many women, such as homemakers and university students, who were not associated with feminism (Hole & Levine, 1971), and their use spread to other groups, such as gay liberation organizations.

Among their many activities and demonstrations, members of the radical feminist wing of the women's movement picketed the Miss America beauty pageant in Atlantic City in 1967 to protest the perpetuation of myths about women. East (1975) says: "Although no bras were burned, as alleged, members of women's liberation groups were thereafter called 'bra burners', and the term 'women's liberation' has been applied by the press to the entire women's movement" (p. 4).

By the late 1960s, the floodgates were open for the resurgent women's movement to flow into the mainstream of public awareness. After the creation of NOW, other organizations (such as the Women's Equity Action League [WEAL]) were formed. The founders of WEAL were dissatisfied with NOW and its position on repeal of criminal abortion laws. WEAL focused on eradicating sex discrimination in higher education, taxation, and employment (Banner, 1974; East, 1975).

The women's movement also gained the attention of the general public through a proliferation of courses on women's history, sociology, and psychology in colleges and universities across the country (by 1975, there were women's studies programs at approximately 900 institutions of higher education) and through an outpouring of feminist books, journals, and magazines (Banner, 1974; East, 1975). Like Betty Friedan's *The Feminine Mystique*, Kate Millet's (1969) *Sexual Politics* spread like wildfire. Other influential books were Robin Morgan's (1970) *Sisterhood Is Powerful*, an anthology of important writings from the women's liberation movement, including Mary Daly's "Women and the Catholic Church," Noami Weisstein's "'Kinde, Kuche, Kirche' as Scientific Law: Psychology Constructs the Female," and Roxanne Dunbar's "Female Liberation as the Basis for Social Revolution"; Shulamith Firestone's (1970) *The Dialectics of Sex*; Carolyn Bird's (1971) *Born Female*; Germaine Greer's (1971) *The Female Eunuch*; Toni Cade's (1970) *The Black Woman*; and Judith Hole & Ellen Levine's (1971) *Rebirth of Feminism*. In 1972, *Ms*, the first militant feminist magazine, was first published and three scholarly journals on women's studies were begun (Banner, 1974). Also, in the early 1970s, the Feminist Press began to issue a newsletter, "Feminist Studies" (East, 1975), and many women's centers, support groups, and programs were established.

Social changes began to occur that would have been unthinkable just five years earlier. For instance, in December 1969 a women's caucus was formed in the National Council of Churches, and the organization elected its first woman president, Dr. Cynthia Wedel. Then in January 1970, Dr. Bernice Sandler, a WEAL officer, filed the first formal charges of sex discrimination (under Executive Order No. 11246) against the University of Maryland. By the end of 1971, charges of sex discrimination had been filed against 300 colleges across the country, largely due to Sandler's and WEAL's efforts. In the same year, Congresswoman Edith Green of Oregon held hearings on discrimination in education and published a two-volume report that provides a classic documentation of discrimination in education (East, 1975).

The National Black Feminists Organization was founded in August 1973. One of the leaders was Eleanor Holmes Norton, an attorney and chair of the New York City Human Rights Commission (East, 1975). In the same year, Frankie M. Freeman (1973), a black feminist and commissioner on the U.S. Commission on Civil Rights, made a plea for understanding that achieving "the rights of minorities and women are parallel in many ways" (p. 1). She continued:

> I believe that the achievement of women's rights is essential to the achievement of racial justice. This is true for two reasons. First, if the notion of *any* human inequality is sanctioned and institutionalized, then other human inequities are predictable and inevitable. . . .

We and others must clearly understand that both the Civil Rights Movement and the Women's Movement are addressing the White male club—that system which gives preference to White men and which operates to maintain a *status quo* in which all women and minority men are at the bottom, hopefully, fighting each other. (pp. 2, 5)

THE WOMEN'S MOVEMENT FROM THE LATE 1960S TO THE PRESENT

By the late 1970s, the women's movement had become a fact of life in the U.S., with a broad base of support among diverse groups of women and with pervasive effects in institutions at local, state, and national levels. However, in the late 1960s, the women's movement had a very narrow base of support and participation, consisting largely of white, middle-class, professional women. Efforts were made by many of these women to attract women of color, but as Seifer (1976) writes:

> Those efforts were largely ill-fated. The style of communicating, the organizing tactics, the priority concerns all seemed to alienate the majority of American women. . . . But as the Movement dug deeper and deeper into all the areas of American life where women face discrimination—from employment to the courts' handling of rape cases; from education to the ability to obtain credit—the fight for equal rights gained new adherents and new constituencies. . . . Many of the new constituencies did not join the original organizations established by early Movement leaders. Instead, they formed their own. (p. 4)

The movement gained strength and momentum throughout the 1970s because of broad goals that addressed the needs of a wide spectrum of women. For example, a high priority was placed on issues that affect families and children, such as domestic violence, reproductive rights, comprehensive child care, the ERA, equal employment and educational opportunity, welfare reform, equitable social security benefits, and access to credit. Seifer (1976) writes:

> Obviously there was much in the message of the Movement that struck a sympathetic chord in American women of all backgrounds. . . . The Movement was saying that traditional women's roles no longer fit the reality of women's daily lives and society had to begin to respond to that change. (p. 4)

By the end of the 1970s, the women's movement had taken hold as a mainstream social movement that had initiated far-reaching social changes. That it would become the most important force for social change in the United

States would not have seemed possible to its detractors in the general public, who saw it as a "flash in the pan" doomed to fail, or to many of the early movement leaders who had struggled for decades against seemingly impenetrable walls of cultural and social resistance to change. Seifer (1976) says that even Betty Friedan, considered by many to have ignited the contemporary women's movement, "never anticipated the extent to which the Movement would take hold" (p. 1).

Following this period of phenomenal growth for women's rights (1965 to 1979), major changes in political power took place that ushered in an ultraconservative backlash against feminism and women's rights (Faludi, 1991) and against civil rights in general. Beginning with the election of Ronald Reagan in 1980 and continuing through the Bush administration, advancement for women and people of color was set back tremendously both by their lack of support for existing civil rights legislation and by overt actions to undermine civil rights (see Chapter 2 for specific examples from the last 10 years).

With the shift in political power in 1980, the Moral Majority and other New Right groups wielded their influence in Washington and across the country for the cause of "saving the family"; however, their activities resulted in a regression on civil rights for women and people of color. This network of conservative groups tried "to divide the public between those committed to equal rights for women and those concerned for families; to them, no one can be both. . . . They are attempting to turn reality upside down by calling their agenda 'pro-family' and labeling the feminist agenda 'anti-family'" (Zeitlin, 1983, p. 274).

CONGRESSIONAL ACTION

The tremendous gains made during the 1960s and 1970s for the rights of all women were supported by a number of significant pieces of legislation and legal actions. However, given the vagaries of political power, much of that legislation was not funded, was underfunded, or not enforced during the Reagan and Bush presidencies. Now, with the Clinton administration in power, the climate in Washington *seems* to be more supportive of the rights of people of color and women.

Following is a discussion of some additional legislation and related political activity that supported the growth of the contemporary women's movement. Some of these efforts were successful; some were not. Hopefully, the time is right for a resurgence of support for women's rights, not only in the legislative branch of government but also in the judicial and executive branches.

The Equal Rights Amendment

1972 was a banner year for positive social action for women's rights: On March 22, 1972, the ERA was finally passed by Congress (49 years after it had first been introduced), but it still required ratification by 38 states. The ERA was pushed through Congress by the combined efforts of women's organizations, civil rights groups, church groups, and a few unions (East, 1975; Ingersoll, 1983; Rawalt, 1983). "Representative Martha Griffiths was the inspiration, the knowledge center, and the gadfly who piloted the ERA through the House—not once, but twice —sending it for the final Senate action in March, 1972" (Rawalt, 1983, p. 66).

Twenty-three states had ratified the ERA before the end of 1972, and by 1975, the total was 35, just 3 short of ratification. Before the seven-year ratification deadline (March 1979) arrived, a massive effort was made to gain an extension of seven more years. NOW organized a parade, which Rawalt (1983) contended was "the largest parade in history on behalf of feminism" (p. 69)— on July 9, 1978, more than 300 state, local, and national groups marched in 90° heat to the Capitol.

A compromise on the time extension to three-and-a-half years was agreed upon by the House and Senate in August and October 1978, respectively. As the new deadline of June 30, 1982, approached, a new organization, ERAmerica, was formed from all active groups supporting the ERA, except NOW, which opted to work independently for the same goal. "NOW achieved a marvel of media support. President Ellie Smeal became the one person, and NOW the one organization, quoted and interviewed by the media on every development" (Rawalt, 1983, p. 71). Even after all these efforts, ratification of the ERA was not achieved by June 30, 1982. A few excerpts from the final report of Suone Cotner, executive director of ERAmerica, summarize the ratification efforts from 1972 to 1982:

> ERA was defeated in spite of overwhelming public support—in spite of a campaign that used all the usual political pressure points—media, constituent phone calls, letters, rallies, editorial endorsements, grass roots lobbying, and polls. *We did not win because those in legislative and power positions did not want us to win.* . . . When all the excuses ran out, legislative sleight-of-hand took over. (quoted in Rawalt, 1983, p. 72; emphasis added)

When will women be admitted into the Constitution? Until that time, women will still be second-class citizens in their own country. The complete text of the Equal Rights Amendment to the Constitution is as follows:

Section I:
Equality of rights under the law shall not be denied or abridged by the United States or by any state on account of sex.

Section II:
The Congress shall have the power to enforce, by appropriate legislation, the provisions of this article.
Section III:
This article shall take effect two years after the date of ratification.

Title IX

In June 1972, Title IX of the Education Amendments of 1972 was passed by Congress. It prohibits discrimination on the basis of sex against students and employees of a school receiving federal financial assistance. Also in 1972, the Equal Pay Act was extended to include federal administrative, professional, and executive employees. Leading proponents of these measures were Senator Birch Bayh of Indiana and Representative Edith Green of Oregon (East, 1975).

Upon rereading the Civil Rights Act of 1964, Representative Green realized that changes needed to be made to ensure sex equality in education. She "found that all education programs were excluded and that it was perfectly legal to discriminate against girls and women in any educational program" (Ingersoll, 1983, p. 204). She also had been concerned about salary disparities between male and female professors and about the unfairness in the distribution of athletic scholarships among male and female students. Thus she held hearings on discrimination against women in education and steered the bill (with Title IX) to final passage.

Title IX has had far-reaching effects on education for women and girls. It prohibits sex discrimination in such areas as admissions to vocational, graduate, professional, and public undergraduate schools; student access to courses and programs; counseling and guidance—tests, materials, and practices; physical education and athletics; student rules and policies; vocational education programs; treatment of married and/or pregnant students; financial assistance; student housing; extracurricular activities; and employment in education institutions (Buek & Orleans, 1973; Council of Chief State School Officers, 1977; Millsap, 1983).

Roe v. Wade

In January 1973, the Supreme Court held in *Doe* v. *Bolton* and *Roe* v. *Wade* [93 S. Ct.739 and 755] that during the first trimester of pregnancy, the decision to have an abortion must be left solely to the woman and her doctor. A state could impose the restriction that the abortion be done by a physician licensed by the state. The state could impose more stringent restrictions in the second and third trimesters of pregnancy (East, 1975).

Women's Educational Equity Act

The Women's Educational Equity Act (WEEA) was passed as part of the Special Projects Act of the Education Amendments of 1974 [Public Law 93-380]. WEEA was shepherded through Congress by Representative Patsy Mink of Hawaii and Senator Walter Mondale of Minnesota. It authorizes support of a broad range of activities targeted on any area of education that perpetuates sex bias and thus "opens many avenues to carry out the purpose of providing educational equity for women" (Women's Educational Equity Act, 1976, p. 1).

The Domestic Violence Prevention and Services Act

In 1980, the Domestic Violence Prevention and Services Act was introduced in Congress in response to the nationally recognized problem of domestic violence. Congressional sponsors were Senator Alan Cranston of California and Representative Paul Simon of Illinois. This act proposed to establish a program of grants to public or private nonprofit agencies seeking to prevent domestic violence and aid its victims. The proposed level of funding was $65 million over three years. Most of the funds "would have gone to local centers that provided emergency shelter to women who left their home because their husbands beat them" ("Conservatives Kill . . . ," 1980, pp. 443–444). The Moral Majority and other ultraconservative groups conducted a massive lobbying effort to defeat the bill, and they succeeded. Senators who carried out the Moral Majority's wishes were Jesse Helms of North Carolina, Gordon Humphry of New Hampshire, Strom Thurmond of South Carolina, and Barry Goldwater of Arizona ("Conservatives Kill . . . ," 1980, p. 445). Zeitlin (1983) analyzes their successful campaign:

> The domestic violence issue was seen by its opponents not as a women's issue, but rather as an anti-family issue. By using the "family" label, the Moral Majority was able to tap into a network of conservative groups, all of whom respond negatively to political issues that allegedly threaten the family. They avoid acknowledging the merits of a particular program by framing the debate in terms of pro- versus anti-family notions. (p. 274)

Zeitlin (1983) pinpoints a major problem of the women's movement: The programs that it advocates (e.g., child care, attempts to reduce domestic violence, welfare reform, etc.) "are not necessarily identified by the public as being pro-family" (p. 274). She concludes:

> Domestic violence is only one of many areas where women's groups have reached out to other family and social service groups. We need to use that experience,

confront the importance of the family issue, and recapture it as an essential element of the women's movement. (p. 274)

ERA REVISITED

As noted earlier, the ERA was not ratified as a part of the Constitution. Phyllis Schlafly, a Moral Majority leader in the fight against the ERA, craftily wielded the "family" issue to defeat it. In her analysis of why the ERA failed to be ratified, Marilley (1989) says that "the 1970s ERA reform leaders failed to make firm ties to traditionally-minded women supporters at the outset; as a result, some state ERA organizations lacked firm foundations" (p. 33). Support for abortion rights and military service for women by some of the reform leaders also widened the gap between them and traditional women.

In her article, Marilley (1989) also makes a comparison between the woman suffrage movement and the ERA movement in order to develop a more successful strategy for the future. She says that "the suffragists vigilantly held to a single-issue strategy; they proclaimed the vote as their only goal, and leaders who wanted a forum for another issue had to go elsewhere" (p. 33). Banner (1974), however, writing 10 years prior to the final defeat of the ERA, analyzed the suffragists' adherence to the single issue of winning the vote as a weakness while viewing the lack of focus on a single goal by the new feminists as a strength. Having the advantage of hindsight, I agree with Marilley (1989) that the current women's movement needs to concentrate primarily on the ERA in a future campaign. For the success of a future ERA, the focus should be kept on these two reasons for its passage: "(1) to reinforce the rights women have gained through legislation and litigation, and (2) to create a powerful sanction against the treatment of women as inferior to men" (Marilley, 1989, p. 38); the focus should not be made murky by other issues such as abortion rights or military service.

Other ideas for the success of a future ERA based on lessons learned from the woman suffrage movement include taking a long-range perspective, remembering that suffragists labored for nearly 50 years before the Nineteenth Amendment was ratified. Thus present-day ERA leaders need to "wait for more accommodating conditions" (Marilley, 1989, pp. 39–40), reassess the reasons for the failure of the ERA, modify strategies, "and rebuild a support base so that they can cultivate a consensus for ERA in the state legislatures as well as in Congress and among the public" (pp. 39–40).

During the woman suffrage movement as well as during the 1970s ERA movement, there was a great fear of and resistance to change in gender roles. "Only after woman suffragists elucidated their aim as political inclusion, not changes in women or society, did they garner the support necessary for victory" (Marilley, 1989, p. 40). In sum, Marilley argues "that the leaders of a future ERA movement must celebrate women's differences, challenge more effectively the notion that women need men's protection, select issues that concern most women, and form firmer alliances" (p. 23).

Given the 1980s regression on women's rights and civil rights in general, the movement for the ERA is "on hold" once again and the women's movement of the 1960s and 1970s is in abeyance, as it was in the years after World War II, but it is not dead. I agree with Taylor's (1989) research, which suggests that

> movements do not die, but scale down and retrench to adapt to changes in the political climate. Perhaps movements are never really born anew. Rather, they contract and hibernate, sustaining the totally dedicated and devising strategies appropriate to the external environment. (p. 772)

While significant problems of inequality still exist, many gains have been made for women since the mid–1960s. During the 1960s and 1970s, women in numerous organizations learned the value of teamwork and coordination of efforts. "Sisterhood" took on a deep and significant meaning that sustains women today and will see us through this period of recidivism on women's rights.

IMPLICATIONS FOR EDUCATION

The significance of the contemporary women's movement and the civil rights movement as well as the realities of our pluralistic society have yet to be reflected adequately in school curricula and practice. However, a persistent demand for changing the white male-as-norm model of education has resulted from the evidence gathered during the last 25 years. This evidence confronts and challenges the androcentrism, sexism, racism, and classism of the old model. Research on women's history and feminist studies indicates that the education of females has not been taken seriously, their voices have not been heard, and their needs have not been met in this male-centered model of education; their history, contributions, values, and perspectives have been excluded.

Many efforts for equal educational opportunity in the schools were developed in response to the women's movement and the civil rights movement of the 1960s and 1970s. These reforms, known as sex-equity education or nonsexist education, are part of a larger thrust to make education reflect our pluralistic society. They seek to integrate accurate information about the history, perspectives, and contributions of women and people of color into the curricula and materials used in school programs and call for the infusion of equity concepts and practices into all parts and levels of education. While laudable, these efforts have had limited success in producing an equitable education for women and people of color, since they still function within a predominantly monocultural and androcentric system.

As Jones (1989) says, "The limits of the adding-women-and-stirring approach were soon recognized and gave way to the more powerful move to reconstruct the enterprise of knowledge itself" (p. 18). In other words, there must be a reconceptualization of the canon of knowledge and a restructuring of the androcentric model of education to one that is gender-balanced, to one that goes beyond the equal educational opportunity model and transforms the whole system of education. Elaborating on Jones's theme, Tetreault (1989) argues for transforming the education system from one of Western male dominance over the "content and substance of knowledge itself to . . . one that interweaves issues of gender with ethnicity, race, and class" (p. 124). When the latter is achieved, the "enterprise of knowledge itself" truly will be transformed.

SUMMARY

This chapter provides a historical overview of the contemporary women's movement and traces its roots to the nineteenth-century social movements of feminism and woman suffrage. Continuities between the different eras are drawn, and it is argued that the social movement for women's rights and liberation has not died when the political climate was hostile but rather been put "on hold" until more favorable conditions arose for its resurgence. The women's movement and concern about the ERA are in abeyance in the early 1990s. Finally, the implications of feminist research for restructuring and transforming education are discussed.

Review Questions

1. Research the lives and contribution of three of the following nineteenth- and early twentieth-century leaders of the woman suffrage movement: Elizabeth Cady Stanton, Lucretia Mott, Lucy Stone, Susan B. Anthony, Frances Willard, Jane Addams, Carrie Chapman Catt, Harriet Tubman, Abigail Scott Duniway, Sojourner Truth, Josephine St. Pierre Ruffin, William Lloyd Garrison, Frederick Douglass, or Ida B. Wells.
2. What is the significance of the Seneca Falls Convention of 1848? Identify the famous document (and its key resolutions) that resulted from this meeting.

3. What is the relevance of nineteenth-century feminism and the woman suffrage movement to an understanding of the twentieth-century women's movement?

4. Discuss continuities, similarities, and differences among the movements for women's rights and liberation in the different time periods covered in this chapter.

5. Compare and contrast the strategies used by leaders of the suffrage movement and those of the ERA movement of the 1970s. What could leaders of a future ERA movement learn from those prior efforts to improve its chances of ratification?

6. What was the social and political climate following World War II (1945–1960) in relation to women? What were the effects of these conditions on women's rights and liberation? Are there any similarities between those years and recent years (1980–1990)?

7. Identify and discuss several key books and writers that laid the groundwork for the resurgent women's movement of the mid-1960s.

8. Review and discuss the key legislation, Executive Orders, and other events that paved the way for the "official" beginning of the women's movement in 1966.

9. What significant legislation advanced the cause of women's rights and liberation in the 1970s?

10. Do you agree or disagree that the advancement of women's rights and civil rights for people of color have been put "on hold" since 1980? Support your position with empirical evidence (based on observation and experience) as well as research evidence (from newspapers, journals, books).

11. Do you think the women's movement and feminism are dead or dormant; relevant or irrelevant to our present time? Why or why not?

| CHAPTER 2 | Sexism: Persisting Problems and Issues |

Men may cook or weave, or dress dolls or hunt humming birds, but if such activities are appropriate occupations of men, then the whole society, men and women alike, votes them as important. When the same occupations are performed by women, they are regarded as less important.

(Mead, 1949, p. 159)

Many of you may wonder why we need to critically examine sex and gender issues in schools of the 1990s. Aren't sexist practices a thing of the past? As the advertisements say, "You've come a long way, baby." Often today's college students say and feel that they have never experienced discrimination and cite examples of people they know who are in nontraditional fields and in positions of leadership as examples of progress toward sex equity.

Recall, for a few moments, your elementary school days. Do you remember the principal and the teacher when you were in the third grade and the sex of each? Reflect on your third-grade classroom: Did the teacher call on boys and girls equally? Were there pink signs for girls and blue ones for boys over the restroom doors? Did you have to line up according to sex to go to the playground? Did the teacher do the "hard" science experiments for the female students, but assist the males only until they could do them independently? Did the boys or the girls get asked to help with moving desks, dusting erasers, or watering plants? Your responses say a lot about whether your early school experiences were sexist.

THE ROLE OF THE CLASSROOM TEACHER

Critical examination of one's own early school experience for sex and race bias can help teachers function more equitably in their classrooms. Since there

is a strong tendency for teachers to replicate the teaching styles and strategies used by their instructors from years past, it is vitally important to be aware
of this likely influence in order not to reproduce sexist and racist practices
unconsciously.

The classroom teacher plays a significant role in the socialization of boys
and girls and may influence development of stereotypic sex-role characteristics
in them. Especially vulnerable are preschoolers whose teachers direct them
into sex-stereotyped activities. In a study of 30 early childhood teachers,
Ebbeck (1984) observed significant imbalances in girls' involvement in the
types of play (climbing, construction, block and sand play) that provide
opportunities for the development of spatial, mathematical, and scientific
skills. Also, Ebbeck's study revealed that the teachers spent 40% of their time
with girls and 60% with boys.

If the teacher calls on boys more, asks boys higher-order questions, and
gives them more positive and definitive feedback and praise, while giving
girls less "air time," ignoring them, asking them lower-order questions, and
responding with more general feedback, she is reinforcing entrenched sex-
role expectations for females to be dependent and passive and for males to
be independent and assertive. These traits have direct bearing on the student's aspirations, self-esteem, achievement, career options, and choices
later in life. Both differential teacher interaction patterns with boys and girls
and sex-segregated classrooms—whether the separate seating arrangements,
lines, work and play groups are devised by the teacher or by the students
themselves—project strong messages about gender expectations and stereotypes.

The teacher–student interaction patterns described above are still prevalent in classrooms and play an important role in maintaining unequal education for students at all levels (Brophy & Good, 1974; Organisation for Economic Co-Operation and Development, 1986; Sadker & Sadker, 1985a, 1985b,
1985c, 1986). Commenting on their research, Sadker and Sadker (1987) say
that an intellectual exchange between the instructor and students occurs most
frequently with white males, with decreasing amounts and quality of interaction and exchange with the following groups in descending order: minority males, white females, and minority females. Interestingly, the Sadkers
observe that this rank order also represents the pay scale, in that white males
receive the most money and minority females, the least. A caveat about the
kind of teacher attention to minority males must be noted. The work of Sadker
and Sadker (1982) and of Jackson and Cosca (1974) indicates that teacher
interaction with black males is characterized largely by reprimands (cited in
Sleeter & Grant, 1988, p. 18). Although these findings are discouraging, there
is a positive aspect to some later research by the Sadkers (1986) and by Whyte

(1984) which demonstrates that teachers can learn how to modify the classroom climate and change their interaction patterns with students so that the instruction is more equitable.

During the last 25 years, there have been many efforts to eradicate sexism and racism in schools. While some notable change has occurred, the effects of deeply ingrained social attitudes, resistance to change, stereotypes, and the recent political and judicial climate have combined to maintain an inequitable system.

OVERVIEW

This chapter provides present and future teachers with an overview of the persisting problems of sexism and sex discrimination, including their multicultural dimensions, in the United States of America and in its public schools. A review of theories and research on gender roles and socialization, on sextyping and stereotypes, and on the effects of sexism on self-concept and achievement are discussed. Implications for education, the teacher's role in nonsexist culturally inclusive education, the issue of color/gender blindness versus color/gender sensitivity, and a rationale for nonsexist, nonracist education round out this chapter. Research activities and reflective exercises are included in this chapter, and in the remaining ones, to make the material more personally meaningful and concrete. Also, questions appearing at the end of this (and other) chapters are designed to help you study, review, understand, remember, and, in some cases, apply the material covered. Recommended readings are included in Appendix B. I think you will find these readings both useful in your class work and personally stimulating.

EVIDENCE OF SEXISM

In the following section, evidence of sexism in education, business and politics, the courts, and the economy is provided for your reflection. To aid the process of reflection, three research activities and a reflective exercise are included.

In Education

Sexism in schools is still alive and well. National events since 1980 have nurtured a climate that negates the egalitarian ideals of our national creed and denies the reality of our multicultural, pluralistic society. The most recent education reform movement—begun in 1983 with the publication of *A Nation at Risk* (National Commission on Excellence in Education) and a number of other national reports—did little to further the cause of equity education. These reports placed a priority on "excellence" in education that left equity concerns in the dust, setting up a false dichotomy between excellence and equity which assumes that the two goals are mutually exclusive. These initial reports were followed by the release of other publications by well-known groups, such as the Holmes Group (Grant, 1990), and by the enactment of more than 700 state statutes pertaining to school reform (Orlich, 1989).

Charol Shakeshaft (1986), a critic of the national reports on school reform, says, "Reagan . . . claimed that one reason that the schools were failing was the attention that had been focused on female, minority, and handicapped students" (p. 499). She astutely observes that, "if these three groups of students are eliminated, only about 15% of the school population remains" (p. 499). Martin Haberman (1987), another critic of the reports, also voiced concern about their disregard for the education of poor students and students of color.

In our democratic society, there is no such thing as an excellent education without equity as its partner in upholding our cherished egalitarian ideals. Students of all races and cultures, all social classes and ability groups, and both sexes must have access to education that provides equal opportunity and results in equal outcomes for all individuals, not just for elite white males.

Mary Futrell (1989), outgoing president of the National Education Association, describes the 1980s as a decade of education debate, not reform. She says the debate appeared in the form of four waves, and the fourth one came from the democratic grassroots of the country. She believes that this wave, begun in 1989, "is predicated on the assumption that schools must offer both excellence *and* equity. I envision schools that will enable *every student*—regardless of race, sex, or socioeconomic status—to reach his or her full potential" (p. 14).

Perhaps the most urgent issue facing educators and the nation as we approach the new century—with the certainty that our public schools will be much more multicultural than they are now—is whether we will persist in our efforts to provide an excellent and equitable education for all our students or whether we will allow education to be used as a tool to separate the "haves" from the "have-nots." Educators need to remember that differential educational opportunity and treatment in schools result in differential outcomes in academic achievement and, later on, in differential occupational and economic achievements for students. These outcomes will have an impact on not only the students' future success but also on our nation's strength and well-being.

While educational and other opportunities have opened up for women and dramatic changes in societal sex-role expectations have taken place since the 1960s, top leadership positions still are held predominantly by white males. In public schools, where there is a preponderance of women teachers (74%), over 62% of principalships are held by men (Gollnick & Chinn, 1994). The percentage of women principals at the secondary level (about 10% percent) in the mid-1980s had declined from that in the 1950s (Harvey, 1986).

At the university level, there is a disproportionate percentage (86%) of male administrators (Metha, 1983). Although there has been a notable increase in the number of women of all ethnic groups earning degrees since 1960 (Grund, 1989a, 1989b), there has not been a similar increase in women faculty. Recent data indicate only 27.6% of all full-time faculty positions in universities and colleges are held by women. Of these, 24.5% are held by white women and 3.1% by women of color (*Digest of Education Statistics,* 1988).

In Business and Politics

Because the school is, in a sense, a microcosm of the larger society, it is important that teachers understand the sociocultural context of problems such as sexism and racism in education. Thus the following discussion on bias in business, politics, and the courts should prompt reflection on some commonalities between those fields and the field of education.

In the corporate world, women are finding that when they make it to middle management positions, that is where they are likely to stay, with the top management positions being nearly impossible to attain. Thirty-three percent of corporate management jobs are held by women, but the percentage of those who are corporate officers at the vice presidential level is comparatively minute (1.65%) ("Corporate Women and the Mommy Track," 1989). Furthermore, these female vice presidents earn 42% less than their male counterparts (Greenberg, 1987).

The iron-clad hold by men on top political offices is equally strong, but there are signs that the political glass ceiling finally may be cracking a bit. For example, in Canada, women make up 13.2% of the House of Commons and 12.5% of the Senate. In the United States, prior to the fall 1992 elections, women made up only 5.2% of the U.S. Congress, but afterwards, the percentage had doubled to 10%. "Women of color more than doubled their numbers in Congress, moving from six seats to 14" ("Women Crack Political Glass Ceiling," 1992, p. 1). Canadian women hold 15.3% of the cabinet appointments and three of the nine positions on the Canadian Supreme Court ("Canadian Women Ahead," 1989; "NOW Organizes Freedom Summer for Women," 1990). In contrast, only two of nine Supreme Court justices in the U.S. are female (Sandra Day O'Connor and Ruth Bader Ginsburg).

Research Activity: Salary Patterns
of Women in Top Management

This research activity is intended for college-level students and preservice teachers.

Conduct several interviews with women in top management positions in a local business or corporation, in the local public schools, and in the university or college to determine whether they have experienced salary discrimination. Next, compare national data (see *Digest of Education* and U.S. Department of Labor statistics) on salaries for the sexes in top management and middle management positions in corporations and in public education institutions. Is there a similar or dissimilar salary pattern between the corporate world and the field of education? Based on evidence from your empirical and library research, what conclusions can be drawn about gender and salary equity in these two arenas?

In the Courts

Title IX. Hard-won progress for women and people of color, gained during the civil rights and women's movements in the 1960s and 1970s, was undermined from 1980 to 1992 by the Reagan and Bush administrations' lack of enforcement of Title IX and other civil rights legislation. Title IX (P. L. 92–318), enacted in 1972, prohibits discrimination on the basis of sex against students and any employee of a school receiving federal assistance.

While Title IX opened many doors for women, it also had some unexpected effects. The lucrative new field of intercollegiate women's athletics—including budgets, recruiting, and public relations—appealed to males. Because of males' more extensive background as coaches, the stereotypic view that males make better coaches, and the established "old boys' network," those already in power placed more males in the new positions that opened up in women's athletics. They have tended to clone the male model of athletics (i.e., win at all costs) for females, and many women have refused to coach in programs with such traditional male values and procedures (Stengel, 1986).

Since the passage of Title IX, there has been a dramatic decrease in the number of female coaches and administrators, while the percentage of male coaches of women's teams has risen dramatically. In 1973, women coached 92% of all women's teams at the collegiate level, but by 1984, that proportion had fallen to 53% (Viverito, 1985, cited in Stengel, 1986). Thus Title IX benefited females by opening up opportunities for them to compete in interscholastic and intercollegiate sports events, but it also opened up new options for males, who had more prior coaching experience, to move into coaching women's sports.

Title IX was weakened considerably by the Supreme Court decision in the *Grove City College* v. *Bell* case in 1984. The Court's decision narrowed the coverage of Title IX so that only the particular unit that was out of compliance, not the whole institution, could be penalized. This decision also threatened the effectiveness of other civil rights statutes, including the Civil Rights Acts of 1964. Efforts to pass a Civil Rights Restoration Act languished in the U.S. Congress for nearly four years before it finally passed in March 1988, with a rider added to satisfy anti-abortion factions ("Title IX Complaints . . . ," 1988).

Research Activity: Coaching Staffs of Women's Athletics— Before and After Title IX

This research activity is intended for college-level students and preservice teachers.

Interview the coaching staff of women's intercollegiate athletics at your college or university. Ask about the ratio of male to female coaches in the programs now and the ratios before Title IX went into effect. Try to arrange an interview with the athletic director. Find out what philosophy the coaches and director hold toward women's athletics. Write a report of your findings for the college newspaper.

Abortion rights. More recent Supreme Court rulings send clear signals that the justices have retreated from civil rights. After the 1988 presidential election, the U.S. Department of Justice asked the Supreme Court to review the 1973 *Roe* v. *Wade* decision that legalized abortion. The Court did not totally dismantle *Roe* v. *Wade*, but its decision on July 3, 1989, in the *Webster* v. *Reproductive Health Services* case pointedly weakened women's constitutional right to abortion by placing more power in the hands of state governments ("States Can Limit . . . ," 1989). Following the Court's lead, the Louisiana legislature passed a law in June 1991, over the governor's veto, that bans abortion in all but the most extreme cases ("Into the Dark Ages . . . ," 1991). In *Rust* v. *Sullivan* the Court ruled by a 5–4 vote on May 23, 1991, that doctors in family planning clinics that receive Title X funds cannot discuss abortion with pregnant women or tell them where to get information about one (Planned Parenthood, 1991).

Now that Bill Clinton is President, the tide has turned back in support of abortion rights. On the twentieth anniversary of *Roe* v. *Wade* (January 22, 1993), Clinton lifted the so-called gag rule imposed on doctors in the *Rust* v. *Sullivan* ruling (Schreiber, 1993).

Racial discrimination. In 1989, the year of the twenty-fifth anniversary of the 1964 Civil Rights Acts, another Supreme Court decision dampened the equity climate for people of color. In the *Patterson* v. *McLean Credit Union* case—in which an African-American woman, Brenda Patterson, charged that she was denied salary increases, subjected to racial slurs, and given demeaning work to do—the Court banned the use of an important 1866 civil rights law to prohibit racial harassment in the workplace. The justices decided by a 5–4 vote that the 1866 law bars racial discrimination in hiring but not racial harassment afterward ("Supreme Court Delivers . . . ," 1989).

The complacency that characterized many civil rights and women's groups in the mid–1980s was jarred by the impact of the 1989–1991 Supreme Court decisions mentioned above. In response to these decisions and other federal actions against civil rights, thousands of women and men across the country organized and marched in protest ("300,000 Rally . . . ," 1989). In another response to these regressive Supreme Court decisions, Congress approved federal legislation, known as the Civil Rights Act of 1990, that would reverse the Court's rulings that weakened federal employment discrimination laws and Title VII of the Civil Rights Act of 1964. President Bush vetoed the legislation in October 1990 ("Bush Proposes . . . ," 1990).

Influence of feminist lawyers. The orientation of the present judiciary seems particularly ironic when we note the increasing number of women in the legal field and their efforts to eradicate sexism and inequality. In 1989, over 40% of law students and 20% of lawyers were women. Since the 1970s, feminist lawyers have challenged the male-centered legal system and have been influential in effecting a number of changes beneficial to women, such as initiating debate on pornography and sexual harassment as violations of civil rights (MacKinnon, 1987) and forging the passage of rape shield laws, which prohibit probing into the victim's past sexual history in the courtroom (Toufexis, 1989).

Some feminist lawyers are for "formal equality" and gender-neutral laws that would give women equal opportunities with men but would not challenge the system *per se*. Other feminist lawyers oppose the gender-blind concept of law and argue that there are some issues—such as violence against women and pregnancy—where conflicts cannot be settled by treating both sexes the same. These lawyers advocate "treatment as equals" with an acceptance of differences between the sexes. The importance of the latter point is made clear by an analysis of inequitable divorce laws, which usually treat men and women the same regarding division of property and other settlements without recognizing the disadvantage of these decisions to women due to their lower earning power based on lack of or lesser education and work experience than men.

In the Economy

While the progress of women during the last 25 years in attaining education and entering nontraditional fields is undeniable, the legal reversals discussed earlier and the persisting wage disparity between the sexes indicate the power and tenacity of the patriarchal system and sexist attitudes.

The wage gap. In increasing numbers, women are working outside the home in all kinds of occupations, but their salaries for comparable work are not equal to males'. Women still earn about 68 cents on the dollar, compared with men. "Minority women earn even less, averaging approximately 50 percent of the wages earned by white males" (Sadker, Sadker, & Long, 1989, p. 117). This grim statistic reflects the combined negative effects of sexism, racism, classism, and ethnocentrism that women of color face in the United States.

Even with the same education as a man, a woman earns less, irrespective of race or class. People expect that the more education they acquire, the greater will be their earnings, but the fact is, women who have finished four years of college make slightly more than men who have only completed elementary school and less than men who have only completed high school (*Digest of Education Statistics*, 1988). Social critic Ivan Illich (1982) puts it this way:

> The wage gap is larger in the States now than it was twenty years ago, even though the country has had a federal pay law since 1963. . . . The current median lifetime income of a female college graduate, even if she has an advanced degree, is still only comparable to that of male high school dropouts. (pp. 25–26)

Just one consequence of sexism, racism, and classism in society is this seemingly intractable wage disparity not only between men and women but also between white males and people of color. Women and people of color have begun to challenge a common practice of government and business— using prior salary as a yardstick to determine pay rates—that results in their being paid lower salaries than white males for doing the same work.

An African-American attorney, Jennifer K. Bell, filed a lawsuit in federal court in April 1989 against the Department of Housing and Urban Development (HUD) for rehiring a former employee, a white male attorney, at a salary two grades above hers because of his prior higher salary, earned while in the private sector, in spite of the fact that their responsibilities and job titles were identical. She brought the charge of sex discrimination under the Equal Pay Act of 1963 and race- and sex-based discrimination under Title VII of the 1964 Civil Rights Act. The *Bell* v. *Kemp* lawsuit is similar to an earlier one, *Kouba* v. *Allstate Insurance Company*, brought by women employees against Allstate for the practice of paying agents and trainees according to their pay in previous jobs. Allstate agreed to stop this practice and established a settlement fund to compensate the women; and the plaintiffs' attorneys established the principle that a salary differential based on past wages is illegal unless justified by the company as a legitimate business reason ("Government's Pay Rates Challenged," 1989).

Feminization of poverty. Despite the increasing number of females in traditional male occupations (such as law and medicine), a greater number of women working outside the home, the passage of the Equal Pay Act of 1963, and greater educational opportunities for women, women make up the majority of the adult population in the federally defined poverty class (Ehrenreich & Stallard, 1982; Jackman, 1987).

Burgeoning numbers of poor women and their dependent children, labeled the "feminization of poverty" in the media, is a sober reminder that economic parity is yet to be attained. The fact that nearly half the families living at the poverty level are headed by single women diffuses many of the popular assumptions about progress made toward sex equality since the 1960s. In 1970, about 16% of children of all races in the United States lived below the poverty level, while in 1985, approximately 21% were in that class. Notable differences in the percentages of children of different races living below the poverty level are worrisome: 17% for white children, 40% for Hispanic children, and 45% for African-American children (U.S. Department of Commerce, Bureau of the Census, 1987). One explanation for the increasing percentage of poor children in the U.S. is the growth of single-parent families, which are often headed by a mother still in her teens (Edelman, 1988). A study conducted in Boston of 100 African-American families headed by women, however, contradicted the stereotypic image of the large, welfare-dependent African-American family by revealing that most of the respondents were single mothers with one child working at a low-paying job (McCain, 1985).

Another reason for the increasing pauperization of children is that women, who usually are awarded custody of children in divorce cases, are still employed primarily in low-paying occupations, such as nursing, secretarial or clerical work, and teaching. In the 1985 salary survey conducted by the magazine *Working Woman*, no field of work was found in which women earned 100% of men's wages. "Even in registered nursing, where 96 percent of the workers are women and most of the seniority is held by women, weekly earnings for men edged ahead by $1.17" (Bodger, 1985, p. 66).

Proposed remedies for reducing pay inequities are varied, but Eleanor Holmes Norton, former head of the Equal Employment Commission and a law professor at Georgetown University, supports raising wages for what is perceived to be "women's work" as well as the principle of comparable worth (Bodger, 1985). Comparable worth goes beyond the principle of equal pay for equal work regardless of sex that was established in 1963 by the Equal Pay Act. It entails comparing various jobs on the basis of factors such as skill, effort, and responsibility, and paying workers accordingly. Comparable worth holds that women and men should be compensated the same for different jobs that have the same intrinsic value.

Research Activity: The Feminization of Poverty

This activity is intended for college-level students and preservice and in-service teachers.

Visit five different social service agencies that provide services for women (e.g., Women, Infants, and Children Program or Homeless Shelter) in your community. Interview service providers, administrators, and several women receiving help. Make a list of interview questions before each visit and analyze your notes after each visit: Were there common patterns of need identified in the different agencies? Were there discrepancies between the perceptions of service providers and the women being served concerning adequacy of support and ease of obtaining it? Do you think there is adequate funding for these programs? What effects of poverty did you observe? On the women? On their children? In your final report, summarize your findings and analyze them. Then, based on your analyses, make some recommendations for improving social services for poor women and their children and discuss some implications for teachers who have poor children in their classroom.

We have looked at evidence of persisting sexism in education, in business and politics, in the legal system, and in the economy. Now, we will briefly examine sexism with a historical lense, peering into past practices of different social institutions, including religion, law, and, of course, education.

THE HISTORICAL ROOTS OF SEXISM

Notice the similarity of thought between the passage from Margaret Mead's (1949) *Male and Female*, quoted at the beginning of this chapter, and the scripture below:

> And the Lord spake unto Moses, saying, ...
> And thy estimation shall be of the male from twenty years old even unto sixty years old, even thy estimation shall be fifty shekels of silver, after the shekel of the sanctuary.
> And if it *be* a female, then thy estimation shall be thirty shekels. (Leviticus 27:1–4)

Devaluation of Women

Since Biblical times, attitudes toward women, "women's work," and their value have not changed appreciably. Not only is "women's work" devalued, but if women gain predominance in a traditionally male domain, it loses prestige. Witness the fields of teaching in the U.S., and medicine in the Soviet Union (Tavris & Offir, 1977). Furthermore, it is not only "women's work" that has been and still is devalued today, but females as persons have historically been, and continue to be, less valued than males in many cultures. Many religious leaders and scientists still say that women are put here "primarily to provide men with children—preferably sons" (Eisler, 1988, p. 81).

The history of the education of women also reflects their devaluation by societies from ancient to modern times. The assumption that biology is destiny permeated the thinking and writing of philosophers from Aristotle to Rousseau on the education of females. However, during the last 125 years, there have been some men, such as John Stuart Mill, George Bernard Shaw, Frederick Douglass, and Havelock Ellis, who supported equality for women in education and in the family.

As late as the beginning of the nineteenth century, women had difficulty in obtaining any education in the U.S. It was believed that girls only needed to learn to read and write and that these skills could be learned from their mothers or at "dame" schools (Banner, 1974). Women who went beyond their "biologically determined" domestic role by getting an education were viewed with suspicion and derision; yet, in spite of these attitudes, women persisted in their search for knowledge and demands for education.

The advantaged position of white males and their dominance has come at a heavy price to our society. Male dominance exists and is supported by the patriarchal system, which enforces it through sexism, racism, and violence (Reardon, 1985). Male dominance and oppression of females dates back thousands of years (Eisler, 1988; S. Johnson, 1986, 1989; Tavris & Offir, 1977), and its main means of perpetuation were and still are economic control, religious and legal sanctions, violence, and homophobia.

Early Common Law

The devaluing of women has many roots (see the discussion of Nancy Chodorow's work on male and female socialization later in this chapter), but one that is immediately relevant can be traced back to early common law. In common law, women and children were placed under legal control of the paternal power. Indicating slaves' low value and status, their legal standing was often equated with that of women and children in the seventeenth century. In building a moral defense for slavery, its advocates repeatedly used the paternalistic construction for their cause (Myrdal, 1944).

Under the common law doctrine known as *femme couverte*, wives were chattels (objects of property) of their husbands and usually had little legal control over their own property, earnings, or children. By 1890, many states had significantly modified such common law practices so that wives gained control over their earnings and inherited property; however, every state still had laws that discriminated against women. Most notably discriminatory were laws that restricted their right to vote in state and federal elections. Because of this restriction, they could neither hold public office nor serve on juries (Banner, 1974).

Rise of Male Dominance

Riane Eisler's (1988) work goes further back in time (before 4000 B.C.) to old Europe (southeastern Europe) to reveal how women were stripped of their responsibility, power, independence, and equality and how they came to be "viewed as male-controlled technologies of production and reproduction" (p. 91). Archaeological discoveries made since World War II, and some as recent as the work by Marija Gimbutas (1980, 1982, 1987), show that in prehistory, civilizations were not dominated by males, warlike, or socially organized by a hierarchy of superiority and inferiority based on sex (Eisler, 1988). The change from a cooperative, partnership model of societies to the familiar dominator, violent model took hold gradually, beginning around 4000 B.C., and was firmly in place by Olympian times. Eisler (1988) says, "after thousands of years of relentless indoctrination, this is simply reality, the way things are" (p. 82).

The basic assumptions of an androcratic society ("the way things are") are that male dominance and aggression are inevitable. Rigid sex-role stereotypes are required to maintain male dominance and support not only warfare but also violence against women and children. Seeing "the other" as "the enemy" is basic to the male-dominator/female-dominated human relations model, and the "war of the sexes" is a direct result of it (Eisler, 1988).

SEX/GENDER ROLES, SOCIALIZATION, AND STEREOTYPING

Gender Identity

The seeds are usually sown for the polarization of the sexes into rigid sex roles as soon as a baby is born. The first question asked is, "Is it a girl or a boy?"; then, gifts and greeting cards are delivered that are "appropriate" to the sex of the baby. Infants are born with biological characteristics that are either female or male; however, aside from the obvious genital differences, male and female babies are very similar in their perceptual development, activity level, temperament, and social behavior. Through early socialization from parents, family, doctors, friends, and early caregivers, the child learns his or her gender identity—the culturally determined feelings, thoughts, and behaviors that are characteristic of "maleness" and "femaleness" in our society. Gender identity reflects the child's unconscious recognition that behaviorally and biologically he or she is either male or female.

Sex-Typing

Differential treatment of females and males, beginning right after birth, provides insight on the formation of both gender identity and sex-typing. Just take time to observe parents' and friends' reactions to baby boys and baby girls the next time you are in a hospital or in a home with newborns. Note differences between their reactions to the male and female infants: What tone of voice is used with each? In what way and how much do they touch each? Do their judgments and expectations differ for each? What kinds of toys are chosen? Studies on how people respond differently to male and female infants give us a partial view of how sex-typing develops. Generally, "the research supports the important role of nurture in sex-typing" (Matlin, 1987, p. 34). Sex-typing refers to how children come to have "sex-appropriate" self-concepts, preferences, behaviors, skills, and personality characteristics (Bem, 1983).

Beyond differential treatment by parents during infancy, factors that influence sex-typing include other family members, peers, the school, the church, and the media. Also, the teacher can look at children's play activities and at a child's own ideas about "masculinity" and "femininity" for clues about how sex-typing develops. The work of Pitcher and Schultz (1983) on children's play and sex-role development shows that female and male differences appear very early and that these differences are reinforced by same-sex exclusivity (e.g., the tendency of girls and boys to play in same-sex groups) and by other peer interactions.

Matlin (1987) reviewed the research conducted since the early 1970s on factors that influence sex-typing and summarized these main findings: Parents' discouragement of feminine activity in their sons is greater than their discouragement of masculine activity in their daughters; promotion of sex-typed play in their children is common; there is little difference in parents' tolerance for aggression in either their sons or their daughters (Maccoby & Jacklin, 1974); parents encourage independence slightly more in their sons than in their daughters (Hoffman, 1972); peers encourage sex segregation and prejudice against the opposite sex (Etaugh, Levine, & Mannella, 1984); there are different expectations for each sex (Conner, Serbin, & Ender, 1978); boys receive more positive and negative attention from teachers than girls, who are often ignored (Brophy & Good, 1974); dependency rather than aggressiveness in girls is preferred by teachers (Levitin & Chananie, 1972); omission of females in texts (Marten & Matlin, 1976) and tests (Saario, Jacklin, & Tittle, 1973) is a problem as well as stereotypic representation when they are included; children's books use biased representations of females (St. Peter, 1979); achievement motivation is greater after children read a story that shows a person of their own sex being successful (McArthur & Eisen, 1976); and stereotypes of women are promoted on television by underrepresentation and by role limitations (Feldstein & Feldstein, 1982).

Theories of Sex-Role Development

A review of some theories that describe sex-role development should aid in understanding the process of acquiring sex-typed attitudes, the persistence of sex-role stereotypes, and how they feed the perpetuation of sex-equity problems in schools. Generally, the three types of psychological theories that describe the content of sex roles and how they are acquired are based on psychoanalytic, social learning, and cognitive–developmental models.

Psychoanalytic theory. Sigmund Freud, in his development of psychoanalytic theory, stressed the biological basis of sex-role development, the critical importance of the early childhood years, and the significance of identification with the same-sex parent. A key component of Freudian theory is the concept of the Oedipus complex, which refers to the unconscious tendency of a young child to be attached to the parent of the opposite sex and hostile toward the other parent. For Freud, the Oedipus complex "constitutes the ultimate formative cause of both health and neurosis. . . . [He] locates the origins of gender differentiation in personality in the oedipal period and in the issues and developmental tasks of this period" (Chodorow, 1978, p. 141). Neo-Freudian Nancy Chodorow (1989) describes Freudian theory as ripe for feminist critique and revision but useful in numerous ways:

> Freud made gender and sexuality central to his theory. Psychoanalysis is first and foremost a theory of femininity and masculinity, a theory of gender inequality, and a theory of the development of heterosexuality. . . . Psychoanalysis makes a feminist argument that women (and men) are made and not born, that biology is not enough to explain sexual orientation or gender personality. . . . Freud's theory is a social and political theory. . . . Psychoanalysis shows that women and men and male dominance are reproduced in each generation as a result of a social division of labor in which women mother. (p. 174)

Freudian theory has strength (over other theories), she writes, in explaining how we live our past in the present and "argues for the replacement of unconscious determination by conscious choice" (Chodorow, 1989, p. 171).

Freud's theory has had considerable impact on our culture: Many of his misogynistic ideas about women (e.g., "genital deficiency" and penis envy) have permeated the popular media as well as the academic and medical press, and his theory has often been used against women (e.g., in calling women "masculine" when they wanted careers). Penis envy is central to Freud's theory of female development: When a little girl notices the difference between her genitals and a boy's, she feels inferior and develops envy for the same equipment. Furthermore, when she realizes her deficiency, the little girl blames her mother for not providing her with a penis and turns to her father in hopes that he will provide one for her. From this transfer of interest to her father grows the female's eventual heterosexual involvement with other men. Freud (1933/1965) wrote that girls "feel seriously wronged . . . and fall victim to 'envy of the penis,' which will leave ineradicable traces on their development and the formation of their character" (quoted in Matlin, 1987, p. 47).

Feminist concerns about Freud's work include: the centrality of Oedipal theory in his view of normal (that is, male) psychological development; his assumption of male physiological superiority; and his conclusions about the lesser moral stature of women—that a woman's personality and character are immutably determined by her envy of the male.

Chodorow (1989) critiques Freud's work:

> He repeated cultural ideology in a context where it can be mistaken for scientific findings. He talks . . . about women's lesser sense of justice, of their jealousy, shame, vanity, and lack of contribution to civilization as if these were clinical findings. (p. 172)

Although Freud (1924) admitted that his understanding of the "developmental processes in girls is unsatisfactory, incomplete, and vague" (quoted in Chodorow, 1978, p. 142), he claimed that girls' superego is not as strong as boys' because girls do not rid themselves of their Oedipus complex in the same way that boys do. Freud concluded, "I cannot evade the notion that for women the level of what is ethically normal is different from what it is in men" (quoted in Chodorow, 1978, p. 143).

Both Matlin (1987) and Klein (1985) warn about the limitations of Freudian theory for explaining sex-role development because of equity considerations. Matlin says that "therapists with a psychoanalytic orientation have a negative view of women that has undoubtedly had an enormous impact on women in therapy. . . . We need to discuss psychoanalytic theory because it has helped to *shape* the development of women, and not because it *explains* gender-role development accurately" (p. 47).

While the work of Carol Gilligan (1982) and Eli Sagan (1988) challenges the Freudian theory of morality as incomplete and flawed, the writing of

Chodorow (1978, 1989) challenges the male bias of his psychoanalytic theory. Her work replaces Freud's negative theory of women's developmental failures with a more positive and realistic one. It is based on her study of the reproduction within each generation of masculine and feminine differences that she says are due not to anatomy but to the simple fact that, almost universally, women provide early child care. Chodorow studies the identity development of males and females and shows how this development, especially the socialization of males, "leads to and perpetuates the devaluation and oppression of women" (1989, p. 23). She writes:

> Until masculine identity does not depend on men's proving themselves, their *doing* will be a reaction to insecurity rather than a creative exercise of their humanity and woman's *being*, far from being an easy and positive acceptance of self, will be a resignation to inferiority. And as long as women must live through their children, and men do not genuinely contribute to socialization and provide easily accessible role models, women will continue to bring up sons whose sexual identity depends on devaluing femininity inside and outside themselves, and daughters who must accept this devalued position and resign themselves to producing more men who will perpetuate the system that devalues them. (1989, p. 44)

Social learning theory. In contrast to psychoanalytic theory, social learning theory focuses on environmental influences on sex-role development and the role of adults in shaping the child's sex-typing. "Social learning theory emphasizes three environmentally-based processes in the sex role development process: direct instruction, direct reinforcement, and modeling" (Klein, 1985, p. 82). A pertinent aspect of this theory is rewards and punishments as mechanisms in learning "sex-appropriate" behavior (Perry & Bussey, 1979); but the greatest amount of social learning, including sex-role learning, comes from observing, modeling, or imitating other people (Mischel, 1970). In addition to imitating real people, students may imitate "symbolic models" whom they have read about or seen on television or in the movies. Matlin (1987) says that exposure to gender-stereotyped models in the media helps explain why children brought up in nonsexist/feminist homes may exhibit very gender-stereotyped behavior from time to time—much to their parents' consternation. Social learning theory has an "intuitive appeal," according to Matlin (1987, p. 49), part of which is its applicability to other aspects of social learning that are closely related to sex-role development, such as self-efficacy (similar to confidence in one's own ability). Bandura (1982), a social learning theorist, suggests that the performance and self-efficacy of students are negatively affected when they are given labels that imply inferiority ("For a girl, that's pretty good problem solving") or place them in subordinate roles ("You girls can watch while the guys demonstrate using the computer"). In contrast to

Freud, however, Bandura "does not think that childhood experiences have any marked or durable effect on adult personality" (Hoyenga & Hoyenga, 1993, p. 220).

Chodorow (1989) critiques social learning theories by saying, "They suggest that changing the social setting and nature of reinforcement should automatically change behavior, which we know from experience is not true" (p. 171). Further, Chodorow (1989) argues that these types of theories "make people (women in this case) into passive reactors to society" (p. 171).

Reflective Exercise: Paul and His Doll

This exercise is intended for college-level students and for preservice and in-service teachers. In-service teachers may wish to adapt this for use with high school students.

Visualize yourself at a family reunion with aunts, uncles, cousins, and other kinfolk enjoying a picnic in the park. Paul, age 3, joins his girl cousins, who are playing with dolls, dressing and undressing them. Soon, he brings a doll over to a group of the men and asks for help buttoning the doll's dress. Imagine what the response of some of the men might be. Would any of the men help him? Maybe so, but it is very likely that at least a few in the group will either laugh, ignore him, tell him to get help from mommy, or say, "What are you doing playing with dolls, Paul? Don't you know boys don't do that?" Imagine the difference in the men's responses to Paul when, instead of a doll, he brings a football to them and starts passing it back and forth with a few of the men. In this case, he is praised for his "strong arm" and asked if he wants to be a professional football star when he grows up.

Reflect on the implications of this vignette for teachers of young children. What would be your response to Paul if he brought his doll to school for "show and tell"?

Cognitive–developmental theory. In cognitive–developmental theory, emphasis is placed on the cognitive processes of the children themselves in forming their own sex-role identity rather than on environmental or adult influences. Numerous studies indicate that acquiring sex-typed attitudes and behaviors is developmental, as are other forms of social learning. Lawrence Kohlberg modeled his theory of sex-role development on stagelike tenets of Jean Piaget's theory (a progression of fixed stages define the developmental changes in children's cognitive capabilities as they mature). Like Freud, Kohlberg (1966) described boys' development first because he believed that "the interpretation of developmental mechanisms of identification in girls is much more complex and ambiguous" (p. 124, quoted in Hoyenga & Hoyenga, 1993, p. 218). After Kohlberg described boys' development, he discussed sex differences. The progression of stages in sex-role development, according to cognitive–developmental theory, is: gender identity, gender stability, and then gender constancy (Klein, 1985).

By the age of 3, children realize their own sex and accurately label themselves; then they come to understand that time does not change the sex of a person; finally, they realize that changes in physical appearance or behavior do not change a person's sex. Kohlberg (1966) believes that after gender constancy is acquired, children start to exhibit preferences for things that are consistent with their established gender identity. In other words, when Susie attains gender constancy, she chooses "sex-appropriate" things and activities because they are self-reinforcing and consistent with her female gender identity, not because of rewards or punishments from others, as social learning theory posits. The weakness of cognitive–developmental theory is that it does not explain why children become sex-typed before a firm gender identity is in place, nor does it explain why sex is used as a method of classification by children (Matlin, 1987).

Feminist Critics of Sex Role Development Theories

Carol Gilligan's (1982) book, *In a Different Voice*, provides a perspective on sex-role development that had been notably missing from prior research, that is, the "voice" of women. As Klein (1985) notes, "Gilligan's work indicates that developmental psychologists and moral behaviorists have taken account of men's lives but not women's" (p. 49). In particular, she, like Nancy Chodorow (1978), challenged the adequacy of research based on male samples and theories derived from male constructs (as in Kohlberg's and Piaget's work) to legitimately describe females' sex-role and moral development.

Building on Chodorow's work, Gilligan's (1982, 1977) perspective on sex-role development is that until the age of 5 most children are dependent on and identify with a female. After that age, a male child is expected to separate and to differentiate from the mother. This enables him to develop a masculine identity. Because it is based on separation, the male identity is threatened by intimacy, and the male "voice" that eventually develops focuses on individuality and self. In contrast, after the age of 5, girls usually continue their identification with the mother. Their identity, based on dependence and connectedness with others, is threatened by separation. They develop a "female voice" that centers on creating and maintaining relationships instead of developing the self and individuality. It is important to observe that she places no value judgment on either "voice"; each sex has both types of "voices," but usually one remains undeveloped until a crisis occurs. Gilligan believes that crises arise for females when they encounter separation from others and for males when they encounter intimacy.

A strength of Gilligan's work is that it goes beyond a concentration on children to include adolescent and young women. Her research has far-reaching implications for understanding and working with females of all ages. For example, women usually learn to take care of others but fail to gain the skills needed to take care of themselves. Gilligan's work helps us reconceptualize women's development so that we can identify sex-role perceptions (such as self-sacrifice) that may be limiting personal and career development in ourselves and in our students. Her work also helps us reconceptualize the meaning of success in such a way that it can validate the lives of women. We come to realize that parts of either "voice" may be useful in developing a more complete self-identity and that by devaluing one sex, as the present patriarchal system does, the development of both is stymied.

The Effects of Sex Stereotyping

Attitudes that determine future choices are formed early in a child's education. It is especially important for teachers to understand sex-typing and to counteract sex or gender stereotypes in the early years of schooling, for they create the false impression in children that activities and interests of boys and girls are mutually exclusive. Sex or gender stereotypes are structured mental categories about males and females that are based on exaggerated, inaccurate, and rigid generalizations (either favorable or unfavorable). They are prejudiced thoughts or beliefs about women and men that have very little correspondence with reality, yet they are used to describe all members of a sex.

Bornstein (1982) indicates that there are "three basic assumptions [about women] that run like an undercurrent through American life, and are reflected in all of our social institutions" (pp. 13–14). These assumptions are: Women's place is in the home; women are physically, emotionally, and intellectually inferior to men; and women should cultivate traditionally feminine characteristics (pp. 13–14). Bornstein also lists three assumptions about men that are woven into our society: Men must participate directly and lead in the civic, political, and economic affairs of the society; men are physically, emotionally, and intellectually superior to women; and men should cultivate traditionally masculine characteristics (pp. 34–35).

The effect that these stereotypic assumptions have on males and females is tremendous, and the implications for education are far-reaching. For women, the impact of sex stereotypes can be seen in their tendency toward lower self-esteem and their ambivalence about success, achievement, and power. Women also are usually overeducated for the jobs they hold and are still at the bottom of the pay scale, with few opportunities for advancement in their work (Bornstein, 1982).

Psychologist Jean Baker Miller's (1976) writing about the "domination–subordination" theme in relation to feminine stereotypes suggests the depth of harm they inflict on women:

> Tragic confusion arises because subordinates absorb a large part of the untruths created by the dominants; there are a great many blacks who feel inferior to whites, and women who still believe they are less important than men. This *internalization* of dominant beliefs is more likely to occur if there are few alternative concepts at hand. . . . It is also true that members of the subordinate group have certain experiences and perceptions that accurately reflect the truth about themselves and the injustice of their position. . . . An inner tension between the two sets of concepts and their derivatives is almost inevitable. (p. 11; emphasis added)

For men, the price of the sex-stereotyped assumptions is also high in that they are deprived of traits and attitudes that have been genderized in favor of women. Bornstein (1982) says: "The pressure on men to compete and succeed results in frustration and stress. Traits of tenderness, sensitivity, and emotionality are underdeveloped in males along with skills in child rearing and homemaking. Unrestrained aggressive behavior causes serious problems in schools and in society" (p. 35). Sadker and Sadker (1982) provide teachers with an excellent overview of the complex nature of male sex-role stereotypes—including some attending problems as well as some instructional approaches and activities to help students understand them. Schau and Tittle (1985) write:

> Masculinity and femininity are not opposites along a single self-concept dimension, as the stereotypes suggest. Rather, they form at least two separate dimensions. A person can vary from highly feminine to not feminine, with a similar dimension for that person's masculinity. . . . To meet the changing conditions and expectations in the United States, adults need to possess a wide variety of skills and traits found in both the traditional masculine and feminine sex role stereotypes which they can use depending upon environmental demands. (pp. 80–81)

Perpetuation of the vicious circle of sexism begins with the commonly accepted sex stereotypes we have just discussed. The assumptions underlying the stereotypes manifest themselves in different expectations for and treatment of boys and girls in the classroom and thus negatively affect their ability to achieve their full potential. Bornstein (1982) says: "As adults, these well-rehearsed students take up traditional functions at home, at work. . . . The perpetuation of these traditions reinforces stereotyped assumptions people hold about what is appropriate and natural for women and men, and the circle of sexism continues" (pp. 10–11).

Reflective Exercise: Sex-Typed Images and Underlying Assumptions

This exercise is intended for college-level students and preservice teachers. Also, in-service teachers may wish to adapt this exercise to use with junior high and high school students.

What are some of the sex-stereotypic mental pictures that you grew up with? Do you remember your first-grade teacher showing the class a colorful poster of an attractive, slender woman in an apron, hair and makeup done perfectly, serving breakfast to her son and daughter while at the same time waving good-bye to her husband, who is at the door, briefcase in hand? Or do you remember the "Blondie" cartoons where Blondie is nagging Dagwood to do the chores that are piling up while he is trying to take a nap on the couch? Constant bombardment with images such as these shape our assumptions about male and female attributes. Thoughtfully consider the assumptions that underlie the stereotypes about males and females in these two examples.

Research Activity: Campus Survey on Female and Male Attributes

This activity is intended for college-level students and preservice teachers (who are the researchers). In-service teachers could adapt it for use with junior high or high school students.

Conduct an informal campus survey on male and female students' assumptions about their sex-role attributes. The researcher goes to a central location on campus where people congregate and interviews as many students as possible in one hour. The researcher asks the students to check all the words on a long list of human characteristics that apply to them. The list would include some of the common stereotypes of women (*passive, patient, emotional, tender, timid, dependent, considerate, fearful, and physically weak*) and men (*strong, tough, active, brave, objective, independent, competent, protective, aggressive, creative, and forceful*), but the words should be scrambled and not be listed or categorized according to gender. Can you think of other words to add to the list?

After each survey is completed, mark whether the subject is male or female. Summarize and tabulate the data from the surveys and critically evaluate the results. Did any stereotypic tendencies emerge from the students' responses? What are some of the rational underpinnings of these stereotypic patterns? In what ways do they reflect the deep-rooted assumptions about the different roles, occupations, and behaviors that are "appropriate" for males and females. Did any of the respondents give you "evidence" (i.e., tell you an anecdote or give an example) to support their choices or try to provide a rationale?

Finally, reflect on the implications of this activity for your teaching. Do you think this kind of activity would be relevant for your students to do? If so, how would you adapt it?

IMPLICATIONS FOR EDUCATORS
AND SCHOOL PROGRAMS

Our role as teachers is to help free students from this vicious circle of sex stereotyping that feeds sexism. When we create school environments that are devoid of sex stereotypes and sexism (see Chapters 3 and 4 for ideas on how to accomplish this), students will be empowered to develop their full academic, personal, and occupational potentials and to explore a wide array of options previously closed to them. We will also be helping them to resist the constant flood of sexist messages and influences they receive from the media, home, and community.

All people (administrators, counselors, coaches, teachers, psychologists, and support staff) in a school system have a responsibility for stopping the cycle of sex stereotyping and sexism. Since sexism has been ingrained in us for centuries, breaking this barrier and changing the system so that it is equitable will not be swift or easy. Such change in schools requires group effort by all educators, not just women. Sexism is a human problem, not a woman's issue.

Color/Gender Blindness versus
New Color/Gender Sensitiveness

The concept of color and gender blindness has been around for some time, as has the idea of color- and gender-free education. "Now, for the first time in 30 years, we have a five-member majority of the justices of the Supreme Court who support the goal of color blindness and gender blindness" (Fein, cited in Sanders, 1989, p. 66). Teachers need to be aware of the assumptions that underlie proclamations of color and gender blindness and to understand the implications for schools.

What research says about gender-free strategies. Researcher Barbara Houston (1985) says that gender-free strategies are likely "(1) to create a context which continues to favor the dominant group, and (2) [undermine] certain efforts which may be needed to realize equalization of educational opportunities" (p. 365). Gender-free strategies do not lead to more active participation by females in athletics or to more student–teacher interactions; in fact, Houston says studies show that gender-free strategies have the effect of lessening educational opportunities for girls (cited in Pai, 1990, p. 115).

What are these findings attributable to? As we saw in the earlier discussion about an unexpected consequence of Title IX—an increasing percentage of males coaching women's intercollegiate athletics—the male-as-norm system of athletics was replicated for women's sports without giving thought to the appropriateness of such a model for women. In a male-dominant society, females are judged by the norms for male behavior, speech, and interpersonal relationships, and "even though the teacher may ignore gender, the students do not disregard gender-related roles" (Pai, 1990, p. 115). These factors largely explain why gender-free strategies may not serve their intended purpose. Research findings indicate that "gender may be excluded as an official criterion, but it continues to function as an unofficial factor" (Houston, p. 363, cited in Pai, 1990, p. 115). Although you may ignore gender in your classroom, your students probably will not. The pervasiveness of the male-as-norm model means that discrimination will very likely occur even when color/gender blindness is proclaimed.

Reflective Exercise: Discovering Pitfalls of Color- and Gender-Blind Education

This exercise is intended for college-level students and for preservice and in-service teachers.

Critically examine the concepts of color and gender blindness for their underlying or hidden assumptions. For instance, what effect might a color- and gender-blind policy have on efforts to hire more teachers of color in a school system? Related to gender blindness is the idea of gender-free education. Think about creating a learning environment that is gender-free, that is, a school setting where gender is irrelevant in determining a person's role or status. What kinds of strategies would you implement? Why use gender-free strategies? What might be some pitfalls of gender-free education?

In place of color/gender-blind strategies, think about other constructs that would better serve education and would help eliminate the pitfalls of color/gender-blind strategies as they are practiced in our male-dominant society. How would a model based on the elimination of gender and racial bias differ from a color/gender-blind model? Where would your energies be directed in each? What kinds of activities would you plan?

A Gender-Sensitive Strategy. Houston (1985) and I recommend that teachers use a gender-sensitive model rather than a gender-blind approach. This model calls for a new color and gender consciousness, not for ignoring color and gender. Think about the implications of a new color and gender consciousness for everyday school practice. Here are a few starters. It would mean that:

- Gender bias is eliminated in language used in the classroom and in learning materials.
- Cross-gender interactions are monitored to equalize opportunities for each sex.
- Gender is taken into account only when doing so will advance equity or prevent sex discrimination.

In sum, a gender-sensitive perspective, in concert with a multicultural perspective, would encourage "constant and critical analysis of the meaning and significance attached to gender" (Pai, 1990, p. 116). Until sexism and racism are eradicated, educators must develop and maintain a high level of gender and race awareness and sensitivity.

Rationale

Justification for education that is nonsexist and culturally inclusive rests on two main premises: first, that diversity is a reality of our society and schools, and second, that equality is a basic ideal of our national creed. The demographic projections of increasing diversity in public schools—students of color are already the majority in many large urban schools and are predicted to represent one in three students by the year 2000—make implementing nonsexist, culturally inclusive education even more urgent. All students—males and females of all groups—need to see themselves, as well as others who are different from them, reflected in the school curriculum. Those who do not often feel detached from school, and doubt their self worth; frequently they fail, drop out, or become underachievers. Students must develop positive self-concepts to grow to their full potential and to develop positive feelings and attitudes toward others.

The second premise undergirding nonsexist, culturally inclusive education is that the ideal of egalitarianism is basic to our national creed. Fundamental to our nation's democratic ideals are equal opportunity for all people, human rights, and social justice. All students need to experience an education that affords them respect and provides both equity and equal opportunity. Thus sex equity that is nonracist becomes a cornerstone of excellence in education that is basic to fulfilling the highest ideals of our democratic society. The teacher's role is critical in making these ideals a reality in schools.

SUMMARY

This chapter examined sexism and sex discrimination in the United States, looked at its historical roots, and found evidence of its persistence in education, in business and politics, in the courts, and in the economy.

The development of gender identity and sex-typing in children and the significant role that socialization and differential treatment of boys and girls play in their development were discussed. A review of theories applied to sex-role development provided perspective on the process of sex-typing. The connection was made between sex-typing, sex-role stereotypes, and how they nurture sexism by devaluing the female and ultimately by limiting both sexes. Some of the negative effects of sexism and rigid sex-role stereotypes on both females and males were discussed.

Finally, the implications of sexism for education and the role of the teacher in eradicating it were explored. Nonsexist, culturally inclusive education is an approach for schools to use in combating sexism, racism, and stereotypes. Color and gender blindness versus a new color and gender consciousness were examined. Justification for nonsexist, culturally inclusive education is based on two premises: Diversity is a reality of our society and schools, and equality is fundamental to our national ideals.

Review Questions

1. What does research say about differential treatment of males and females in the classroom? What are the effects on students?
2. Give several current examples of sexism in society and schools and then analyze them in relation to their historical roots in law, religion, the economy, or education.
3. What kinds of discrimination do women face at work in the 1990s? What special problems do women of color encounter in the world of work?
4. Do you agree or disagree with the practice of using prior salary to determine the pay of a new employee? Why or why not?
5. Discuss the three major psychological theories that describe how sex roles are acquired. Analyze each theory for its weaknesses and strengths and explain which one you think best explains the development of sex-typing.
6. Discuss the work of Nancy Chodorow and Carol Gilligan on sex-role and moral development. How do their views differ with those of other theorists? What contributions have they made to help us better understand male and female development and sexism in society?
7. Reflect on your own experiences in elementary and secondary school. Do you recall instances of sex bias? Were you the recipient of biased treatment? Give some concrete examples and draw parallels with examples you have observed or experienced in the university setting.
8. Reread the last section of this chapter on "Implications for Educators and School Programs." Reflect on why we need education that

is nonsexist and culturally inclusive. Write a one-paragraph rationale (justification) for it.

9. What role does the teacher play in creating a nonsexist classroom environment? Discuss this with a colleague and generate a list of ideas. These could be used with the discussion of sex equity in curriculum and instruction in later chapters.

10. Explain why color/gender-blind education is not compatible with nonsexist, culturally sensitive education.

11. Start writing daily entries in a journal. Record your thoughts, questions, and concerns about sex and race equity and your role in making education fair and unbiased for all students.

Nonsexist, Culturally Inclusive Instruction: Issues and Strategies

CHAPTER 3

When teachers become aware of the nature and cost of sex bias in schools, they can make an important difference in the lives of their students. Teachers can reduce sexism in schools or even make it obsolete. *They can make sex equity a reality for children in our schools. Then tomorrow's children, boys and girls, need not suffer from the limiting effects of sexism in school.*

(Sadker, Sadker, & Long, 1993, pp. 125–126; emphasis added)

While the first two chapters of this book have focused on the foundations of nonsexist education, this chapter turns to more practical considerations of application and implementation in the classroom. Although others in the school (counselors, administrators, and other staff) play important roles in making the total school environment equitable, day-to-day implementation of a nonsexist, culturally inclusive curriculum rests on the shoulders of the classroom teacher. What can a teacher do to assure the delivery of nonsexist, culturally inclusive instruction?

Consider what teachers should know about self-identity, cultural diversity, expectations and self-fulfilling prophecies, classroom climate, learning styles, sex stereotyping, biased language, and the effects of these factors on the differential achievement of males and females. This chapter discusses these issues and presents a number of strategies and activities as well as research studies that should help generate considerable thought. Your ideas are crucial to this exploration, for you will play the central role as facilitator of equity in the classroom.

ISSUES OF NONSEXIST INSTRUCTION

The Teacher's Self-Identity

The first issue for examination is the teacher's self-identity and its significance to effective nonsexist instruction. Gender identity is an important part of one's total self-identity. It, along with ethnicity, race, language, age, lifestyle, physical and mental ability/disability, and religion, defines the person. Having an awareness and appreciation of one's own unique characteristics is the basis for accepting others. The teacher who is self-accepting is better equipped to understand and to deal appropriately with diversity in the classroom.

The socialization experiences that shape gender identity also shape our value system and attitudes toward others. All of these attitudes and values about self and others will have an impact on how teachers handle diversity in their classrooms and on the implementation of nonsexist, multicultural instruction. Depending on their backgrounds (including religious, political, and socioeconomic factors), they may find that their value systems are either vastly different from, partially aligned with, or very closely aligned with the values implicit in nonsexist education. Teachers need to reexamine their values in order to recognize whether there are conflicts between them and those espoused by nonsexist, culturally inclusive education, and to deal reflectively with any areas of dissonance.

Active engagement in discovering for oneself that sex bias exists in textbooks and in classroom interactions is also necessary for change to occur. Tucker's (1989) research revealed that even though teachers in his study knew about the research on "teacher talk"—that is, that more takes place with boys than with girls—and stereotypic portrayals of males and females in reading books, they needed to find this out for themselves by analyzing their own classrooms and textbooks. Tucker concluded that teachers must go through the process of discovery of sex bias in their schoolroom before they can take real action for change.

Reflective Exercise: "Teacher Talk" with Students

This exercise is intended for college students who are preservice or in-service teachers enrolled in teacher education courses (undergraduate or graduate).

In-service teachers will study their interactions with students in their own classrooms; preservice teachers could do this exercise during a field placement prior to student teaching or during student teaching. If this is not possible, the preservice teacher would benefit by simply observing a seasoned teacher's verbal interactions with children. Be sure to obtain the teacher's approval before doing a formal observation (i.e., tallying each observed interaction).

The purpose of this exercise is to determine whether your verbal interactions with both girls and boys are roughly equal and to help you identify potentially biased teaching behaviors. There are several ways of gathering data about your interactions with children in your classroom (or in your cooperating teacher's classroom). Have a peer count the number of times you interact with boys and with girls or set up a videotape or an audiotape to record your interactions. This is a good opportunity to collaborate with another teacher or student teacher by observing in each other's classrooms or by helping with the recording equipment. Each observation period should last from 30 to 40 minutes. The observer marks each time you make a comment to a student, whether it is a direction, a correction, a question, an answer, praise, a reward, a remark about behavior, and so on. Do not count the times when you speak to the whole class. If you are using an audio- or videotape to assess your "teacher talk" with students, mark each interaction with each sex just as an observer would have. Tally all the verbal interactions with each sex and divide each total by the number of girls and boys in the class. For example, in a class with 10 boys and 12 girls, if a teacher has 64 interactions with the boys and 37 interactions with the girls in a 30-minute observation period, the teacher is giving boys over 50% more attention ("teacher talk") than the girls (64/10 = 6.4 interactions per boy; 37/12 = 3.1 interactions per girl) (Sadker & Sadker, 1982).

Reflect on the results of your observation. What insights about your verbal interactions with students have you gained? Is your "teacher talk" distributed more fairly than that of the imaginary teacher in the example given above? Although that example is fictitious, it reflects numerous research findings indicating that boys receive the most teacher attention (Sadker & Sadker, 1982).

You may wish to follow up this exercise by using similar observational techniques that are fine-tuned to yield more specific information about your teaching behaviors. You could, for example, model your observation categories on those developed by Sadker and Sadker (1982) that distinguish between: teacher interactions that criticize and those that praise students; praise or criticism that relates to academic comments and that which relates to non-academic comments; questions that are either low level (memorization) and those that are high level (evaluation and application); and academic interventions that facilitate independent student learning and those that short-circuit it.

Cultural Diversity

Educators and the general public have been showered with information from popular and academic presses concerning demographers' projections about the "browning" of U.S. society and of its schools. Projections about the school-age population indicate that, by the year 2010, 38% of all students will be students of color. Along with this growing diversity in the student population, an unfortunate decline in the already small percentage of teachers of color in the public schools is occurring (Carnegie Forum on Education and the Economy, 1986; Hodgkinson, 1989, 1990). The need for teachers of color is greater now than ever before in order to accurately reflect the social reality of an increasingly multicultural society and to provide role modeling for students of color.

Meeting the needs of students of color is reaching the crisis point in urban public schools, where there are high dropout and suspension rates and low teacher expectations. Efforts are underway in a number of U.S. cities where students of color already are the majority to develop African-American immersion schools or special programs in public schools to meet the needs of African-American males. For example, in September 1990, the school board of Milwaukee voted to create two new schools specifically for black boys (Daley, 1990, p. B-8). In an analysis of this development, Walteen Truely (1991) writes:

> Often absent from this discussion, or parenthetical to it, is discussion of the educational needs of African American girls and the potential impact of these programs on them. . . . African American girls are also tragically underserved by urban public school systems. . . . Conclusions that girls are better off in the school system because of the presence of female role models in the classroom ignore the social class, ethnic, racial and power differences between African American girls and their teachers, even when those teachers are predominantly female. (p. 4)

This effort to establish public schools solely for African-American boys is a clear example of the lack of concern for and the invisibility of female students of color in school systems. It reinforces the truism that women and girls of color are in double jeopardy in U.S. society because of their race and sex and that racism and sexism are linked (in spite of their different histories) as forms of oppression that support the white, patriarchal system. Thus, in an exploration of sex equity in education, racism needs to be examined as a concomitant obstacle that female students of color must overcome in order to attain their aspirations. Butler (1993) suggests:

> Teaching about women of color should result in conveying information about a group of people largely invisible in our curricula in a way that encourages students to seek further knowledge and ultimately begin to correct and reorder the flawed perception of the world based on racism, sexism, classism, and ethnocentrism. (pp. 163–164)

By analyzing the well-known and markedly different socialization patterns, historical experiences, and statuses of women of color and Anglo women, one can begin to understand the complexities of attaining sex equity in a white, androcentric school system.

Unfortunately, in our pluralistic society, there is a "dread of difference" that becomes a barrier blocking access to the strengths and resources available from other people who are different from oneself. Not only are ignorance and poor interpersonal communication the result of this dread and avoidance of difference, but they are also significant taproots of sexism, racism, and homophobia. Nonsexist education, like multicultural and multiethnic education, is based on a celebration of diversity. It is aligned with a belief that education must reflect the diversity in our pluralistic society. To implement nonsexist, culturally inclusive education successfully, teachers need to understand and reflectively handle the contradictions that result from our U.S. ideal of equality and the sexist and racist practices that they will encounter in school and in the larger community. Also, teachers need to look inward to examine their own self-identity in relation to issues of diversity and to recognize that one's values and attitudes—which might be at odds with the values and philosophy of nonsexist, culturally inclusive education—strongly influence behavior toward others who are different from ourselves.

Expectations as Self-Fulfilling Prophecies

Differential treatment of students for whom teachers hold low expectations is likely to have a negative effect on their learning and behavior. Since the publication of Rosenthal and Jacobson's landmark work on teacher expectations in 1968, well over 100 studies have been conducted on the topic (McCormick & Noriega, 1986). Educational researchers have examined the degree to which teacher expectations seem to affect students, and they have debated the implications of this for classroom practice and teacher education. Dolores Grayson (1987), the developer of the Gender/Ethnic Expectations and Student Achievement program, writes:

> "*Effort*" *statements* are *used* more frequently *with males*, than with females. (i.e., "Carlos, if you tried harder in this class, you could do it. You just need to *put forth more effort!*) With females, the emphasis is frequently on whether or not they have exerted any effort at all. (i.e., Maria, you had trouble with this homework, didn't you? Well, you *tried!*) In the example, Carlos is given the message that he has the ability, but is not using it. Maria is given the message that she doesn't have the work, because she doesn't have the ability. The message is that less is expected and accepted. (p. 4)

In a study of Mexican-American students, it was found that they experienced more interaction with teachers than Anglo students in only two ways: being criticized and receiving directions. The Anglo students experienced more interactions with teachers in all of the positive categories (U.S. Commission on Civil Rights, 1973).

Reflective Exercise: Differential Teacher–Student Interactions

Reflect on the educational implications of lower teacher expectations for female students as well as Mexican-American and other students of color. Why do you think the teacher expected less of Maria? Could there be a connection between the type of teacher interaction cited in the study (criticizing and giving directions) and the high dropout rate for Mexican-American students? What other effects might there be?

Those who are concerned about educational equity have an acute awareness of the harmful effect of low expectations on the academic and social attainment of females and students of color. When they feel that teachers have low expectations of them, students of color and female students are more likely to become passive spectators (or drop out) rather than to be active participants in the process of their education.

Does this mean that teachers should hold the same expectations for all students—males and females, Anglos and students of color, those who are proficient in English and those whose English is limited, those who are able-bodied and those who are physically challenged? Should we not consider the students' own motives, their likes and dislikes? A critical element in understanding teacher expectations of student performance is that they affect the ways that teachers treat students. Differential treatment of students is appropriate when it is based on their genuine individual needs (e.g., José needs to learn to add and subtract before he can learn multiplication; therefore, the teacher does not expect him to use multiplication just because most of the children in the class are doing so) or on their interests or talents (e.g., Anna, who is artistically gifted, is given the option of presenting her project on Mayan influences on mathematics either as a written report or as a painted mural). However, the effects of differential treatment are harmful and inappropriate in cases where teachers' decisions are based mainly on the student's ascribed characteristics (e.g., sex, skin color, body type) rather than on an accurate assessment of the student's academic or social needs.

A case that illustrates the effects of both low and high teacher expectations on students' achievement occurred in the 1980s at Garfield High School in Los Angeles. Low teacher expectations for the Hispanic students were producing record numbers of failures and dropouts. A complete turnaround in their achievement and attendance came about when a new math teacher, Jaime Escalante, treated the students differently: He provided a challenging learning environment and held high and rigorous expectations for them. Their high scores on the A.P. Math (Calculus) test were challenged by the Educational Testing Service (ETS), with the implication that they had cheated (i.e., Hispanic students were not expected to be able to make such high scores in calculus). They took the test again under the scrutiny of ETS personnel and came away with the same high scores. This story was dramatized in the film *Stand and Deliver*, which is now available as a videotape. A caveat is in order for preservice teachers who are considering using this film with prospective students: You should preview *Stand and Deliver*—a good practice with any instructional media—before showing it to your students. For the in-service teacher: Consider whether or not you think Escalante's tactics are appropriate for replication in your classroom (e.g., critics think that some of his methods are too harsh). The teacher educator might want to use *Stand and Deliver* as a springboard for small-group discussion of expectations as self-fulfilling prophecies in the classroom.

Gender and Achievement/Attainment

Differential teacher expectations and interactions with female and male students help explain why gifted girls are less likely to exhibit commitment to careers, even though they make better grades than boys, and why the self-esteem of college women in mixed-sex schools declines throughout their academic careers. These disparities in educational achievement patterns are especially disquieting in view of the data indicating that girls start out academically ahead of boys and generally receive better grades throughout their schooling than boys do (American Association of University Women, 1992; Maccoby & Jacklin, 1974).

In addition to understanding the power of teacher expectations and self-fulfilling prophecies on the achievement of female students, teachers need to recognize the "double bind" that females are enmeshed in because of their socialization. Bell (1988) describes the reality of most girls' experience:

> One aspect of this bind is that girls are caught between feminine sex role expectations and achievement norms for which boys, not girls, are socialized. When measured by this male standard, girls are found deficient in many areas considered important to high achievement motivation. This framing of the problem leads to solutions that require girls to adopt the achievement behaviors characteristic of a male sex role stereotype. (p. 1)

Girls are caught in a very real conflict between female-centered values and a competitive and individualistic school culture that violates those values. Adding insult to injury, the problem of girls' lesser achievement is often attributed to their "deficiency." Bell (1988) argues, and I agree, that the "deficiency" of girls is not the problem, "but that schools fail to respect and support the different values girls bring to school. . . . The solution lies in changing school culture rather than female behavior" (p. 2).

The previous discussion indicates that the causes and sources of differential educational achievement between female and male students are complex and diverse. By being aware of the kinds of problems discussed above and reflecting on different ways to handle them, teachers take the first steps toward creating more equitable classrooms. They realize that nonsexist education nurtures the development of the feminine aspect—which has traditionally been devalued—in all students; thus male students as well as female students will reap benefits.

Reflective Exercise: Creating an Equitable Climate

This exercise is intended for college students and for preservice and in-service teachers. Changing school culture to be more equitable and supportive of female students requires that teachers attend to a number of problem areas that have been shown to influence interaction patterns and achievement. Think about what you would want to do in your classroom to create an equitable environment. Then reflect on the problems listed below and write some suggestions for ways to avoid these situations in teaching your own students.

> 1. *Discipline/classroom control:* "Quantitatively and qualitatively, *Black, Hispanic or Latino, and low socioeconomic white males receive the most negative types of discipline.* . . . Studies have shown that *even when males and females are misbehaving equally, the males are more likely to get harsher reprimands.*" (Grayson, 1987, p. 3)
> 2. *Self-concept:* "Studies indicate that both males and females are taught that being male is inherently better than being female. . . . The *messages* children receive *about* their *gender, race, class, etc.* greatly *influence how they perceive their own worth* and *how others perceive them.*" (Grayson, 1987, p. 3)
> 3. *Evaluation of performance:* "Generally, *males* are *given feedback* directly *related to the task,* content or thought process involved. More often than not, *females* are *given feedback related to* the *appearance* of their work." (Grayson, 1987, p. 4)

Research Activity: Teacher Interviews on Equity Issues

This exercise is intended for college students and preservice teachers. Try to generate more ideas for dealing with the three equity problems listed above.

Interview several in-service teachers and find out their perceptions of these and other equity problems in their schools. Do you think that these teachers effectively challenge inequitable practices, situations, and behaviors? What would you do if you were in their positions?

Classroom Climate

Creating a classroom climate that is equally supportive of learning for both sexes and students of color is exciting and challenging. The excitement comes from realizing that when daily choices are made for nonsexist, culturally inclusive education, you are part of a larger movement intent on making education more equitable for all students. The most common sex inequalities of society found in the classroom "are sex segregation, male dominance, and interpersonal interactions designed to subtly reinforce sex differences and sex stereotyping" (Lockheed & Klein, 1985, p. 189). These sex inequalities may be present in either the formal curriculum or the "hidden curriculum," which, in turn, influences the teacher's instruction and the classroom climate. According to Gollnick and Chinn (1994), "the hidden curriculum includes the norms and values that undergird the formal curriculum. . . . It includes the organizational structures of the classroom and school as well as the interactions of students and teachers" (p. 312). See Chapter 5 for a discussion of evaluating the "hidden curriculum."

An example of overt bias in the formal curriculum is when a teacher uses curriculum materials that show only male role models of leadership without any critical discussion of the absence of females as leaders. A hidden curriculum aspect of sex bias that affects the classroom climate might be the unwritten rules in the school about "appropriate" discipline and punishment for males and females or different racial groups. Other aspects of the hidden curriculum are the teacher's nonverbal messages conveyed through body language and eye contact and the verbal messages delivered through the actual content of lessons, units, and/or courses. How does the individualistic competition that dominates most classrooms function as a hidden curriculum element that could impede students' achievement? Think about other aspects of the hidden curriculum that determine whether the classroom climate is equitable or not. What could you do to defuse those hidden aspects of the curriculum? (See Ginsburg and Clift [1990] for a penetrating analysis of the hidden curriculum of preservice teacher education.)

Learning Style

Another construct to examine for its effect on equity and classroom climate is learning style, which describes the student's characteristic pattern or strategy for acquiring and processing information. "It is the composite of characteristic cognitive, affective, and physiological behaviors that serve as relatively stable indicators of how a learner perceives, interacts with, and responds to the learning environment" (Keefe & Languis, 1983, p. 1), according to the National Task Force on Learning Style and Brain Behavior. Learning style is independent of ability to learn or intelligence (Witkin, Moore, Goodenough, & Cox, 1977), but it is an important equity issue for teachers to understand since it helps them design instructional strategies to fit diverse students' learning modalities (Bennett, 1990).

Learning style is an equity issue because current teaching methods and determinants of school success are fine-tuned to benefit students with an analytical learning style (Cohen, 1968)—mostly white males. They are not, however, as responsive to the varied learning styles and intellectual modes of females (Belenky, Clinchy, Goldberger, & Tarule, 1986; Gilligan, 1982; Noddings, 1984), students of color (Decker, 1983; Gollnick & Chinn, 1994), students of non-Anglo ethnicities (Longstreet, 1978), and those with nonverbal, global learning modalities (Sperry, 1973).

Some students process information by using an analytic approach that is linked to the idea of field independence, while others demonstrate a global/relational orientation that is related to field dependence (Kagan, Moss, & Sigel, 1963). Strengths of the field-independent student are the verbal and mathematical/logical intelligences associated with left-brain functions, while strengths of field-dependent student lie in the nonverbal and global intelligences of the right brain. In Betty Edwards's (1989) *Drawing on the Right Side of the Brain*, Chapter 3 is devoted to left- and right-brain research and provides an excellent comparison of the characteristics of the left-mode and right-mode. Field-independent students seem to be more at ease with independent activities and impersonal abstractions, whereas field-dependent students are more receptive to group work and close personal interactions.

Research on field independence–dependence as a dimension of learning style is extensive and dates back to the psychological research done in the late 1940s on people's distinctive perceptual characteristics. Herman Witkin was the first researcher who extended "the study of psychological sex differences into the area of human perception" (Haaken, 1988, p. 312). Observing that people vary greatly in their abilities to differentiate objects from their backgrounds, Witkin and his associates studied the extent to which an individual's perception of an item is influenced by the context (field) in which it appears (Guild & Garger, 1985). Bennett (1990) says that diagnosis of field independence–dependence is now determined by use of a simple embedded-figures test (in contrast to the original procedure, in which the subject was placed in a dark room and asked to place a luminous rod that was suspended within a tilted frame into a vertical position). Bennett (1990) continues:

> If we visualize people along a continuum from extreme field dependence to extreme field independence, we find that people at the field-dependent end are unable to locate simple figures embedded in the complex pattern. Field-independent people, on the other hand, can quickly separate the simple figure from the background. (p. 143)

A caveat about field independence–dependence. These concepts about learning styles are now widely accepted and their importance in education is recognized; however an analysis and a warning about the history of the development of field independent–dependent constructs are crucial to a discussion of sex equity and classroom climate. Feminist concerns about the constructs center on these points:

- The social conditions that make them so pervasive now
- The social milieu during the time that the constructs gained acceptance in psychological research
- The political implications of the constructs
- The assumptions underlying the naming of the constructs
- The use of the constructs to determine school success or failure

Haaken (1988) conducted an in-depth case study of Witkin's 30-year research record that helps illuminate these concerns. She reports that field dependence, although not appearing in the literature until 1954, was valued positively in the early research of Witkin and his coinvestigator, Solomon Asch (1948). However, following World War II, Wilkin changed the focus of his work to personality factors in perception and gender, and this is when field dependence began to be viewed negatively in relation to field independence. Haaken (1988) argues:

> Witkin's conception of field independence had specific political implications. Field independence was presented as the higher form of development, indicating higher levels of differentiation between self and environment. Independence represented a reliance on "internal frames of reference" and a concomitant freedom from environmental influence. Field-dependent people, in contrast, "tend to be submissive to authority, to require environmental support, to deny inner events—a mechanism of defense especially characteristic of children—to have difficulty in impulse control and to make childish drawings of the human figure. The presence of such characteristics seems to suggest an 'arrest' in progress toward emotional maturity." (p. 325)

Haaken's (1988) critique of Witkin's research places it within the social context of the postwar years. Although during the war women worked in many traditionally male jobs, after it, the "natural" division of labor was to be restored, along with the belief in "natural" sex differences and emphasis on the "domestic mystique" (p. 316). Haaken believes that the results of Witkin's research "provided a scientific rationale for the exclusion of women from industrial jobs after the war because perceptual abilities are closely related to technical job skills" (pp. 316–317), even though he probably did not condone this social application of his work on field dependence.

Haaken (1988) continues: "The social assumptions that were embedded in Witkin's research are also evident in the naming of the phenomenon. In a society that valued independence and individual autonomy, field dependence had negative connotations" (p. 318). Finally, she suggests that "Witkin over-interpreted his findings in a direction that was consistent with prevailing stereotypes of women during a postwar shift in ideas about essential differences between the sexes" (p. 318).

The purpose of analyzing learning style constructs is not to throw them out or to devalue using knowledge about them for improving instruction—many studies (e.g., Dunn, Beaudry, & Klavas, 1989, and Ramirez & Castaneda, 1974) have been conducted since Witkin's work that are very useful. Rather, the purpose of the analysis is to reinforce the idea that all research and researchers (no matter how impeccable their credentials) are embedded in the social and historical contexts and constraints of the times in which they exist; there is no "pure" scientific research when human subjects are involved. For example Witkin was influenced by prevailing stereotypes of women and work and by the government sources (military-related programs) that funded his research. Their program policies "encouraged quantitative, clinically based research and refinement of assessment tools. . . . The emphasis on testing and measurement gave psychology greater scientific and social legitimacy as a part of the effort to prepare the armed forces for the defense of American interests abroad" (Haaken, 1988, p. 319).

A major theme of this book is that contemporary education functions to maintain a system that supports and perpetuates sexism (as well as racism). One way that oppression is maintained relates to the learning style that predominates in classrooms, that is, the field-independent mode that primarily favors white males. School success is awarded to the student with an analytical, cognitive learning style, one who is individualistic, independent, competitive, and able to engage in highly abstract, analytical, linear, and logical thinking.

We must ask, as Witkin did not, "What social conditions make the continued dichotomy between independence–dependence in mode of learning so prevalent?" and "Why does the reward system in schools favor the field-independent cognitive learner rather than the field-dependent affective learner?" Studies by Gilligan (1982) and Noddings (1984) suggest that relational styles of problem solving may be preferred by some males and by numerous females. Using alternative teaching styles and honoring various learning styles, including the field-dependent, relational mode, strengthens the field-dependent aspect in both males and females, in students of color as well as in Anglo students. These are important efforts because of past practices that skewed success in favor of the field-independent learner.

Belenky and colleagues (1986) believe that females and males differ in their ways of knowing and challenge current individualistic approaches to teaching and learning that encourage "separateness" as being less appropriate for females who prefer "connectedness" and cooperation. Below is a discussion of two approaches—cooperative learning and intuitive learning—that provide alternatives to traditional competitive instruction.

ALTERNATIVE INSTRUCTIONAL APPROACHES

Cooperative learning and intuitive learning are not panaceas, but they are alternatives to behavioristic/reinforcement, objective-driven instruction that favors the field-independent student with a left-brain mode of information processing. Also, and of major importance for our discussion here, these approaches address the needs of students whose mode of information processing is nonverbal, global, and relational.

Cooperative Learning

The strength and intrinsic quality of cooperative learning is that by teaching content to a peer, the student becomes more engaged in the learning process, learns the material more effectively, takes more responsibility for individual and group learning, and develops interpersonal and intergroup skills that are usually restrained in traditional competitive learning environments. Nearly 20 years of research on cooperative learning strongly suggests that it encourages higher academic achievement and more prosocial interactions among students than does individualistic/competitive learning (Bell, 1988; R. T. Johnson & D. W. Johnson, 1989/1990; Prescott, 1989/1990; Slavin, 1989). Specifically, Johnson & Johnson (1981) found that cooperative learning in small groups helped reduce sex and race inequities in the learning environment.

In *The Nature of Prejudice*, Gordon Allport (1954) explained his contact theory of interracial relations in this way: If people of different races are to develop positive interpersonal relations, they need to be engaged in frequent cooperative activities as equal partners. When each member of the group contributes importantly to the task at hand to achieve an agreed-upon goal, the people learn to respect and like one another. Allport's theory also reminds educators that simply providing unstructured contact between diverse groups does not improve intergroup relations. Contact must be carefully structured for students' attitudes to change toward a different racial group.

Lee Little Soldier (1989), in advocating the use of cooperative learning methods to reach Native American students and to increase cross-racial acceptance, writes:

The potential benefits of cooperative learning for Native American students are clear. Cooperative learning appears to improve student achievement, and it also matches such traditional Indian values and behaviors as respect for the individual, development of an internal locus of control, cooperation, sharing, and harmony. Cooperative learning can improve the attitudes of students toward themselves, toward others, and toward school. (p. 163)

The cooperative learning movement has helped raise teachers' awareness—in a time of perceived conflict between equity and excellence in education—of the significant social consequences of learning that are frequently ignored in traditional classroom instruction. Curriculum and instruction in schools are structured according to a Eurocentric and competitive model with values and reward systems that are founded on the traditional male version of knowledge and way of knowing. To restructure curriculum and instruction with structured and well-monitored cooperative learning methods would help redress the present imbalance and appeal more to the need for relationships and interconnection voiced by many students of color and female students. This is not to say that white male students will not benefit from cooperative learning activities. Ideally, they would benefit by having the opportunity to exercise their feminine traits (e.g., care, feelings, and emotions), which, for the most part, are devalued by society. On the other hand, cooperative learning activities offer female students the opportunity to exercise their female "voice" and to integrate elements of the male "voice," such as decisiveness, leadership, and objectivity. However, few schools operate under ideal conditions. Some research studies indicate that cooperative learning may not be a positive strategy for girls because of social dominance by males in any size or type of group (Lockheed & Harris, 1984) and because of the dominance of male communication patterns (Lakoff, 1976). Some researchers are still debating important issues surrounding the purposes and theoretical frameworks of cooperative learning (Noddings, 1989; Sapon-Shevin, 1991), and others call for more research into cross-gender learning (Lee & Bryk, 1986; Thorne & Luria, 1986). To overcome these and other barriers to success for female students, Scott (1985, cited in Grant [1991]) suggests:

that teachers use small, mixed-sex groups more frequently, monitor and remediate problems, demonstrate a strong commitment to mixed gender work groups, and teach directly about the restrictions of sex stereotyping and different gender communication patterns. Scott and others believe that without intentional teacher behaviors such as these, equitable relationships and interactions may not be fostered in cooperative learning environments. (p. 307)

While problems still exist in relation to sex equity and cooperative learning, there are a wide array of approaches that have been used and evaluated.

These approaches differ in some ways, yet all have the goal of bringing students together to work in structured small groups to help one another learn academic material or acquire social skills. Slavin's work (1991) emphasizes the importance of group goals and intergroup competition between teams, rewards, and individual accountability. The goal of the group task is to learn something (academic material) rather than to do something. While including some of the same elements as Slavin's work, R. T. Johnson and D. W. Johnson's research (1989/1990) places more emphasis on the acquisition of social skills in small groups and engaging students in cooperative work on a single problem or assignment. Their approach to cooperative learning does not include intergroup competition between teams; in fact, D. W. Johnson (1982) has voiced concern about team competition functioning to elevate "the destructive aspects of competition from an interpersonal to an intergroup level" (p. 147).

Classroom Activity: Learning Cooperatively About the Contributions of Women in the U.S.

This classroom activity is intended for use in the upper elementary grades (grades 4–6) by preservice teachers. In-service teachers may adapt this activity for upper elementary, middle school (grades 7–9), or high school students.

Step 1: Individuals in small groups: Number off, 1 to 12; then form small "home" groups of 6 members. Students in each "home" group collaborate in researching the contributions of the following women:

a. Margaret Chase Smith	g. Eleanor Roosevelt
b. Sally K. Ride	h. Rita Moreno
c. Katherine D. Ortega	i. Rosa Parks
d. Harriet Ross Tubman	j. Helen Keller
e. Margaret Sanger	k. Sacajawea
f. Geraldine Ferraro	l. Susan B. Anthony

Step 2: Individuals in expanded groups: Each individual focuses on only one woman in order to gain more knowledge in an expanded group to take back to her "home" group, in which she becomes the "expert" on that contributor. In the expanded group, all number 1s from the different "home" groups get together and focus only on "a" above (Margaret Chase Smith); all number 2s, on "b" above (Sally K. Ride); and so on, through "f" (Geraldine Ferraro). The following day, the focus will be on "g" (Eleanor Roosevelt) through "l" (Susan B. Anthony). Within the expanded group, each person shares and discusses information gleaned from the "home" group collaborative research and, of course, learns new information from other group members on the assigned woman.

Step 3: Cooperative exchange: Each individual returns to the original "home" group of 6 members as an "expert"—explaining and discussing his new knowledge and insight about the life, nuances of character, and contributions of the woman who was assigned for study with the expanded group. This cooperative exchange expands both the individual's and the group's knowledge and understanding of women's lives and contributions to U.S. history and culture.

Step 4: Large-group closure: After repeating the cycle as indicated above ("g" through "1") on the following day, the total class evaluates the knowledge gained about the twelve women contributors and generates a new list (with the teacher's help) of women to research later in the month. The class is encouraged to reflect on the process of working together in the small "home" group and in the expanded group. What were the benefits of sharing the research duties in the small group? Did all members do their share? How did it feel to be an "expert"?

Intuitive Learning

Recall our earlier discussion of field independence and analytical thinking and their strong linkage to success in most schools. Usually, school systems do not recognize that this is a "hidden" form of discrimination against students who have a field-dependent learning style. Strength in the left-brain functions of verbal and mathematical intelligence mark the field-independent student who is rewarded over the field-dependent student whose strength is the right-brain functions that are global and nonverbal. Roger Sperry (1973), a pioneer in brain research, believes that both science and our educational system neglect the nonverbal form of intellect and actually discriminate against those in whom the right brain is dominant.

Rationale for intuition in education. The examination of intuition in education for its affinity to the mode of learning of field-dependent students as well as for expanding the learning horizons of field-independent learners is a fertile area to explore in the context of nonsexist education. Edwards (1989) argues that most educational systems neglect half of the brain of every student, because these systems have "been designed to cultivate the verbal, rational, on-time left hemisphere" (p. 36). She describes the right-hemisphere mode as "the intuitive, subjective, relational, holistic, time-free mode" (p. 36). These descriptors are similarly used to describe the field-dependent learning style. Edwards continues: "This [right-hemisphere] is also the disdained, weak, left-handed mode which in our culture has been generally ignored" (p. 36). Intuition, being a function of the right-hemisphere mode, has also been ignored or treated "contemptuously as a catchall for any process not easily described as logical or linear" by some educators (Noddings & Shore, 1984, p. 2). In agreement with Edwards, the noted psychologist Jerome Bruner (1960/1977) says: "Unfortunately, the formalism of school learning has somehow devalued intuition" (p. 58). Bruner builds a rationale for intuition in education: "The complementary nature of intuitive and analytic thinking should . . . be recognized. Through intuitive thinking the individual may often arrive at solutions to problems which he would not achieve at all, or at best more slowly, through analytic thinking" (p. 58). He also argues for the importance of establishing "an intuitive understanding of materials before we expose our students to more traditional and formal methods of deduction and proof" (p. 59). Noddings and Shore (1984) contend that "by ignoring intuition and regarding it as an unimportant part of learning, educators avoid a process that has been credited with producing some of the most important advances in the sciences and one that has contributed immeasurably to the arts and humanities" (p. 2).

What is intuition? Intuition is a way of knowing that is parallel with the intellect. Illustrating this point, Edwards (1989) says, "The history of science is replete with anecdotes about researchers who try repeatedly to figure out a problem and then have a dream in which the answer presents itself as a metaphor intuitively comprehended by the scientist" (p. 34). It is a function of right-hemisphere processing of information that does not rely on logic and linear reasoning to solve problems. It is "the ah-ha! response" (Edwards, 1989, p. 35), a flash of insight, a gut feeling that something is right (or not right). Bruner (1960/1977) adds to our understanding by saying:

> Intuitive thinking, the training of hunches, is a much-neglected and essential feature of productive thinking not only in formal academic disciplines but also in everyday life. The shrewd guess, the fertile hypothesis, the courageous leap to a tentative conclusion—these are the most valuable coin of the thinker at work. (p. 14)

How does intuitive thinking work? Intuitive thinking does not proceed in the same measured, stepwise fashion that characterizes analytic thinking. Rather, "it tends to involve maneuvers based seemingly on an implicit perception of the total problem. The thinker arrives at an answer, . . . with little if any awareness of the process by which he reached it" (Bruner, 1960/1977, p. 58). Although intuitive thinkers may not be aware of the exact aspect of the problem they were unscrambling, Bruner (1960/1977) says, "usually intuitive thinking rests on familiarity with the domain of knowledge involved and with its structure, which makes it possible for the thinker to leap about, skipping steps and employing short cuts . . ." (p. 58). The intuitive thinker immediately apprehends or grasps the significance, the meaning, or the structure of a problem without using formal strategies of analysis and proof (Bruner, 1960/1977).

Curriculum, instruction, and intuition. Noddings and Shore (1984) describe the application of intuition in the curriculum in this way:

> An intuitive arrangement or presentation of subject matter is one that takes into account the functioning of intuition, of an intuitive faculty. It does not begin with well-defined objectives for the student. . . . Rather it provides setting, background, multiple paths barely to clearly discernible. (pp. 116–117)

Their exposition of the intuitive in education charges contemporary curricula with two major errors: "dictatorial prespecification of learning objectives, together with bland and uniform instruction to achieve them" and the "emphasis on the general, cognitive, and rational over the concrete, affective, and nonrational" (p. 129).

In intuitive learning arrangements, feeling, emotion, and the senses are critical filters that the learner uses in attaining meaning and understanding. An element that is commonly used in intuitive arrangements is metaphor. Noddings and Shore (1984) write: "The idea here is to focus the attention of the student on particular conceptual operations and roles in a familiar domain and then move to a domain of new objects in which moves and roles are sufficiently alike to preserve critical operations and identities" (p. 118). Intuitive learning arrangements also use concrete examples. It does not matter, according to Noddings and Shore (1984), whether the student moves from concrete cases to generalization or vice versa, for "both moves must be made if understanding is to be attained" (p. 119).

An intuitive approach to teaching and learning functions well in small-group settings in which peer interactions occur. "Awakening the inner eye" in students involves a quest for meaning and understanding that is based on their own logic (i.e., children require a working demonstration of a concept), not the logic of the subject matter or of the computer (Haroutunian-Gordon, 1988). This approach to teaching and learning insists on students making choices, setting their own goals and purposes in order to engage their intuition and enhance "their quest for meaning" (Noddings & Shore, 1984, p. 149).

Bruner (1960/1977) believes that it is very important to establish "an intuitive understanding of materials before we expose our students to more traditional and formal methods of deduction and proof" (p. 59). He specifically states that "the early teaching of science, mathematics, social studies, and literature should be designed to teach these subjects with scrupulous intellectual honesty, but with an emphasis upon the intuitive grasp of ideas and upon the use of these basic ideas" (p. 13).

Conditions and elements that nurture intuitive responses. Bruner (1960/1977) conjectures that there are some predisposing factors that are correlated with individual differences in the use of intuition. He poses the following five questions for reflection:

1. *Is the development of intuitive thinking in students more likely if their teachers think intuitively?* Yes. Teachers who take risks by being willing to reveal their intuitive interpretations to the class encourage such habits in the students. Noddings and Shore (1984) believe that "effective intuitive arrangement and presentation of subject matter depends ultimately on the teacher. . . . The instructor must have a belief in the value of intuitive insights and should also have experienced intuitive processes personally. Above all, a tolerant, encouraging attitude is essential" (pp. 130–131).

2. *Does the structure or connectedness of knowledge increase facility in intuitive thinking?* Yes. Bruner (1977) cites cases of numerous math and physics teachers who emphasize the importance of the students' understanding the structure and order of the disciplines as evidence "that such understanding of structure enables the student, among other things, to increase his effectiveness in dealing intuitively with problems" (p. 63).

3. *What is the effect of teaching so-called heuristic procedures on intuitive thinking?* Consider the following: According to *Webster's New Twentieth Century Dictionary* (1978), *heuristic* means "to discover or learn; specifically, designating a method of education or of computer programming in which the pupil or machine proceeds along empirical lines, using rules of thumb, to find solutions or answers" (p. 856). Bruner's (1960/1977) definition of *heuristic* is "in essence a nonrigorous method of achieving solutions of problems" (p. 63).

In response to the question posed above about heuristic procedures, Bruner (1977) provides an example of a "rule of thumb": Tell students having trouble solving a problem to think of a simpler but similar one; "then use the method for solving the simpler problem as a plan for solving the more complicated problem" (p. 63). He warns of the pitfall of becoming so aware of heuristic rules to make intuitive interpretations that the process is reduced to an analytic one. He writes:

> On the other hand, it is difficult to believe that general heuristic rules—the use of analogy, the appeal to symmetry, the examination of limiting conditions, the visualization of the solution—when they have been used frequently will be anything but a support to intuitive thinking. (p. 64)

4. *Does guessing facilitate the development of intuitive thinking?* Possibly. Bruner (1977) says that although guessing is often penalized in school and

the student who guesses is thought to be slow, there are certain situations in which it is desirable and may facilitate the development of intuitive thinking. For instance, he thinks it is "better for students to guess than to be struck dumb when they cannot immediately give the right answer" (p. 64). Also, he thinks students are at an advantage when they realize that there are alternatives to choose from that fall some where between truth and total silence. Noddings and Shore (1984) warn that, "Students should be made aware from the start that intuition yields knowledge and insight, not immutable truth" (p. 131).

5. *Is effective intuitive thinking fostered by the development of self-confidence and courage in the student?* Yes. Bruner (1984) observes that an intuitive thinker may often obtain the correct solution to a problem but might also be proven wrong when the solution is checked. "Such thinking, therefore, requires a willingness to make honest mistakes in the effort to solve problems. One who is insecure, who lacks confidence in himself, may be unwilling to run such risks" (p. 65).

Classroom strategies that foster intuitive responses. One effective strategy that I observed in an alternative high school (also used in some U.S. hospitals) which nurtures students' intuitive faculties is pet therapy. The teacher said that many students who had been withdrawn, passive, and unmotivated to learn began to "come alive" intellectually and emotionally when they cared for a classroom pet and received its unconditional love in return.

In my multicultural nonsexist education class I use a strategy that is designed to generate affective and intuitive responses from students, focusing on the internment of Japanese-Americans following the bombing of Pearl Harbor. I want the students to learn more than the facts and figures about the internment: I want them to feel as much as possible what it would be like to be ordered to leave home—on short notice, carrying only two duffel bags of belongings to an unknown destination for an unknown period of time—and to be incarcerated behind barbed wire in your own country, when your only offense was being born of Japanese descent with Oriental features. I support Noddings and Shore's (1984) contention that "an intuitive treatment aimed at inducing affective response will have the correlative result of producing more lasting learning of facts, principles, and concepts" (pp. 126–127).

I use a variety of visual images, newspaper clippings, old magazines, and photographs to help the students grasp the meaning of the Japanese-American internment to those whose civil liberties were violated as well as to unaffected citizens. The capstone visual material that helps the students realize that this really happened to approximately 110,000 Japanese-Americans, nearly two-thirds of whom were U.S.-born citizens, is an original videotape that a colleague and I produced, *Our Story: The Japanese American Internment*

(McCormick & McKay, 1989). It is an interview, conducted by three students, with a Japanese-American couple who were incarcerated in 1942, shortly after President Roosevelt signed Executive Order 9066, which required all persons of Japanese ancestry living on the West Coast to be transferred by the U.S. Army to areas deep in the interior of the country. In the video, the couple share their personal experiences of loss, grief, anger, humiliation, and recovery. They also discuss the significance of the restitution measures that were signed into law on August 10, 1988, by President Ronald Reagan, 42 years after the last internment camp closed. The reparations program includes a formal apology from the U.S. government and a $20,000 payment to each victim of the internment. Finally, they remind us to be eternally vigilant in guarding our civil rights by saying: "Incarceration? In our own country? Yes! But may it never happen again."

A third strategy that is used to elicit intuitive responses from students is visualization or guided imagery, a strategy that is widely used among sports trainers to enhance the performance of athletes. This strategy can inspire teachers who are ground down by a bland, objective-driven curriculum and instruction to try a sensory, imaginative approach to teaching—one that respects students' diverse styles of learning and generates intuitive thinking.

Kieran Egan (1992), a professor and writer whose work on imagination earned him the 1991 Grawemeyer Award for Education, skillfully explains the use of visualization as a *teaching* strategy:

> The teacher can encourage students to form mental images of whatever is the subject of a lesson, concentrate on the images, elaborate them or move them, and then turn to writing or experimenting or whatever is the appropriate activity. This kind of visualization has found favour in the use of the technique commonly called Guided Imagery. As the name suggests, the images are stimulated by the teacher's descriptions, and the students follow a verbal account that details sights, sounds, tastes, and smells, creating for themselves as vivid images as they can. Students can be encouraged to employ this kind of visualizing on their own to achieve a better grasp on whatever area of knowledge is being dealt with. (p. 61)

Commenting on the successes with the use of visualization in athletic training, Egan (1992) says: "The results in terms of improved performance have encouraged educationalists to import the technique into teacher pre-service and in-service programmes" (p. 62). He believes that visualization overlaps with the capacity that is reported in numerous accounts of mathematicians' and scientists' "breakthroughs," "as evident in cases such as Einstein's where visualizing led to his theories of relativity" (p. 62). Further, Egan warns that visualization should not be seen as a paradigm of imaginative activity, "but to see it as a species of thinking of the possible is obviously sensible" (p. 62).

Reflective Exercise: Thinking of the Possible—My Ideal Classroom

This exercise is designed for college students and preservice or in-service teachers.

The purpose of this visualization is to generate intuitive thinking about your ideal classroom and to stimulate reflection about classroom climate, teacher attitudes, values, and behaviors in working with both sexes and students of diverse racial, ethnic, ability, and social groups. It is intended to evoke visual imagery of yourself in an ideal setting, communicating effectively with all students.

Close your eyes, breathe deeply, and relax. This is an opportunity to let your imagination run free. Imagine an ideal classroom setting. Visualize details of the room as vividly and concretely as possible: the colors, textures, aromas, lines, and shapes in the physical surroundings. Next, picture the students in the age range and grade that you would like to teach. Imagine them going about their school work in an energetic and responsible manner, typical of students of that age and grade. Is there a buzz of excited chatter, occasional laughter, and enthusiasm in the air? Are they exchanging ideas, helping one another as they explore the subject matter and learn about one another? The students represent a "salad bowl" of diverse ethnic, racial, social, language, and ability groups.

Now, place yourself—a recent recipient of your state "Teacher of the Year" award—in the classroom. Evoke an image of the teacher you would like to be in all respects. Imagine yourself as this ideal teacher in your ideal classroom. Notice how easily you work with the students and facilitate learning. Picture yourself interacting with them: The rapport is positive and reciprocal. What are you doing with the students? What kind of nonverbal and verbal messages are you sending? What kind and level of questions are you asking? What is the quality of students' responses to you and to one another? Take plenty of time to move about your ideal classroom.

Continue sitting with your eyes closed and be receptive to the mental pictures, intuitive flashes, and creative ideas that float through your consciousness. Let the images flow; do not allow the analytic mind to "edit" anything out. Learn all you can about yourself teaching a diverse student group in an equitable manner.

Take several deep breaths, slowly open your eyes, stretch, and slowly come to a standing position, wide awake and refreshed. Now, while the imagery and intuitive hunches and ideas are fresh in your mind, write several pages in your journal about your experience as an ideal teacher in your ideal classroom. What did you learn about yourself and your ideals of equitable teaching from this visualization? How did you as the ideal teacher interact with the students? Based upon what you just learned about your ideal self, which of your actual values, attitudes, and behaviors would have to be modified or changed to be more like the ideal nonsexist teacher you just imagined?

Finally, to stimulate your reflection on ways to work with both sexes and with students of color, write responses to the following questions in your journal. To what extent did you as the ideal teacher

- Avoid stereotyping students based on their ascribed characteristics?
- Recognize different learning styles and use appropriate teaching strategies for the different modalities?
- Know the name of each student and what name each preferred to be called in class?
- Treat each student as an individual with unique needs, interests, history, and beliefs?
- Include contributions of diverse groups and women as integral parts of the curriculum?
- Know the traditions, history, and perspectives of the diverse groups in the class?
- Acknowledge the influence of group identification and membership?

SEX STEREOTYPING AND CLASSROOM INSTRUCTION

The common sex-role stereotypes of males and females, as well as their harmful effects on students' self-concept and achievement, were thoroughly explored in Chapter 2, which forms the background for the following discussion, activities, and exercises concerning some ways to counteract sex-stereotyping in classroom instruction.

To maximize students' achievement and growth, the teacher needs to create a learning environment that is free of sex-stereotyping in instructional organization, interactions, materials, and activities. Along with their new book bags, pencils, and notebooks, children come to school armed with well-established sex-role stereotypes about "appropriate" female and male behavior. In addition, they self-segregate according to sex in their play groups, seating, and friendship choices (Lockheed & Klein, 1985).

Sex-segregated classrooms perpetuate sex-role stereotypes. Unfortunately, the voluntary self-segregation of children is rarely counteracted by teacher interventions that would encourage cross-sex interactions. Lockheed and Klein (1985) encourage teachers to refute sex-role stereotypes by presenting a contradictory reality to the children:

Children's stereotypes about substantial differences between the sexes could be reduced by interacting with cross-sex classmates. A highly sex-integrated classroom would provide many opportunities for sex stereotypes to be confronted by contradictory evidence and subsequently minimized. (p. 193)

Strategies for sex-integrated instruction that will confront sex stereotypes with "contradictory evidence" include cross-sex cooperative learning groups, small-group activities (e.g., games, learning centers, and computer stations), and role playing in which helping behavior is rewarded. Following are 10 strategies to help teachers achieve a classroom free of sex stereotypes.

TEACHER STRATEGIES
TO COUNTERACT SEX STEREOTYPES IN K–12 CLASSROOMS

1. Provide leadership opportunities for both sexes.
2. Organize classroom activities that encourage cross-sex cooperation.
3. Avoid sex-segregating practices, such as having academic teams (e.g., Science Fair Team) made up of one sex only or designating parts of the playground or classroom for one sex.
4. Use instructional materials that are nonsexist. If this is not possible, then point out the sex bias in the material; encourage the students to critically examine materials for sex and race stereotypes.
5. Use unbiased visuals and media in instruction to illustrate nonstereotypic roles of males and females.
6. Monitor your own behavior for sex-stereotyped expectations, language, and practices.
7. Analyze all of the content areas for sex- and race-stereotyping.
8. Infuse information about sex-stereotyping and sex equity throughout your instruction.
9. Infuse your instruction in all subjects with accurate information about women of all ethnic, age, ability, and socioeconomic groups and their contributions and perspectives.
10. Examine tests for sex and cultural bias and sex stereotypes. Employ multiple forms of evaluation of students' work.

Classroom Activity: Role Playing—Who's the Leader?

This classroom activity is appropriate for use at the middle school level through college level with preservice teachers. In-service teachers may wish to adapt this for use in their classrooms.

Conduct a role-play exercise in which each student takes turns being the leader (executive) in a scenario such as this: In a bank setting there are two females and two males—two are customers, one is a bank executive, and the fourth is a teller. One customer is angry about an entry on her recent bank statement that she thinks is a mistake. The teller has called the bank executive on the phone for advice. This takes some time, and the second customer is getting very upset about the long wait in line. Role-play this scenario (add a resolution to the conflict situation, if you wish) with the four roles played according to the stereotypes ("males are leaders"; "females are followers"); then switch roles and play the scene again with the assumption that both sexes can be leaders (i.e., without the stereotypes).

Lead a discussion of stereotypic expectations of males and females relative to leadership in this role-play exercise. End the exercise by sharing your feelings and reactions. Generate a list of all the men and women you know who are employed in nontraditional occupations and, later, invite several of them to visit the class and talk about their work experience.

Reflective Exercise: Thinking About Stereotypes

This exercise is intended for college students and preservice or in-service teachers. In-service teachers could adapt these scenarios for use with middle school to high school students.

This exercise is a springboard for reflecting on real-life situations that might occur; in fact, many of these ideas were adapted from newspaper reports. Doing this exercise will put you in touch with your feelings about gender, race, sexual preference, age, and sex roles and can be used to stimulate discussion of the psychological and sociological roots of stereotypes and prejudice.

Each of the following scenarios has a stereotype embedded in it. After identifying the stereotype, respond to the situation by indicating your rating on a scale of 1 to 4, with 1 being "very comfortable" and 4 being "very uncomfortable." Analyze your ratings, and then do the follow-up research activity. There are no right or wrong responses.

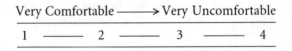

Very Comfortable ———→ Very Uncomfortable

1 ——— 2 ——— 3 ——— 4

1. You are flying to China via a 747 jet. When airborne, a female voice says over the intercom, "Hello, this Mildred Poe, your captain, speaking."
2. It is your week to drive the four neighborhood children and your cousin to child care. Upon arrival, you discover that two of the three child-care aides are males.

3. Your car broke down on the interstate, so you sent for help. The garage sends a 60-year-old female mechanic.
4. A female student with pronounced scars and burns on her neck, face, and hands explains to classmates that she has not yet mastered the art of using electric curling rods and combs.
5. In a newspaper article about a young woman who was wearing shorts and a cut-off T-shirt when she was raped while out jogging, the writer commented, "She was asking for it."
6. Anna and Emilio were good friends in college. After graduating with the same grade-point average and degree, they both went to work for the same insurance firm. They have identical jobs but, unbeknownst to them, Emilio's salary is 10% more than Anna's.
7. Two young children watch an hour of the *Garfield* cartoon show on television on Saturday. During that hour, the children see three times as many male characters as female ones.
8. Katrina works at an advertising agency 40 hours per week and her husband, Klaus, puts in similar hours each week as an insurance salesman. Klaus helps Katrina with the home chores by carrying out the trash and washing dishes.

Research Activity: Follow-Up Thinking About Stereotypes

This activity is intended for college students and for preservice or inservice teachers.

In order to counteract stereotyping, teachers need to understand its roots and to reflect on their own ingrained attitudes and stereotypic thinking about different groups.

In small groups of four people, discuss and analyze your responses to the eight scenarios in the preceding exercise. Is there agreement or disagreement on the stereotype embedded in each one? Have you ever come face to face with such stereotypes? What is the source of your discomfort with specific scenarios? What are some plausible alternatives for various reactions?

As a group, generate responses to the following questions:

1. What are five stereotypes about each gender? about gays and lesbians? about African-American women? about Mexican-American women? about elderly women? about sexually abused women?
2. Is there any rational basis for the stereotypes you identified? If so, justify your position on this issue; if not, explain why.
3. Do you agree or disagree with a person who says that stereotypes correctly provide group norms? Explain your answer.

4. Discuss the statement, "All stereotypes are incorrect and harmful because, by definition, they diminish individuality and diversity."
5. Stereotypes that express favorable attitudes are not harmful. Do you agree or disagree? Give an example.
6. What can be done to eliminate these stereotypes? Would you confront a teacher in the teachers' lounge who was heard expressing a generalization that was not factual about Asian-American girls, African-American girls, or another group?

Do some brainstorming with the group to arrive at several "best possible" actions to take in each of the following settings to eradicate sex-role and racial stereotyping: the home, the school, and the workplace.

NONSEXIST LANGUAGE AND INSTRUCTION

This section focuses on issues and implications of sexist language in classroom interactions between teacher and students and student and student. Some activities for middle school and senior high school classrooms are provided; future teachers or practitioners, however, might benefit by doing the activities in advance. The reflective exercise that follows should provide a starting point for discussion of the widespread, everyday use of sexist language.

Reflective Exercise: Sexist Language Is No Joke

This exercise is intended for college students and preservice or in-service teachers. In-service teachers could adapt it for use with high school students.

What is your reaction to the following phrases:

"The girls in the office"; "I pronounce you man and wife"; "Mary is a foxy chick"; "Meet Dr. Jones and his wife, Susan"; "Jobs Available for Seamstresses and Handymen"; "Women make terrible drivers"; "Women henpeck their husbands"; "Myrtle is an old biddy"; "Married women at hen parties sound like a gaggle of geese"; "All men are created equal"; "This fabric is man-made"; "She is a lady doctor"; "That was a bitchin' movie"; "What do you guys think?" (to a mixed-sex audience); "She's a dried-up old prune"; "Free drinks for skirts, Wednesday night, 10:00 P.M. to midnight"; "Miss Allen and Dan arrived"; "A woman who achieved high marks"; "The average man on the street was surveyed"; "Lady of the house"; " This is a co-ed college"; "So, I see you're babysitting today!" (Comment to a father out for a stroll with his baby); "Log in your man-hours for the week"; "The flood waters spewed out of the manholes!"

How do you feel about these words that are often used to describe or address women: *broad, sweetpea, honey, sugar, baby, buttercup, female, girl, chairman,* or *lady?*

Which of the above examples do you consider to be sexist? Which ones are demeaning or inaccurate? Does the context in which the descriptor is used make a difference? Does sexist language affect people's attitudes and behavior toward others? Common comments and questions about sexist language are: "What's the big deal anyway? There are more important things to worry about, like unequal salaries"; "That's just the way things are"; "Relax—can't you take a joke?" Sexist language is no joke.

Language as Power

Women are disempowered by being equated to food and compared with animals: "A woman is not a person as a chicken is not a bird" (Russian proverb). As the proverb and the following passage illustrate, sexist language hurts:

> Reporting on "The Chickenization of Women," author Anne-Jeanne D'Arcy notes that women are frequently referred to as poultry. Young women are chicks, married women cluck at hen parties. They egg men on. Mothers watch their broods. Child rearing ends with the empty-nest syndrome. Husbands at home are henpecked by their wives. At sixty, a woman is an old biddy. . . . D'Arcy then asks, "Is it just a coincidence that so many women's wages are chicken feed?" (Women's Center, 1989/1981, p. 1)

Language is a powerful tool that can reflect either the devaluation and trivialization of women or human equality for women and men. Sexist language is not a given in a child's language development; it is *learned*. Language is a mirror of social attitudes, values, and models of human behavior and relations. Sexist language reflects sexism, just as racist language reflect racism. Language not only reflects people's attitudes and values; it also helps shape them. Biased language is not ordained on high, nor is it an inevitable force of nature that is beyond our control. We have a choice in the words we use or do not use.

Those who say that sexist language is "no big deal" may also argue that the English language is innately sexist, so why bother to try to change it. However, the extreme androcentric (i.e., male-as-norm) quality of present-day English did not become systematized until the 1700s. Male-as-norm attitudes were imposed on language users by male usage authorities and grammarians of the eighteenth century. So, the language is *not* innately sexist; it was made that way (Vann, 1990). As Susan Melnick (1977) writes:

Bias is apparent in two major dimensions of linguistic discrimination against women: (a) Male dominance, reflected in general linguistic use, which treats women as objects and appendages, as a subculture of the male; and (b) sex differences in language use, . . . which characterize "women's language" as different (and presumably deficient) from that of men. . . . These stereotyped linguistic habits should be understood as images that tend more to socialize our thinking than to reflect inherent traits of women and men. (p. 61)

Our written and spoken language changes with the times and reflects the social climate of those times. Thus it is neither timeless nor neutral. Defining the way we think, act, and perceive ourselves and others, language has powerful social and psychological effects. Ultimately, language is power to define who we are and power to control our lives.

Teachers have the power to choose the words they use or do not use. These suggestions are intended to raise awareness about sex bias in language and to provide some practical guidelines for practitioners.

TEACHER STRATEGIES TO COUNTERACT SEXIST LANGUAGE

1. Use parallel language when referring to females and males: Say "Ms. Allyn and Mr. Jay," not "Susan and Mr. Jay"; "husband and wife," not "man and wife"; "girls and boys," not "young ladies and boys."
2. Avoid linguistic marking that assumes male-as-norm, such as a teacher referring to a principal as a "lady principal." Instead, say "Maria Martinez, the principal."
3. Grant equal respect to males and females: Say "Bobby is a good student and Susan is a good student," not "Bobby is handsome and Susan is a good student"; "Elio is a top executive and Maria is an attorney," not "Elio is a top executive and his wife is charming."
4. Talk about qualities of the person, not about qualities of the sex: Say "Lu Liu achieved high marks," not "a Chinese boy achieved high marks."
5. Use titles for jobs that imply that they are for females as well as for males: Say "supervisor" instead of "foreman"; "work-hours" rather than "man-hours"; "police officer" instead of "policeman"; "chairperson" instead of "chairman."
6. Avoid using the so-called generic male pronouns to refer to women and girls.

Sexist language patterns can be *unlearned* with awareness and sensitivity training that clarifies how sexist language distorts reality and puts women down; for example, if you think male pronouns really do refer to both sexes and women are just being "testy" to object to that usage, try using only female pronouns to refer to all students (boys and girls) in the next class that you teach. You will see, I think, that the male students do not think you are referring to them, nor do they think it is funny. Sexist language patterns can also be unlearned by participating in experiences that are specifically designed to reduce the use of biased language in classroom interactions as well as by exposure to role models who use sex-fair and inclusive language.

The following activities are designed for middle school through college students to help raise awareness about bias in language and ways to encourage sex-fair language.

Classroom Activity: Rewriting Everyday Language

This exercise is intended for middle school through college students and for preservice teachers.

In the right column, write an alternative to the sexist word in the left column. The new word should be sex-inclusive.

SEXIST WORDS	ALTERNATIVE WORDS
Aviatrix	
Airman	
Cavemen	
City fathers	
Girls (in reference to adult females)	
Libbers	
Mankind	
Manpower	
Little old lady	
Repairman	
Spinster, old maid	
The wife	
Office girl	

Follow-up: Discuss the implication and effect of the words in the left column. Why are the words considered sexist? Explain to a friend why you chose the alternative word and be prepared to discuss in class.

Classroom Activity: Newspaper Analysis

This exercise is intended for middle school through college students and for preservice teachers.

Conduct a five-day analysis of your local or school newspaper for sexist language. Look at the news stories, editorials, photographs, cartoons, and advertisements. Record your findings (specific instances of sexist language) on a form that includes: (1) the name of the newspaper, city and state; (2) the date; (3) the sexist language example listed under one of these categories: news story, photo caption, cartoon, advertisement, editorial; (4) the day's total number of sexist examples; and (5) the week's total number of sexist examples under each category. At the end of five days, tally the totals from each day to obtain the weekly total of sexist language examples in each category. Save some examples for use in the follow-up activity.

Follow-up: Choose five of the most blatantly sexist items from your week's collection and rewrite the item so that it is nonsexist. Make a class bulletin board of the "before" and "after" news items or create a class newspaper that uses sex-fair language.

SUMMARY

In this chapter, issues and strategies of nonsexist instruction were covered. Issues examined were the teacher's self-identity in relation to gender and diversity; cultural diversity and the interrelation between different forms of oppression; the self-fulfilling nature of teacher expectations on student growth and achievement; gender achievement and sex bias; classroom climate and equity considerations; learning style dimensions and implications; stereotyping in instruction; and linguistic bias.

Reflective exercises, research activities, and classroom activities were provided to raise awareness, to extend knowledge about sex-equity concepts and contributions of women and people of color, and to develop skills that enable students and teachers to participate actively in eradicating sexism in their lives and in the classroom.

Review Questions

1. Write a paragraph about your own self-identity (including gender) and discuss the implications of your growing gender awareness for dealing with diversity in the classroom.
2. When/If students self-segregate themselves according to gender, what can you do to create opportunities for them to experience mixed-sex groups?
3. Review the section on teacher expectations as self-fulfilling prophecies. Then recall instances in your school days when such preconceived expectations had a negative effect on your achievement or attainment. Are there situations when expectations functioned positively in your school or personal life?

4. What are some of the "costs" of sex bias and differential treatment for female students? for male students?
5. Discuss aspects of the overt curriculum and the hidden curriculum that can affect classroom climate and sex equity in instruction.
6. What are the general characteristics of field-dependent and field-independent learners? Which learning style is rewarded most often in schools?
7. How do sex stereotypes negatively affect males?

Curriculum Development for Sex Equity and Cultural Inclusion

CHAPTER 4

The feminist challenge to the mainstream curriculum re-visions and rewrites the future in ways that promise or threaten, depending on how one looks at it, the mainstream curriculum in fundamental, and not merely incidental or tangential, ways.

(*Warren, 1989, p. 46*)

Like the previous chapter, this one focuses on practical considerations, but now the focus is on curriculum: How can educators transmit components of nonsexist education (attitudes, knowledge, and skills) to students through the formal or overt curriculum? What can teachers do to transform the curriculum so that it is gender balanced? How can educators infuse sex equity into the structure, content, materials, and strategies of the curriculum? How can the curriculum be changed to promote social action that confronts the problems of sexism and racism and encourages active participation in a democratic society? What are the existing and emerging models of curriculum? This chapter probes these questions and includes a section on student objectives and applications and teacher resources and strategies for infusing equity content into the curriculum in six subject areas.

MODELS OF EDUCATION AND CURRICULUM

As mentioned at the end of Chapter 1, feminist critiques of education reveal three dominant models: male-as-norm (androcentric); equal educational opportunity; and nonsexist, culturally inclusive. These models are discussed separately, but this should not be interpreted to mean that they are discrete alternatives. Rather, when these models of thinking about education and curriculum are identified in practice, they often overlap.

Male-As-Norm Model

This model, both as an ideal and a reality of practice in education and curriculum development, is one in which there is a white, Western, male monopoly of knowledge, skill, and power (Noddings, 1990). Based on an orientation to curriculum that Schubert (1993) refers to as "intellectual traditionalist" (pp. 81–82), this androcentric model has historically dominated education in the United States—and still dominates in many schools. Females and people of color are viewed as deficient and marginal. The assumption of this model is that "outsiders" (i.e., females, students of color, homosexuals, or the physically or mentally challenged) have to mold themselves to fit into the mainstream (androcentric) system of education. In the process of "fitting in" and adapting to the androcentric curriculum, they, of necessity, deny their own social and cultural identity (Lewis, 1989).

The exclusivity of this model of curriculum denies opportunities to females to take courses or participate in programs that are defined along strict gender lines. For example, school girls in New York City, not unrepresentative of the whole country in the early 1970s, could not take classes in metal working or mechanics because there was not "freedom of choice" according to School Board Policy (National Organization of Women, 1972).

In the male-as-norm model, gender is a dominance construct in the sense of MacKinnon's (1987) analysis. She describes gender in terms of power between males and females, with male supremacy and female subordination defining relationships between them. I believe that MacKinnon's construct can be applied to relations between teachers (predominantly women) and administrators (predominantly men) in that males enjoy a clear power and status dominance and that these power inequalities are reflected in the curriculum. In this model, women and people of color (students and teachers) are devalued and disempowered.

Equal Educational Opportunity Model

In this equalitarian model, there is an emphasis on quantitative equality between males and females (and between racial groups) in education. It is epitomized by the equal educational opportunity (EEO) philosophy, curricula, and programs that emphasize sameness for all students and assimilation into the mainstream curriculum. Historically, this politically liberal model grew out of the civil rights and women's rights movements of the 1960s and 1970s, which pushed for equal opportunity in employment and educational and legal equality. The goal of this model, described in terms of equal access, participation, and outcomes, is to adapt the standard androcentric curriculum to the needs of women and people of color but not to change its basic structure or tenets. EEO programs seek to remove barriers, such as policies or social conditions, that impede access to or participation in various activities by specific "protected" groups. They have been federally supported for nearly 25 years.

Curriculum revisions typical of the EEO model include "adding on" courses about women or ethnic groups; including contributions of excluded groups; critiquing and revising teaching materials and texts to eliminate race and sex stereotypes; and changing policy to allow boys and girls to take non-traditional courses. Some schools broaden their knowledge base to include non-Western, multicultural nonsexist content, but the more common assumption is that females and students of color are to be assimilated into standard, androcentric school programs and curricula after equity adjustments have taken place. In her critique of the education profession, Noddings (1990) observes that "most of the work cited in mainstream literature accepts, implicitly or explicitly, the idea of assimilation: Women are just like men; they can and should be equally represented in all the fields men have dominated until now" (p. 416).

A Nonsexist, Culturally Inclusive Model

This emerging model focuses on restructuring the whole of education to create a system that is gender balanced and culturally inclusive. It seeks to integrate principles of equity (e.g., social justice, fairness, and gender and cultural balance) with an ethic of care rather than seeking quantitative equality. While the model's overriding goal is to transform the entire androcentric education system to reflect the perspectives, concerns, values, and contributions of women and diverse groups along with those of men, this chapter chiefly addresses the formal curriculum relative to the model.

Drawing on Carl Grant's (1978) conceptualization of "education that is multicultural," I apply his description to the model for education that is nonsexist and culturally inclusive: "Rather than being one of several kinds of education, it is a different orientation toward the whole education process" (pp. 45–49).

Those who support education that is nonsexist believe that a truly equitable education is not possible within the framework of the male-as-norm model and cannot be fully realized within the EEO model. After 25 years of the EEO model, mounting evidence shows that education still functions to winnow the "haves" from the "have-nots," to perpetuate sexism, racism, and ableism (Klein, 1987; Grant & Sleeter, 1986, 1988; Sadker, Sadker, & Long, 1993; Tetreault & Schmuck, 1985).

Feminists contend that the weakness of the EEO model is that it does not question the basic goals and assumptions of today's education system. The nonsexist, culturally inclusive model supports the continuation of EEO efforts (e.g., hiring more women and people of color and infusing the curriculum with equity content) but goes beyond them to critically examine, challenge, and promote change of the basic orientation, assumptions, curriculum, and structure of androcentric education.

This model envisions a curriculum that includes women and people of color and thereby affirms their lives and experience. The curriculum fits the "experientialist" orientation that, according to Schubert (1993), is rooted in ideas of John Dewey and integrates diverse ideas and groups. It is concerned with

> everyday dilemmas . . . [that] surely relate to today's increased consciousness of persons who are oppressed or silenced because of race, class, gender, health, age, place. . . . The central assumption is that curriculum reform is enhanced by grass roots participation of those who will be affected most directly by the reform. (p. 84)

This emerging curriculum model is rooted in feminist pedagogies that incorporate the multiple voices of women, their experiences, concerns, ethic of care (Gilligan, 1982), and ways of knowing (Belenky, Clinchy, Goldberger, & Tarule, 1986). Conceptually, this curriculum draws on the work of Darling-Hammond (1990), Giroux, J. B. (1989), Laird (1988), Martin, J. R. (1982, 1984, 1985), Noddings (1986, 1990, 1992), Tetreault (1989, 1993), and Warren (1989).

A CURRICULUM FOR SEX EQUITY AND CULTURAL INCLUSION

Warren (1989) believes that "the implementation of feminist pedagogies is central to any feminist curricular transformation project" (p. 50). Elaborating on feminist pedagogy, Warren continues:

> [It] encourages cooperative learning, classroom interactions that are free of gender biases, critical thinking in the classroom, . . . use of examples that grow out of the student's own experiences, recognition of different "learning styles" and "thinking styles" . . . appreciation of diversity and life experiences, and legitimate use of human emotion and experience. (p. 50)

Feminist issues are not just theoretical and political; they have direct relevance to classroom pedagogy. Jeanne Brady Giroux (1989) argues that "feminist theory needs to be critically appropriated and understood as a central concern for creating within schools a political community free of injustice and sexism" (p. 10).

The curriculum for the nonsexist culturally inclusive model presented in the next section is based on the following principles:

- It integrates the concept of gender with race, ethnicity, class, age, and social class (see the Introduction for my rationale).
- It is interdisciplinary.
- It incorporates a reconceptualization of knowledge that shifts from an androcentric perspective to a more holistic one that includes both females and males.
- It recognizes that knowledge is a social construction that must be viewed in a contextual framework.
- It recognizes different learning and thinking styles and is structured to accommodate them.
- It incorporates a variety of instructional strategies that attend to the needs and values of girls and women (see Chapter 3 for more on instructional strategies).
- It takes the "experientialist" orientation to curriculum discussed earlier in this chapter.
- It incorporates feminist perspectives on pedagogy.

Developing a Nonsexist Curriculum That Is Culturally Inclusive

Transforming the curriculum is an ongoing process. As the structure and content of the curriculum are changed to reflect diversity, students are more likely to perceive issues, events, problems, innovations, and trends from the perspective of the opposite sex or a different cultural group. An important goal of curriculum for education that is nonsexist is to enable students to understand significant social issues (such as sexism, racism, homophobia, ageism, and ableism) and their interrelation (Butler, 1993); to make decisions about these persistent problems; and to take individual and group actions to help eradicate them.

The following guidelines for *beginning* to transform the male-as-norm curriculum to one that is gender balanced and multicultural are provided to illustrate how nonsexist, multicultural content can be embedded in the structure of different curricular areas. They are not intended to be followed rigidly, nor are they a "recipe" for a successful sex-equity curriculum.

An *ideal*, fully implemented nonsexist curriculum incorporates feminist pedagogies that draw on students' experiences and enables them to make choices and decisions concerning their own goals, objectives, and actions. Therefore, as you begin the process of curriculum reconstruction, use the following guidelines as "starters" and move toward the ideal of students developing their own purposes and direction for action.

Finally, it is necessary to define the interdisciplinary concepts (of selfhood, cultural/gender adaptation, cultural pluralism, etc.) that form the foundation for a curriculum that is nonsexist and therefore appear repeatedly in the guidelines in the next section. From them, goals in five major areas are developed, and appropriate student objectives are devised in relation to each goal. Briefly stated, the concepts are as follows:

Selfhood: A concept of self-identity derived from early socialization and influenced by one's gender, ethnic group, social class relationships.

Cultural/Gender Adaptation: The ability to retain one's own cultural/gender identity while successfully participating in the mainstream culture.

Cultural/Gender Awareness: Consciousness of cultural and gender similarities and differences; cognizance of one's own culture and gender and that of others.

Cultural/Gender Literacy: Knowledge of the history, contributions, and perspectives of different cultural groups and of both sexes.

Cultural Relativism: Recognition of the worth and role of women and diverse cultural groups, with no implication of the superiority of one group over another.

Gender Sensibility: Receptiveness and responsiveness to the values, beliefs, and perspectives of each gender.

Cultural Pluralism: A characterization of U.S. society as a universal (common) culture with ethnic and cultural subgroups. A view of society as a "salad bowl" rather than a "melting pot." The philosophic basis for education that is nonsexist and multicultural.

Cultural Democracy: The relationship between the ideals of U.S. democracy and the historical and social realities of our pluralistic society.

Individual and Institutional Bias: Inequalities created by institutions (banks, schools, courts, etc.) and individuals that result in discrimination against a microcultural group. The institutional type is usually a result of established practices, or "business as usual," whereas individual bias is usually rooted in low self-esteem and ignorance.

Social Action: Participation in activities to help solve the problems of inequality. Implementation of strategies to help eliminate intergroup conflict. Brings democratic political skills to bear on issues of gender, race, and class inequalities.

GUIDELINES FOR DEVELOPING
A NONSEXIST CURRICULUM

Goal 1: To understand self and others as cultural beings acting within a cultural context.

Selfhood: Identifies self and others as members of several groups by virtue of sex, race, age, ethnicity, language, culture, ability, social class, and religion.

Cultural/Gender Adaptation: Chooses and uses a variety of interaction and learning styles as tools for self-actualization and effective interpersonal and intergroup relations.

Cultural/Gender Awareness: Understands that women and men are both alike and different; distinguishes between the similarities that define individuals as human and the differences that make them unique.

Cultural/Gender Literacy: Applies a nonsexist, multicultural knowledge base to understand individuals, groups, and events.

Cultural Relativism: Demonstrates understanding that cultural and gender differences do not imply cultural or gender deficiency.

Gender Sensibility: Analyzes own feelings and behaviors toward people of a different gender or sexual orientation.

Goal 2: To recognize U.S. (and world) diversity.

Cultural Pluralism:
- Defines the U.S. as a multicultural, multiethnic, multiracial society.
- Analyzes U.S. diversity as a source of vitality, strength, and richness.

Cultural/Gender Literacy:
- Identifies and describes the basic history, demographics, and contributions of one's own identity groups and those of others, including the opposite sex and the major racial, ethnic, and cultural groups in the U.S.
- Recognizes ways that U.S. culture is shaped by experiences, contributions, and perspectives of diverse women and men.
- Knows that all individual groups are distinct but interrelated parts of the U.S. macroculture.

Cultural Democracy:
- Relates cultural pluralism to the democratic identity, ideals, and principles of the U.S.
- Analyzes the relationship between cultural pluralism and the ideals of democracy; recognizes the contradiction between the ideals and realities of U.S. society.

Goal 3: To understand how group membership helps determine values, attitudes, and behaviors.

Cultural/Gender Literacy and Cultural Relativism:
- Compares the positive and negative experiences of females and males of different backgrounds and recognizes similarities and differences between and within genders and cultural groups.
- Recognizes how different experiences can influence males and females and cultural groups to view events, trends, and innovations from various perspectives.
- Identifies current and historical perspectives of gender and cultural groups on issues, events, situations, and developments.
- Traces specific influences of gender and culture on verbal and nonverbal interaction styles.
- Predicts the effect of trends, events, and innovations on gender and cultural groups.
- Demonstrates open-mindedness about the roles, rights, and responsibilities of persons regardless of gender, sexual orientation, race, ethnicity, ability, religion, language, class, or age.

Goal 4: To understand the dynamics of discrimination, bias, prejudice, and stereotyping.

Individual and Institutional Bias:
- Differentiates between individual and institutional sexism, racism, elitism, and ableism and knows how inequity is institutionalized.
- Identifies how prejudice, discrimination, bias, and stereotyping impede interpersonal and intergroup relations.
- Identifies how prejudice, discrimination, bias, and stereotyping impact the aspirations and achievements of individuals and groups.
- Detects beliefs and actions based on prejudice and bias in self, others, and institutions.

Cultural/Gender Sensibility:
- Tests cultural/gender information and generalizations for accuracy; uses accurate information as clues for understanding individual and group behaviors and perspectives.
- Interacts without overgeneralizing (stereotyping) or overcompensating (patronizing).

Cultural Relativism:
- Understands that no individual or group is inherently superior or inferior because of sex, race, culture, class, age, sexual orientation, religion, or language.

Goal 5: To demonstrate skills for effective social action and interaction among gender, racial, culture, ethnic, and ability groups.

Social Action:
- Identifies, describes, or predicts the impact of historical and current events, trends, and innovations on different groups.
- Considers sex equity and multicultural dimensions in problem solving and decision making.
- Reconciles points of view in conflicts arising within and among sex, race, ethnic, socioeconomic, and ability groups.
- Confronts individual and institutional bias, prejudice, and discrimination in school and community.
- Identifies, describes, and practices basic civil rights and responsibilities as defined by the Constitution and legislation.
- Extends own cross-gender and cross-cultural experiences and understandings.
- Resolves interpersonal and intergroup conflicts across sex, cultural, racial, and ability groups.
- Resists impact of stereotypes on self and others in expanding career and economic horizons.
- Demonstrates respect for physical and cultural differences by modeling nonsexist, culturally sensitive language and interaction patterns.

Some general teacher strategies for achieving the goals and objectives in the preceding guidelines are listed below. Special attention should be paid to these, for they address the kinds of teacher behaviors that are required for transforming education from the mainstream male-dominant model to a gender-balanced, multicultural one.

TEACHER STRATEGIES FOR TRANSFORMING THE CURRICULUM

1. Vary instructional strategies to meet the needs of both sexes and of diverse groups of students.
2. Infuse each subject area of the curriculum with nonsexist multicultural content, including the contributions and perspectives of women, people of color, the disabled, and the aged.
3. Provide diverse role models in the classroom, gymnasium, playing field, and other sites and in different field-related occupations.
4. Provide an equitable quantity and quality of attention and questioning to both sexes and diverse groups of students.

5. Review and supplement textbooks, workbooks, computer software, supplementary materials, and media used in all classes and school activities for accurate, balanced, and specific representation of females, people of color, the disabled, and the aged.
6. Provide access to all courses, programs, and activities for students regardless of their race, sex, socioeconomic status, or disability.
7. Assure participation in courses, programs, and activities that are desired by female students, students of color, disabled students, and poor students.
8. Include the accurate cultural origins of music, art, games, dances, inventions, discoveries, literature, and so forth when introducing them in a class or in an extracurricular activity.
9. Monitor self and other faculty members and administrators for familiarity with the requirements of Title IX, Title VI of the Civil Rights Act, Section 504 of the Vocational Rehabilitation Act, and P.L. 94-142.
10. Use nonsexist, unbiased, nonderogatory language in the classroom, the gymnasium, locker room, playing field, on field trips, and at performance and exhibition sites.
11. Provide a nonsexist, culturally inclusive instruction and learning climate through teacher example, expectation, and support; through classroom materials, media, software, and bulletin boards; through integrated instructional groupings and task assignments; and through varied teaching strategies and evaluation methods.
12. Use direct and indirect methods to reduce computer, science, and mathematics anxiety, avoidance, or indifference among female students and students of color.
13. Infuse instruction with unbiased career information that includes the status of females, people of color, and the disabled in each field of study.
14. Vary methods of teaching concepts, skills, and problem solving to meet the needs of diverse students, to develop interpersonal and intergroup interaction skills, and to provide practice in citizenship and social action.
15. Monitor placements of students at community training sites to discourage rigid sex-role vocational stereotyping and to widen job opportunities and options for all students.
16. Interact with counselors, psychologists, curriculum committee members, administrators, school board members, parents, and other teachers about the goals and content of nonsexist, culturally inclusive curriculum.

CLASSROOM APPLICATIONS

The guidelines for classroom applications in the six different content areas
that follow are not intended to serve as a complete curriculum guide, since
the examples do not cover everything that should be infused into the curriculum. Students' interests will help give form and direction to the curriculum.
These strategies and applications represent some possibilities for exposing
students to basic equity education concepts and competencies, rather than
precise directives about what to teach and how to teach it.

As you begin to implement these ideas, draw on your own knowledge,
skills, and resources. Be guided by your students' intuition and imagination,
by their needs, interests, and life experiences, and involve them in goal setting and selection of materials and activities. Examples of classroom strategies and resources are provided throughout the guidelines for you to use as
points of departure for deciding how to plan and deliver a nonsexist, multicultural curriculum.

The Arts

*Goal 1: To understand self and others as cultural beings acting within a
cultural context.*

ELEMENTARY LEVEL

Objectives: To understand that people are both alike and different; to distinguish between the similarities that define us as human and the differences that make us unique.

Strategy: Help the children explore how similarities and differences, as a natural part of the school and community environment, are reflected in the
artwork of other children in their class. Have a schoolwide exhibit of all
children's artwork. Use student docents to explain the works during the
exhibit to encourage peer interaction, receptivity to others' ideas, and a
broadened understanding of art.

Resources:

Carson, J. (1985). Tell me about your picture. *Instructor, 94,* 40. [Emphasizes
how art lessons can develop students' self-confidence when time is included for talk about their artwork.]

Day, V. (1987). A guided encounter with art. *School Arts, 86,* 26. [Describes
the use of student docents by the Milwaukee Art Museum.]

SECONDARY LEVEL

Objective: To understand the significance of cultural perspective in understanding self and others.

Strategy: Have the students study the various forms of artistic expression of women and cultural groups in the United States; observe and discuss similarities and differences of themes or content and of artistic style, such as use of color, symbols, texture, form, and line.

Resources:

Beckett, W. (1988). *Contemporary women artists.* New York: Universe.

Grigsby, J., Jr. (1977). *Art and ethnics—Background for teaching youth in a pluralistic society.* Dubuque, IA: Brown.

Mid-America Arts Alliance. (1984). *Through the looking glass: Drawings by Elizabeth Layton.* Kansas City, KS: Lowell.

Rozelle, R., Wardlaw, A., & McKenna, M. (Eds.). (1990). *Black art ancestral legacy—The African impulse in African-American art* (catalogue for the exhibit). Dallas, TX: Museum of Art; New York: Abrams.

Tufts, E. (1974). *Our hidden heritage—Five centuries of women artists.* New York: Paddington.

Goal 2: To recognize U.S. (and world) diversity

ELEMENTARY LEVEL

Objective: To define the U.S. as a multicultural, multiethnic, multiracial society.

Strategy: Teach the students to sing songs from different countries and cultures that are reflected in U.S. music.

Resources:

Baker, G. (1985). Teaching strategies for music. *Planning and organizing for multicultural instruction.* Reading, MA: Addison-Wesley.

Blood-Patterson, P. (Ed.). (1988). *Rise up singing.* Bethlehem, PA: Sing Out Corp.

Boette, M. (1971). *Singa hipsy doodle.* Parsons, WV: McClain.

Lloyd, R., & Lloyd, N. (1969). *The American heritage songbook.* New York: American Heritage.

Reck, D. (1977). *Music for the whole earth.* New York: Scribner.

SECONDARY LEVEL

Objective: To define the U.S. as a multicultural, multiethnic, multiracial society.

Strategy: Assign research projects on the origins of musical instruments; plan and present a musical program that demonstrates the many different influences on instruments used today. Choose musical selections that reflect a diversity of composers, including women and members of different cultural groups.

Resources:

Colwell, R. (1969). *The teaching of instrumental music.* New York: Appleton-
    Century-Crofts.
Hughes, L. (1955). *Famous Negro music makers.* New York: Dodd, Mead.
Ritchie, J. (1963). *The dulcimer book.* New York: Oak.
Warren, F., & Warren, L. (1970). *The music of Africa.* Englewood Cliffs, NJ:
    Prentice-Hall.

ELEMENTARY LEVEL

Objective: To relate cultural pluralism to the democratic identity, ideals, and
    principles of the U.S.
Strategy: Research the dance contributions of women and different cultural
    groups and have the children practice the dance(s) of a selected group.
    An example is a West Indies dance called the Limbo. Any number of chil-
    dren can participate, and the only equipment needed is a seven-foot pole,
    music, and a soft mat to dance on (in case someone falls while trying to
    slither backwards under the lowered pole).
Resources:

Eldridge, M. (1985). Points of departure. *Design for Arts in Education, 86,* 20.
    [Explores teaching multicultural awareness through the performing arts.]
Joyce, M. (1980). *First steps in teaching creative dance to children.* Palo Alto,
    CA: Mayfield.
Nelson, E. (1973). *Dancing games for children of all ages.* New York: Sterling.

SECONDARY LEVEL

Objective: To relate cultural pluralism to the democratic identity, ideals, and
    principles of the U.S.
Strategy: Using a theme, such as "With Liberty and Justice for All," let the
    students create a mural that shows the contributions to U.S. society by
    women and people of color as well as white men.
Resources:

Murals in public buildings, such as U.S. Post Offices, government and
university buildings. Many artists were commissioned to create public art-
works during the Great Depression through a federal work program called
the Works Progress Administration (WPA).

**Goal 3: To understand how group membership helps determine values,
attitudes, and behaviors.**

ELEMENTARY LEVEL

Objective: To trace specific influences of gender and culture on verbal and
    nonverbal interaction styles.

Strategies: Have the children read stories, poems, and plays written by and about different gender and cultural groups. Role-play characters in these selections.

Resources:

Tafolla, C. (1992). *Sonnets to human beings and other selected works.* Santa Monica, CA: Lalo Press. [Includes "Selected Works for Children," pp. 155– 163.]

Vargas, M. (1984). Studying nonverbal communication through creative dramatics. *English Journal, 73,* 84.

SECONDARY LEVEL

Objective: To trace specific influences of gender and culture on verbal and nonverbal interaction styles.

Strategies: Have the students analyze plays with themes that reflect different gender and cultural perspectives, such as those by playwrights Amiri Baraka, Lillian Hellman, Eudora Welty, and Carson McCullers. One choice might be the recently produced play *Abundance,* written by a contemporary playwright, Beth Henley. It is a revisionist Western epic that shows history through the eyes of women. Present scenes from the selected plays in a school assembly.

Study the relationship between music and religion among African-Americans.

Resource:

Henderson, C. (1985). The music of black America in arts education. *Design for Arts in Education, 86,* 29.

Goal 4: To understand the dynamics of discrimination, bias, prejudice, and stereotyping.

ELEMENTARY LEVEL

Objective: To understand that neither sex and no cultural group is inherently superior or inferior.

Strategy: In small groups, have students discuss photographs in art magazines of artwork by women of different cultural, age, and ability groups. Explain the historic exclusion of women artists from museums, exhibits, and books.

Resources:

The National Museum of Women in the Arts *News,* 1250 New York Avenue, N.W., Washington, DC 20005-3920; (202)783-5000.

Schuman, J. (1981). *Art from many hands—Multicultural art projects for home and school.* Englewood Cliffs, NJ: Prentice-Hall.

SECONDARY LEVEL

Objective: To understand that neither sex and no cultural group is inherently superior or inferior.

Strategy: Have students analyze an art appreciation textbook for inclusion of artwork by women and people of color. Research the artistic contributions of several of these artists: Elizabeth Layton, Alma Thomas, Frida Kahlo, Helen Frankenthaler, Juanita Martinez, Isabel Bishop, Blanche Lazzell, Georgia O'Keefe, John Biggers, Edward A. Love, and Richmond Barthe.

Resources:

Council on Interracial Books for Children. (1980). *Guidelines for selecting bias-free textbooks and storybooks.* New York: Racism and Sexism Resource Center for Educators.

Rodriguez, F., & Sherman, A. (Eds.). (1983). *Cultural pluralism and the arts.* Lawrence, KS: University Press of Kansas.

Goal 5: To demonstrate skills for effective social action and interaction among gender, racial, ethnic, cultural, and ability groups.

ELEMENTARY LEVEL

Objective: To extend one's own cross-gender and cross-cultural experience and understandings.

Strategies: Help the students learn that all cultural groups have contributed to dance in the United States and that it is an artform through which all people can communicate. Study the life of Isadora Duncan and her contribution to modern free-form dance.

Invite an ethnic or women's dance troup to perform at the school and to conduct dance workshops with the children.

Resource:

Weiner, J., & Lidstone, J. (1969). *Creative movement for children.* New York: Van Nostrand Reinhold.

SECONDARY LEVEL

Objective: To extend one's own cross-gender and cross-cultural experience and understandings.

Strategies: Guide the students in exploring dance as employed in theater arts with its varied cultural and regional influences. Research these groups for their contributions to dance: Dance Theater of Harlem, Martha Graham Dance Company, the Paul Taylor Dance Company, or the Ko-Thi Dance Company.

Arrange for the students to attend a theater performance by an ethnic or women's dance group at a local college or university.

Resource:

Ko-Thi Dance Company, "A Milwaukee Treasure," established in 1969, is the only professional arts organization in Wisconsin dedicated to the preservation, documentation, and promulgation of African, African-American, and Caribbean traditional dance and music. For workshop or performance information, contact Bess Pruitt & Associates, Inc., Artists Management, 819 East 168th St., Bronx, NY 10459; (212)589-0400; FAX (212)617-4551.

Health and Physical Education

Goal 1: To understand self and others as cultural beings acting within a cultural context.

ELEMENTARY LEVEL

Objective: To choose and use a variety of interaction and learning styles as tools for self-actualization and for functioning across genders and cultures.

Strategy: Help the students organize a cooperative game in which there are no winners or losers based on physical abilities, such as the game of "Knots," where the objective is to "untie" a chain of people using physical and verbal cooperation. After the knot is "untied," lead a discussion about the feelings of the students in response to this cooperative game.

Resources:

Michaelis, B., & Michaelis, D. (1977). *Learning through noncompetitive activities and play.* Palo Alto, CA: Education Today Co. ["Knots" is described in this book, pp. 75–76.]

Sandoval, R., & Strick, D. (1977). *Games, games, games—Juegos, juegos, juegos.* Garden City, NY: Doubleday.

SECONDARY LEVEL

Objective: To analyze one's own feelings and behaviors toward those who are different.

Strategy: Have the students conduct interviews with low-income families that are headed by single females regarding health needs, foods, and how nutritional requirements are met on a limited budget. Then plan a week of menus and prepare a shopping list (actual grocery store prices of items needed to prepare the meals) for a low-income family of one adult and two preschool children on a budget of $20.00.

Resources:

Baker, G. (1985). *Planning and organizing multicultural instruction.* Reading, MA: Addison-Wesley. [See pp. 216–227 on foods.]

Mindel, C., & Habenstein, R. (Eds.). (1977). *Ethnic families in America—Patterns and variations.* New York: Elsevier.

Goal 2: To recognize U.S. (and world) diversity.

ELEMENTARY LEVEL

Objective: To understand ways that U.S. culture is shaped by the contributions, experiences, and viewpoints of diverse groups and women.

Strategy: Help the children research the ethnic, religious, or other influences on clothing worn by some cultural groups in the U.S. For example, some women from India who are now U.S. citizens still wear the traditional dress called a sari. If possible, get an Indian-American woman to come to class and demonstrate how to wrap a sari. Then get large pieces of fabric for the children to use for dressing up in their own saris.

Resources:

Community members with an Indian heritage.

Singer, M., & Spyrou, M. (1989). *Textile arts: Multicultural traditions.* Radnor, PA: Chilton.

Pitt, V. (1967). *Let's find out about clothes.* New York: Franklin Watts.

SECONDARY LEVEL

Objective: To understand ways that U.S. culture is shaped by the contributions, experiences, and viewpoints of diverse groups and women.

Strategy: Assist the students in analyzing the family living styles of various ethnic groups as well as the different family patterns across the U.S., then help them assess possible effects of these factors on future health care of women, children, and the elderly.

Resources:

Baum, C., Hyman, P., & Michel, S. (1977). *The Jewish woman in America.* New York: New American Library.

Takaki, R. (1994). *From different shores—Perspectives on race and ethnicity in America* (2nd ed.). New York: Oxford University Press. [See Part IV, "Gender," pp. 161–223.]

Willie, C. (1976). *A new look at black families.* Bayside, NY: General Hall.

Goal 3: To understand how group membership helps determine values, attitudes, and behaviors.

ELEMENTARY LEVEL

Objective: To predict the effect of trends, events, and innovations on women and people of color.

Strategy: Assign research projects on different forms of health care, including the perspective that modern concepts of health care are culturally conditioned. Discuss folk medicine, remedies, and practices (e.g., midwifery) that still affect the health of women and different ethnic and cultural groups in the U.S.

Resources:

Doane, N. (1980–1985). *Indian doctor book—Nature's method of curing and preventing disease according to the Indians.* Charlotte, NC: Aerial Photography Services.

Thiederman, S. (1986). Ethnocentrism: A barrier to effective health care. *Nurse Practitioner, 10*(8), 52–59.

Wiggington, E. (Ed.). (1972—ongoing). *Foxfire* (series). Garden City, NY: Doubleday/Anchor.

SECONDARY LEVEL

Objective: To predict the effect of trends, events, and innovations on women and people of color.

Strategies: In small groups, have the students discuss the effect of Title IX and P.L. 94-142 on physical education and athletic programs.

Assign students to monitor local newspaper coverage of the participation in sports events of males, females, the disabled, and students of color.

Resources:

Griffen, P. (1983). *Fair play in the gym: Race and sex equity in physical education.* Amherst, MA: University of Massachusetts Press.

Uhlir, A. (1987). *Physical educators for equity.* Washington, DC: Women's Educational Equity Act Program, U.S. Department of Education.

Goal 4: To understand the dynamics of discrimination, bias, prejudice, and stereotyping.

ELEMENTARY LEVEL

Objective: To identify how prejudice, discrimination, bias, and stereotyping impact the aspirations and achievements of women and diverse groups.

Strategy: After the students have collected jokes and cartoons about athletes and sports, have the class evaluate them for stereotypes, inaccuracies, and omissions and lead a discussion of the results relative to race, sex, age, and disability in sports and athletics. Study outstanding women athletes of color, such as Wilma Rudolph (the first U.S. woman to win three Olympic gold medals) and others (e.g., Althea Gibson, Alice Coachman, Vivian Stringer, Wyomia Tyus, and Leslie Allen) who overcame great odds to excel in their sports.

Resources:

Hine, D. (Ed.). (1993). *Black women in America: An historical encyclopedia.* Carlson.

Spenser, C., & Sams-Wood, J. (Eds.). (1984). Black women—Achievement against the odds (catalogue for the exhibit). Washington, DC: Smithsonian Institute.

SECONDARY LEVEL

Objective: To integrate sex, race, abilities, and culture as part of a positive, realistic identity for self and others.

Strategy: Research the availability and quality of health care and social services for disabled, elderly, ethnic, and low-income women in the community.

Resources:

Orque, B., Bloch, B., & Monrroy, L. (1982). *Ethnic nursing care: A multicultural approach.* St. Louis: Mosby.

Ulin, R. (1982). *Teaching and learning about aging.* Washington, D.C.: National Education Association.

Goal 5: To demonstrate skills for effective social action across sex, racial, ethnic, cultural, and ability groups.

ELEMENTARY LEVEL

Objective: To confront individual and institutional bias, prejudice, and discrimination in school and society.

Strategy: Have the children collect a file of advertisements for health care products and services. Evaluate them for fair inclusion of females, people of color, the elderly, and the disabled in illustrations, language, and content. Redesign the ads in class, then write letters to the product advertisers suggesting changes where bias is found.

Resource:

Media Watch, 1803 Mission St., Suite 7, Santa Cruz, CA 95060. (408)423-6355. (A watchdog group that monitors media advertising industry for bias; contact person, Ann Simonton.)

SECONDARY LEVEL

Objective: To confront individual and institutional bias, prejudice, and discrimination in school and society.

Strategy: Write to publishers of physical education textbooks to criticize or praise the exclusion/inclusion of females, the disabled, and people of color.

Resource:

Council on Interracial Books for Children. (1988). *Guidelines for selecting bias-free textbooks and storybooks.* New York: Racism and Sexism Resource Center for Educators.

Language Arts

Goal 1: To understand self and others as cultural beings acting within a cultural context.

ELEMENTARY LEVEL

Objective: To integrate sex, race, abilities, and culture as part of a positive, realistic identity for self and others.

Strategy: Encourage the students to collect rhymes and sayings that they know and use. For example, they can recite rhymes used for counting. Explore other forms of children's folklore (e.g., jump-rope jingles) and language games unique to a cultural group, such as the ritual African-American verbal game, "Playing the Dozens." Make a class folklore book using the contributions of all children in the class.

Resources:

Shepard, M., &. Shepard, R. (1975). *Vegetable soup activities.* New York: Citation.

Worstell, E. (1972). *Jump the rope jingles.* New York: First Collier Books.

SECONDARY LEVEL

Objective: To integrate sex, race, abilities, and culture as part of a positive, realistic identity for self and others.

Strategies: Engage the students in a study of the oldest form of literature—poetry. Study its history and forms among different cultural groups and among women. Read and discuss examples of different types of poetry (lyric, narrative, and dramatic). Focus on the narrative poems of a specific ethnic group or of individual women poets in the U.S. (such as those by African-American poet Phillis Wheatley) or on the dramatic poetry of a Mexican-American poet (such as Carmen Tafolla).

Introduce a unit on "Poetry as Protest" and focus on women poets from 1960 to the present such as Sylvia Plath, Anne Sexton, Karen Swenson, and Adrienne Rich. Compare their poetry with that of nineteenth-century poets, such as Margaret Fuller and Emily Dickinson, and early to mid-twentieth century poets, such as Amy Lowell, Hilda Doolittle, and Marianne Moore. Students try to determine which poets were/are feminists.

Resources:

Baker, G. (1983). *Planning and organizing for multicultural instruction.* Reading, MA: Addison-Wesley. [See Chapter 8, Generalizations and teaching strategies for language arts, pp. 147–171.]

Morgan, R. (1970). *Sisterhood is powerful.* New York: Vintage Books. [See Chapter V, The hand that cradles the rock: Protest and revolt-poetry as protest, pp. 557–574.]

Goal 2: To recognize U.S. (and world) diversity.

Objective: To analyze U.S. diversity as a source of vitality, richness, and strength.

Strategy: Guide the children in an exploration of oral storytelling traditions of a specific ethnic group of women, such as Native American Indians, Mexican Americans, or African-Americans. If possible, invite a local woman to share stories with the class. Also, invite grandparents to visit the class to tell "old-time" stories. Using the language experience approach, have the children make up their own stories and tape-record them. Or you can transcribe them as they are told.

Resources:

Allen, P. (Ed.). (1989). *Spider women's granddaughters: Traditional tales and contemporary writing by Native American women.* New York: Fawcett Columbine.

Association of Black Storytelling, P.O. Box 11484, Baltimore, MD 21239. Contacts: Mary Carter Smith or Linda Goss.

Chase, R. (Ed.). (1948). *Grandfather tales.* Boston: Houghton Mifflin.

Miles, M. (1971). *Annie and the old one.* Boston: Little, Brown.

Neuenschwander, J. (1976). *Oral history as a teaching approach.* Washington, DC: National Education Association.

Ralph, J. (1971). (Adaptation). *Rabbit and coyote—A Mexican folk tale.* New York: Macmillan.

Objective: To analyze U.S. diversity as a source of vitality, richness, and strength.

Strategy: Initiate a study of the literary traditions, folklore, and the oral arts (storytelling and singing) from a particular region of the country. Trace the contributions of women to these regional forms of expression. For example, examine the work of the Appalachian folklorists Jean Ritchie and Betty Smith. Have a panel of Appalachian "experts" (students) lead a discussion on the important beliefs, values, and practices that are embodied in Appalachian folklore.

Resources:

Chase, R. (Collector & Editor). (1971). *Jack tales.* Boston: Houghton Mifflin. (Original work published 1943)

Williamson, J. (Ed.). (1977). *An Appalachian symposium.* Boone, NC: Appalachian State University Press. [See Ritchie, J., Living is collecting—Growing up in a southern Appalachian "folk" family, pp. 188–198; and Smith, B., The gap in oral tradition, pp. 199–205.]

Goal 3: To understand how group membership helps determine values, attitudes, and behaviors.

ELEMENTARY LEVEL

Objective: To demonstrate open-mindedness about the roles, rights, and responsibilities of persons regardless of sex, race, culture, ethnicity, ability, language, or religion.

Strategy: Use the comics as a resource that depicts real-life situations and the universal language of humor. Organize the students into small groups for these activities. Have the children examine comic strips and tally the sex, race, age, and disability of the characters and record whether the person plays a main or supporting role and the kind of role he or she plays. Have the groups share their results with the whole class. Finally, have each group create an original nonsexist, multicultural comic strip. Then compile all of them into a class "funny paper."

Resource:

Cheney, A. (1984). *Teaching reading skills through the newspaper.* Newark, DE: International Reading Association.

SECONDARY LEVEL

Objective: To demonstrate open-mindedness about the roles, rights, and responsibilities of persons regardless of sex, race, culture, ethnicity, ability, language, or religion.

Strategy: Encourage students to do creative writing on themes such as sisterhood/brotherhood, experiences of acceptance and rejection, cooperation and competition, belonging to groups, and cultural adaptation. Let students edit each other's writing for use of biased language.

Resources:

Allen, P. G. (1992, 1986). *The sacred hoop—Recovering the feminine in American Indian traditions.* Boston: Beacon.

Carlson, R. (1979). *Sparkling words.* Geneva, IL: Paladin House.

Spandel, V., & Stiggins, R. (1990). *Creative writers.* White Plains, NY: Longman.

Goal 4: To understand the dynamics of discrimination, bias, prejudice, and stereotyping.

ELEMENTARY LEVEL

Objective: To test cultural information and generalizations for accuracy; to use accurate information as tentative clues for understanding individual and group behaviors and viewpoints.

Strategy: Have the students select their favorite television program and then analyze the portrayal of characters and their roles for bias and stereotyping. Help the children create their own TV program using puppetry to portray a gender-balanced, multicultural cast of characters who use unbiased language.

Resources:

Lewis, S. (1960). *Fun with kids.* Garden City, NY: Doubleday. [Explores puppetry with children.]

McCaslin, N. (1990). *Creative drama in the classroom.* White Plains, NY: Longman. [Includes sections on creative drama and puppetry.]

SECONDARY LEVEL

Objective: To test cultural information and generalizations for accuracy; to use accurate information as tentative clues for understanding individual and group behaviors and viewpoints.

Strategy: Have the students watch the evening news for a week, track coverage of the issues of poverty and homelessness in the U.S. and record information related to women, children, and people of color. After compiling the week's news notes, have the students conduct further research on the topic, then write a paper that analyzes the accuracy of news reports on the issues.

Resource:

Fletcher, J., & Surlin, S. (1973). *Mass communication instruction in the secondary school.* Urbana, IL: ERIC Clearinghouse on Reading and Communications Skills (ED 157 137).

Goal 5: To demonstrate skills for effective social action and interaction among gender, racial, ethnic, cultural, and ability groups.

ELEMENTARY LEVEL

Objective: To consider nonsexist, multicultural dimensions in problem solving and decision making.

Strategy: Read stories to the children about past and present leaders in the women's rights movement who are representative of different ethnic and cultural groups in the U.S. Role play a discussion between one leader from the past (e.g., Susan B. Anthony) and one contemporary leader (e.g., Shirley Chisholm) about their dreams, concerns, and perceptions related to the social issues of their eras.

Resources:

Calkins, C. (Ed.). (1975). *The story of America* [Chapter 24: Women's role in the making of America, pp. 426–441.] Pleasantville, NY: The Reader's Digest Association.

Schneir, S. (Ed.). (1972). *Feminism: The essential historical writings*. New York: Vintage.

SECONDARY LEVEL

Objective: To analyze U.S. diversity as a source of vitality, richness, and strength.
Strategy: Stimulate the students to analyze literature (e.g., Charlotte Perkins Gilman's *Herland* or Edith Wharton's *The House of Mirth* and *The Age of Innocence*) for social, political, and economic issues of the past that are still concerns to women and people of color today. Brainstorm to discover whether the social conditions of the past (as portrayed in the selected literature) are the same today, have improved, or have regressed. Make two lists on the chalkboard for the students to respond to: (1) What forces in society have limited the improvement of social conditions? and (2) What forces have promoted improvement in social conditions?
Resources:
Candelaria, C. (1980). Six reference works on Mexican-American women: A review essay. *Frontiers, 5*(2), 75–80.
DuBois, E., & Ruiz, V. (Eds.). (1990). *Unequal sisters: A multicultural reader in U.S. women's history*. New York: Routledge.
Walker, A. (1989). *The temple of my familiar*. New York: Pocket Books/Washington Square.

Mathematics

Goal 1: To understand self and others as cultural beings acting within a cultural context.

ELEMENTARY LEVEL

Objective: To distinguish between voluntary and involuntary group membership.
Strategy: Using Venn diagrams, help the students to place themselves on the basis of such attributes and variables as color of eyes, hair, or skin; glasses/no glasses; gender; home language; interests; and skills. Analyze which characteristics are changeable (voluntary) and which are fixed (involuntary).
Resources:
EQUALS Project. Lawrence Hall of Science, University of California at Berkeley, Berkeley, CA 94720; (415)642-1823.
Strauss, S. (1988, October). Girls in the mathematics classroom: What's happening to our best and brightest? *Mathematics Teacher*, 533–537.

SECONDARY LEVEL

Objective: To identify self and others as members of several groups by virtue of sex, race, age, ethnic group, language, culture, and ability.

Strategy: Construct Venn diagrams from such sets of statements as: "Some women are not engineers"; "Some engineers are not women"; "Some engineers are electrical engineers."

Resources:

EQUALS Project. Lawrence Hall of Science, University of California at Berkeley, Berkeley, CA 94720; (415)642-1823.

Hart, L. (1989). Classroom processes, sex of student, and confidence in learning mathematics. *Journal for Research in Mathematics Education, 20*(3), 242–260.

Willoughby, S. (1990). *Mathematics education for a changing world.* Alexandria, VA: Association for Supervision and Curriculum Development. [See Chapter 4, Problem solving, pp. 37–59.]

Goal 2: To recognize U.S. (and world) diversity.

ELEMENTARY LEVEL

Objective: To know that all individual groups are distinct but interrelated parts of the U.S. macroculture.

Strategy: Using tessellating shapes, the children will contribute to a multicolored design such as a quilt or mosaic. Compare the design to U.S. society—each person and group is unique and identifiable and contributes to the character of the whole.

Resources:

EQUALS Project. Lawrence Hall of Science, University of California at Berkeley, Berkeley, CA 94720; (415)642-1823.

Hannon, A. (1988, January). Should math be multicultural? *Mathematics in School,* pp. 28–30.

SECONDARY LEVEL

Objective: To identify and describe the basic history, demographics, and contributions of his or her own identity group and those of others, including the opposite sex and the major racial, ethnic, and cultural groups in the U.S.

Strategy: Facilitate the students' creation of a "Trivial Pursuit" board or card or computer game based on biographies of women, people of color, and the disabled in mathematics and related fields. Try to elicit some examples from the U.S. and from your state.

Resources:

Perl, T. (1978). *Math equals—Biographies of women mathematicians + related activities.* Menlo Park, CA: Addison-Wesley.

Zaslavsky, C. (1991). Multicultural mathematics education for the middle grades. *The Arithmetic Teacher, 38,* 8–13.

Goal 3: To understand how group membership helps determine values, attitudes, and behaviors.

ELEMENTARY LEVEL

Objective: To predict the effect of trends, events, and innovations on women and other diverse groups.

Strategy: On individual "lifelines," have the students estimate the years to be spent in various life activities such as preschool, years in school, paid work, marriage, parenting, and retirement. Help the students analyze the lifelines for group differences, then compare to U.S. demographic data, such as average work-life expectancies of men and women, percentage of women in the labor force, and percentage of full-time homemakers.

Resources:

Campbell, P. B. (1991, June). Girls and math: Enough is known for action. *Women's Educational Equity Act Center Digest,* pp. 1–3.

EQUALS Project. Lawrence Hall of Science, University of California at Berkeley, Berkeley, CA 94720; (415)642-1823.

Fox, L. (1981, January). Mathematically able girls. *The Arithmetic Teacher,* pp. 22–23.

SECONDARY LEVEL

Objective: To recognize how different experiences can influence groups to view events, trends, and innovations from various perspectives.

Strategy: Arrange for the students to interview several adult men and women about their experiences, opinions, attitudes, and behaviors concerning math. Have the students summarize the interviews and draw inferences about whether or not their gender roles influenced their opinions, attitudes, and behaviors.

Resources:

Chavez, A., & Widmer, C. (1982, February). Math anxiety. *Educational Leadership,* pp. 387–388.

Holmes, N. (Ed.). (1991). The road less traveled by girls—Educators seek ways to boost female achievement in math and science. *The School Administrator, 10*(48), 8–19.

Jacobs, J. (1978). *Perspectives on women and mathematics.* Columbus: Ohio
    State University Press.
National Council of Teachers of Mathematics, 9806 Association Drive, Reston,
    VA 22091; (703)620-9840.

Goal 4: To understand the dynamics of discrimination, bias, prejudice, and stereotyping.

ELEMENTARY LEVEL

Objective: To detect beliefs and actions based on prejudice and bias in self,
    others, and institutions.
Strategy: Assess the students' attitudes about math and math-based occupa-
    tions and activities on a questionnaire that probes their experiences (in
    and out of school) and feelings. Let the students compare their experi-
    ences and discuss how they can affect feelings, attitudes, and behaviors.
Resource:
Hall, C., & Hoff, C. (1988, August). Gender differences in mathematical per-
    formance. *Educational Studies in Mathematics,* pp. 395–401.

SECONDARY LEVEL

Objective: To understand how prejudice, discrimination, bias, and stereotyp-
    ing affect the aspirations and achievements of women and people of color.
Strategy: Provide students with problems to solve that teach math skills and
    simultaneously convey information about the participation of females
    and students of color in mathematics. Help students become aware that
    math is a "critical filter" for entry into many occupations, from archi-
    tecture to zoology.
Problem Example: In 1986, 6% of all U.S. engineers were women. There were
    1,749 female engineers. How many male engineers were there? Make a
    graph showing the five occupational areas with the highest average start-
    ing salary offered in 1987. Show the percentage of women entering each
    of those areas.
Resources:
EQUALS Project. (1982). *SPACES: Solving problems of access to careers in engi-
    neering and science.* [Presents 32 classroom activities using mathematics
    and career information to develop problem solving abilities for grades
    4–10.]
EQUALS Project. (1980). *Use EQUALS to promote the participation of women in
    mathematics.* Berkeley, CA: EQUALS Project [Lawrence Hall of Science,
    University of California at Berkeley, Berkeley, CA 94720; (415)642-1823].

[Provides methods and materials for elementary, secondary and pre-service, inservice courses.]

Goal 5: To demonstrate skills for effective social action across gender, racial, ethnic, cultural, and ability groups.

ELEMENTARY LEVEL

Objective: To demonstrate respect for physical and cultural differences by modeling nonsexist, culturally sensitive language and interaction patterns.

Strategy: Have the students listen to or read biographies of women, people of color, and disabled individuals, such as Maria Mitchell, astronomer; Sally Ride, astrophysicist; Elijah McCoy, inventor; Lillian Gilbreth, engineer; Charles Drew, physician; and Kathryn Green, inventor. Enact skits based on real or imaginary incidents in their lives, such as Sally Ride applying to be the first woman in space or Kathryn Green applying for a patent and being denied.

Resources:

Krause, M. (1983). *Multicultural mathematics materials.* Reston, VA: National Council of Teachers of Mathematics.

National Women's History Project, 7738 Bell Road, Windsor, CA 95492-8518; (707)838-6000.

Perl, T. (1978). *Math equals—Biographies of women mathematicians + related activities.* Menlo Park, CA: Addison-Wesley.

SECONDARY LEVEL

Objective: To resolve interpersonal and intergroup conflicts across ethnic, cultural, and gender gaps.

Strategy: Have the students compete in heterogeneous groups to see which one can build the tallest structure (using only paper, tape, scissors, and paper clips) that can be moved intact to a measurement site. Encourage the students to analyze the team process and the relationship of competition to cooperation.

Resources:

EQUALS Project. Lawrence Hall of Science, University of California, Berkeley, Berkeley, CA 94720; (415)642-1823.

Stand and Deliver. [A film of the true story of Jaime Escalante, math teacher at Garfield High School in Los Angeles, and his dedicated work with Hispanic students. Originally produced by L.A. Public Education Television; now available on video.] (Be sure to preview this video to determine its appropriateness for use with your students.)

Science

Goal 1: To understand self and others as cultural beings acting within a cultural context.

ELEMENTARY LEVEL

Objective: To understand that people are both alike and different; to distinguish between the similarities that define us as human and the differences that make us unique.

Strategy: Make a collection of pictures of diverse people for use in the classroom, with both students and the teacher contributing to the collection. Have the students describe physical differences and classify them as "physical" or "acquired"; then make a collage of the pictures.

Resource:

Baker, G. (1983). *Planning and organizing for multicultural instruction.* Reading, MA: Addison-Wesley. [See Chapter 10, Generalizations and teaching strategies for science, pp. 203–227.]

SECONDARY LEVEL

Objective: To understand that people are both alike and different; to distinguish between the similarities that define us as human and the differences that make us unique.

Strategy: Help the students generate definitions of specific physical and mental disabilities. Decide how these differences are similar to and different from race and sex differences.

Resource:

Heward, W., & Cavanaugh, R. (1993). Educational equality for students with disabilities. In J. Banks & C. McGee Banks (Eds.). *Multicultural education—Issues and perspectives* (pp. 239–261). Boston: Allyn & Bacon.

Goal 2: To recognize U.S. (and world) diversity.

ELEMENTARY LEVEL

Objective: To define the U.S. as a multicultural, multiethnic, multiracial society.

Strategy: Have the children read or listen to stories from many cultures about different natural phenomena, such as "How the Camel Got Its Hump," "Thor's Hammer," "Pecos Bill," and "The Loon's Necklace." Trace the origin of popcorn to Native American peoples. Share Indian legends concerning what makes the corn pop. Discuss scientific explanations of why corn pops. Conclude that there are many groups of people in the U.S. with varied myths to explain natural phenomena. Be careful not to characterize myths and legends as silly or superstitious.

Resource:

Tiedt, P., & Tiedt, I. (1990). *Multicultural teaching—A handbook of activities, information, and resources.* Boston: Allyn & Bacon.

SECONDARY LEVEL

Objective: To identify and describe the basic history, demographics, and contributions of one's own identity group (including gender) and that of others, and of the major racial, ethnic, and cultural groups in the U.S.

Strategy: Facilitate the formulation of a science history "question of the day" with content from biographies of people of color, females, and the disabled who have contributed to the sciences (e.g., Rita Levi-Montalcini, a neurobiologist who received the Nobel Prize for her discovery of nerve growth factor, and Barbara McClintock, a research scientist in cytogenetics and a Nobel Prize winner in medicine). Then have the students create a collage, scrapbook, or bulletin board of diverse people working in science-based fields.

Resources:

Alcoze, T. (1993). *Multiculturalism in mathematics, science, and technology: Readings and activities.* Menlo Park, CA: Addison-Wesley.

Gornick, V. (1983). *Women in science: Portraits from a world in transition.* New York: Simon & Schuster.

Herzenberg, C. (1984). *Women scientists from antiquity to present: An index.* Connecticut: Locust Hill Press.

Keller, E. (1983). *A feeling for the organism: The life and work of Barbara McClintock.* San Francisco: W. H. Freeman.

Levi-Montalcini, L. (1988). *In praise of imperfection: My life and work.* New York: Basic Books.

Rossiter, M. (1982). *Woman scientists in America: Struggles and strategies to 1940.* Baltimore: Johns Hopkins University Press.

Goal 3: To understand how group membership helps determine values, attitudes, and behaviors.

ELEMENTARY LEVEL

Objective: To identify current and historical perspectives of women and various groups on situations, issues, and developments.

Strategy: Facilitate an investigation into the reasons that some Asian-Americans and other people of color do not like or cannot digest milk. Initiate a brainstorming session among the students to generate ideas about nutritional alternatives to milk (e.g., soybean products).

Resources:

Catholic Daughters of America. (1971). *Cooking 'round the world and at home.* Morgantown, WV: Author.

Mattson, S. (1987). The need for cultural concepts in nursing curricula. *Journal of Nursing Education, 26*(5), 206–207. [Discusses various cultural beliefs and practices, including dietary considerations, that impact on health.]

SECONDARY LEVEL

Objective: To identify current and historical perspectives of women and various groups on situations, issues, and developments.

Strategies: Involve the students in comparing and contrasting the attitudes of women and various groups toward nature and the environment (e.g., Asian-Americans, Native Americans, Hispanic-Americans, the Amish, Euro-Americans, African-Americans).

Help the students plan and implement an Earth Day event at your school.

Resources:

Going Green. (1990). *World Press Review, 37*(8), 1–76. [Special issue on the environment.]

Ruether, R. (1975). *New woman—New earth.* New York: Seabury. [See Chapter 8, New woman and new earth: Women, ecology, and social revolution, pp. 186–214.]

Warren, K. (1987). Feminism and ecology: Making connections. *Environmental Ethics, 9,* 3–20.

Goal 5: To demonstrate skills for effective social action and interaction across gender, racial, ethnic, culture, and ability groups.

ELEMENTARY LEVEL

Objective: To resist the impact of stereotypes on self and others in order to expand career and economic horizons.

Strategy: Help reduce mechanical and science anxiety of students by setting up "tinkering" stations in the classroom. They will take apart old (simple) appliances and reassemble them. Then have the students write and illustrate instruction manuals for disassembling and reassembling the appliances.

Resources:

Backyard Scientist. An independent science curriculum for ages 4–14. Contact Jane Hoffman, PO Box 16966, Irvine, CA 92713; (714)551-2392.

Sprung, B., Froschl, M., & Campbell, P. (1985). *What will happen if. . . . Young children and the scientific method.* New York: Educational Equity Concepts. [An early childhood curriculum guide for the physical sciences, including equity issues.]

Tobin, K., & Garnett, P. (1987, January). Gender related differences in science activities. *Science Education,* pp. 91–103.

SECONDARY LEVEL

Objective: To identify, describe, or predict the differential effect of historical and current events, trends, and innovations on women and diverse groups.

Strategy: Help the students generate a list of areas in need of scientific research (such as the ideas below), including ones that may be viewed from different perspectives by each sex and by different ethnic groups, social classes, age groups, and the disabled. In heterogeneous groups, rank the listed areas, then attach dollar amounts to each one and defend the group decisions. Speculate on how homogeneous groups might prioritize the list. Analyze whether research money is allocated on a logical basis or on the basis of vested interests.

Example List: Tay-Sachs disease, sickle-cell anemia, global warming, hemophilia, osteoporosis, breast cancer, thalassemia, AIDS, toxic shock syndrome, infant mortality, agriculture, aquaculture, Alzheimer's disease, herbal medicine.

Social Studies

Goal 1: To understand self and others as cultural beings acting within a cultural context.

ELEMENTARY LEVEL

Objective: To analyze one's own feelings and behaviors toward those who are different.

Strategy: Have the students write on topics such as, "If I Were a Girl, I Would . . ."/"If I Were a Boy, I Would . . ." and "If I Were White, I Would . . ."/"If I Were a Person of Color, I Would . . ." Discuss the ways that being male or female and white or a person of color affects what we do and how we are treated. This kind of activity typically reveals gaps in self-esteem and understanding between males and females and between whites and people of color that can help you select activities that increase self-esteem and intergroup understanding, remove limitations, and widen options for all students.

Resources:

Canfield, J., & Wells, H. (1976). *100 ways to enhance self-concept in the class-room.* Englewood Cliffs, NJ: Prentice-Hall.

Chapin, J. (1992). *Elementary social studies—A practical guide.* White Plains, NY: Longman. [Includes information on various cultural groups, problem exploration, and conflict resolution.]

McCormick, T. (1990). The multicultural life of the child. In C. Sunal (Ed.). *Early childhood social studies* (pp. 107–129). Columbus, OH: Merrill.

SECONDARY LEVEL

Objective: To apply a nonsexist, multicultural knowledge base to understand individuals, groups, and events.

Strategy: On U.S. maps, have students trace the movements over the years of their mothers, grandmothers, and great-grandmothers and write or tell brief descriptions of who went where, why they moved, and what they did in each place. The focus in this assignment is more on women's history than on family history. Be sensitive and accommodating to students who are attached to foster mothers, stepmothers, adoptive mothers, or have no mothers. They can be encouraged to choose any adult woman who is significant to them and trace her movements and her maternal ancestors to and within the country.

Resources:

Hilts, L. (1977). *How to find your own roots.* Mattson, IL: Great Lakes Living Press.

National Women's History Project. 7738 Bell Road, Windsor, CA 95492-8518; (707)838-6000.

Goal 2: To recognize U.S. (and world) diversity.

ELEMENTARY LEVEL

Objective: To define the U.S. as a multicultural, multiethnic, multiracial society.

Strategy: Facilitate the building of shoe box dioramas depicting events in the lives of diverse women in the history of the U.S. or in your state. Let the students share their creations by exhibiting them in the school's hallway showcases or library.

Resource:

National Women's History Project. (1993). *Women's history catalog.* 7738 Bell Road, Windsor, CA 95492-8518; (707)838-6000. [Includes outstanding multicultural women's history resources—books, gifts, teaching materials.]

SECONDARY LEVEL

Objective: To analyze the relationship between cultural pluralism and the ideals of democracy; to recognize the contradiction between the ideals and realities of U.S. society.

Strategy: In small cooperative groups, have the students develop a computer game, quiz, card game, or trivia game concerning the status and participation of women, the disabled, and people of color in federal and state governments.

Comparative Questions: In what year did Native American Indians first vote at the national level? What group of citizens were placed in concentration camps during World War II? Which president used a wheelchair? Who was the first woman Supreme Court justice? How many women legislators are there in the U.S. Congress? In what year did women gain the right to vote? To help students draw conclusions, ask some *comparative questions,* such as: In what year did white/black men first vote at the national level? Were black women able to vote when black men won that right? How many men legislators are in the U.S. Congress?

Resources:

Banks, J. (1987). *Teaching strategies for social studies.* Boston: Allyn & Bacon.

McCormick, T., & McKay, J. (1989). (Video with teacher's guide). Our Story: The Japanese American Internment. Ames, IA: Iowa State University Research Foundation. Rental from Iowa State University Media Resource Center, 121 Pearson Hall, Ames, IA 50011. [An interview with a Japanese-American couple who experienced the internment during World War II.]

Goal 3: To understand how group membership helps determine values, attitudes, and behaviors.

ELEMENTARY LEVEL

Objective: To compare the positive and negative experiences of individuals and groups of different backgrounds; to recognize similarities and differences between and within the sexes and various groups.

Strategy: Let the students listen to storytellers—who come to class in costume as different historical women and people of color—relate tales of "their" lives. Then have the students draw pictures or write stories to tell how they would have acted in the story, and why they would or would not have acted differently from the story characters.

Resources:

Gross, S. H. (1987). Women's history for global learning. *Social Education,* *51*(3), 194–198.

Newlon, C. (1972). *Famous Mexican Americans.* New York: Dodd-Mead.
Tan, A. (1991). *The kitchen god's wife.* New York: Putnam. [A fictional characterization of Chinese-American experience with historical flashbacks to China.]

SECONDARY LEVEL

Objective: To identify current and historical perspectives of women and diverse groups on situations, issues, and developments.
Strategy: Involve all class members in creating a press conference, newscast, or TV interview in which they or resource people impersonate famous historical women and people of color and their surmised views on issues of contemporary times. For example, Chief Standing Bear (a Sioux born in 1868) might give his perspectives on present-day groundwater pollution and destruction of the rain forests, while Anne Hutchinson (born 1591; the first female theologian in the United States) would give her views on the objection (still prevalent in many locales) to women serving as pastors and priests.
Resources:
Bailey, J. (1977). *Those meddling women.* Valley Forge, PA: Judson. [See Chapter 1, Prophet in the wilderness—Anne Hutchinson, pp. 13–25.]
Jameson, E. (1988). Toward a multicultural history of women in the western United States. *Signs: Journal of Women in Culture and Society, 13*(4), 761–791.

Goal 4: To understand the dynamics of discrimination, bias, prejudice, and stereotyping.

ELEMENTARY LEVEL

Objective: To identify how prejudice, discrimination, bias, and stereotyping impact the aspirations and achievements of women and diverse groups and impede interpersonal and intergroup relations.
Strategy: Have the children experience methical and deliberate discrimination in the classroom along the lines of the "brown eyes/blue eyes" experiment conducted by the third-grade teacher, Jane Elliot, in Riceville, Iowa, to give students firsthand experience with prejudice. Following the assassination of Martin Luther King, Jr., she methodically discriminated against her all-white students on the basis of their eye color, giving brown-eyed children dominance one day and blue-eyed children dominance the next. Reactions (including academic performance) to both oppression and privilege were dramatic and instructive. After the experiment, have students analyze their feelings, behaviors, attitudes, and

academic performance as both the oppressors and the oppressed. I offer one caveat: Due to the highly charged nature of this activity, teachers should view the following films and carefully plan and think through this experiment before implementing it, since it can, and usually does, bring out very strong emotional responses from students.

Resources:

Eye of the Storm (motion picture). ABC Films. Color. 30 minutes. [Describes Jane Elliot's experiment to teach children about prejudice based on their eye color.]

A Class Divided. [This 60-minute segment of "Frontline" is shown periodically on educational TV channels. Fifteen years after the original experiment on prejudice, Jane Elliot held a reunion with her former third graders to discuss its effect on their lives.]

SECONDARY LEVEL

Objective: To differentiate between individual and institutional sexism, racism, elitism, and ethnocentrism; to understand how inequity is institutionalized.

Strategy: Facilitate an in-depth examination among students about how anti-Semitism led to the Nazi Holocaust. How and where did people learn anti-Semitism before World War II? What about in our present time?

Resources:

Anti-Defamation League of B'nai B'rith, 823 United Nations Plaza, New York, NY 10017.

National Conference of Christians and Jews, 71 Fifth Avenue, Suite 1100, New York, NY 10003.

Quinley, H., & Glock, C. (1983). *Anti-Semitism in America.* New Brunswick, NJ: Transaction.

Wyman, D. (1984). *The abandonment of the Jews: America and the Holocaust, 1941–1945.* New York: Pantheon.

Goal 5: To demonstrate skills for effective social action across gender, racial, ethnic, culture and ability groups.

ELEMENTARY LEVEL

Objective: To reconcile points of view in conflicts arising within and between sex, race, ethnic, and ability groups; to confront individual and institutional bias, prejudice, and discrimination in school.

Strategy: Have the students generate and use rules about sex harassment and name-calling, covering language dealing with sex, race, ethnicity, religion, age, and mental and physical disabilities.

Resources:

Day in the Life of Bonnie Consolo. (Film). 16 minutes, color. Rental from University Film and Video, University of Minnesota, 1313 Fifth Street, S.E., Suite 108, Minneapolis, MN 55414, 1-800-847-8251. [Tells the sensitive story of Bonnie, who was born without arms yet leads a normal and productive life.]

Moulton, J., Robinson, G., & Elias, C. (1978). Sex bias in language use: "Neutral" pronouns that aren't. *American Psychologist, 33,* 1032–1036.

SECONDARY LEVEL

Objective: To identify, describe, and practice basic civil rights and responsibilities as defined by the Constitution and legislation.

Strategy: Guide the students in the use of case studies—of unresolved civil rights problems related to sex, race, ethnicity, and disability—to develop solutions, make decisions based on facts, and predict consequences of decisions. Have the students compare the issues in actual cases, such as the grape workers' strike in 1965, the grape boycott in the 1980s led by Cesar Chavez, and the 1988 demonstration of deaf students at Gallaudet University to protest the appointment of a hearing person as president.

Resources:

Mi Vida: The three worlds of Maria Gutierrez. (Film and video). Available from One West Media, P.O. Box 5766, Santa Fe, NM 87502-5766. [Tells the success story of the daughter of Hispanic migrant farmworkers.]

The Wrath of Grapes. (Video). Produced by the United Farmworkers of America. 15 minutes, color; order from El Taller Grafico, P.O. Box 62, Keene, CA 93531. [Promotes the boycott of table grapes because of pesticide poisoning of the farmworkers.]

SUMMARY

This chapter discussed three approaches to education and curriculum: the male-as-norm model; the equal educational opportunity model; and the nonsexist, culturally inclusive model. The latter model is most appropriate and effective for meeting the goals of education that is nonsexist and multicultural. A guide for beginning to transform the male-as-norm and EEO models to a nonsexist, culturally inclusive one is presented. It provides teacher strategies, resources, and materials; key concepts, goals, and objectives; and some examples of student activities for application in the classroom. Ideas for infusion of nonsexist, multicultural content into six discipline areas are given.

Review Questions

1. What are the similarities and differences between a male-as-norm and an EEO model of curriculum? between an EEO and a nonsexist, culturally inclusive curriculum?
2. With a partner, make a list of two additional nonsexist, multicultural strategies for each of these discipline areas: the arts, health and physical education, language arts, science, mathematics, and social studies.
3. Develop a nonsexist, culturally inclusive lesson plan for your discipline area, including the following:
   A key concept
   A goal
   Student objectives and activities (at least two of each)
   Teacher strategies
   Teacher and student resources and materials
   Evaluation (See Chapter 5)

CHAPTER 5

Ongoing Considerations and Connections

Our Future Is Now

All institutions, not only those specifically designed for the socialization of children, will have as their goal the actualization of our great human potential.... For above all, this ... will be a world where the minds of children—both girls and boys—will no longer be fettered.... They will be taught new myths, epics, and stories in which human beings are good; men are peaceful; and the power of creativity and love ... is the governing principle.

(Eisler, 1987, pp. 202–203)

While the delivery of nonsexist, culturally inclusive instruction is ultimately the teacher's responsibility, others in the school, such as counselors, administrators, psychologists, and librarians play important roles in making the total school environment equitable. Administrators and support staff carry special responsibility for providing an empowering environment where students can fulfill their potential. This kind of learning environment includes unbiased career counseling and materials, equitable school policies, staff development sessions on sex/race equity, ongoing evaluation for sex/race equity in the school, fair testing of students, and unbiased library and curriculum materials. The first part of this chapter focuses on the internal factors that have an impact on equity in the schools, and the second section discusses forces that are external to the school but greatly affect equity in schools. Some examples are homelessness, violence against women and children, sexist media advertising and programming, and sex-role stereotypes of ideal beauty in popular culture. The third section presents an analysis of other movements that overlap in significant ways with the move toward a nonsexist, culturally inclusive curriculum. Last, concluding thoughts about making a new world in which there is hope for a better, more equitable education system are offered for teachers' consideration.

INTERNAL FACTORS THAT AFFECT EQUITY IN SCHOOLS

Empowerment of Students

Is there a climate of respect for gender and ethnic differences in the school? Do teachers, administrators, and staff support people hold high expectations for *all* students? If you answered positively, your school probably would receive high marks for empowering its students to fulfill their full potentials. For example, anyone who is different from the white, middle-class, male norm is not viewed as deviant or "a problem." Nor is that person's voice silenced in the classroom or office. There is a comfortable feeling among people in the school about diversity. They feel that diversity adds richness and expands learning opportunities, that all students have potential that must be nurtured. These feelings and behaviors among educators are likely to be reified in their students, who will fulfill the educators' expectations for them (Rosenthal, 1987).

Basic principles. Creating a climate that is conducive to empowerment of all learners requires educators to examine their own behaviors and practices. According to Wilbur (1989), principles that are basic to an equity climate include:

1. *Inclusive language:* All communication (oral and written) allows each student to positively identify with the intended message. Language usage is nonsexist and nonracist. (See Chapter 3 for a discussion of nonsexist language.)
2. *Accuracy:* Information that is collected, disseminated, and processed is substantiated by verifiable data. The school environment encourages the critical analysis of information and of personal and social beliefs, attitudes, and actions. Distortions of truth or myths are confronted and challenged by pertinent data.
3. *Individuality/variation:* The characteristics that embody the uniqueness of students are expressed in the classroom. Despite perceived role expectations, individuals acknowledge, promote, and value similarities and differences among peers.
4. *Visibility/affirmation:* There is validation of the worth of each individual and group by acknowledging and valuing their needs, experiences, and contributions.
5. *Representation:* Multiple perspectives of events and phenomena are presented throughout the learning process. The diverse needs and interests of individuals and groups are mediated, and alternative views and experiences of individuals and groups are sought.

6. *Integration:* In all parts of the educational program, the diverse needs, experiences, and historical contributions of individuals and groups are "woven into a unified structure" (Wilbur, 1989, p. 2).

Counseling

Reflect on any encounters you may have had with your high school counselor. Were you told things that began with "Well, since most women quit work after a few years to have babies, I would recommend that you . . . "; "Females always are . . ."; "Don't you think you'd be happier doing secretarial work than going into chemistry?" Whether biases and expectations are conveyed openly ("As the research shows, girls just aren't good in math") or more covertly (as in the examples above), career counseling has a significant impact on students' career aspirations. A sex-fair counselor does not impose a double standard for male and female student career aspirations. The counselor must not focus solely on male career development, nor treat women's development as trivial or irrelevant (McCormick, 1990). Counseling theories need to expand to include material on the psychology of women, sex-role stereotypes, sex differences, and norms for acceptable male and female behavior. "Theories must admit that the client doesn't need to adjust—rather the change is needed in society and sex-role expectations" (National Advisory Council on Women's Educational Programs, 1977, p. 7).

The counselor must guard against labeling sex and cultural differences that vary from the white male model as deficient or pathological (McCormick, 1990). A noted author and professor of counseling psychology, Derald Wing Sue, says that counselors need to become more culturally aware of their own biases, values, stereotypes, and assumptions about human behavior. He believes that counselors must examine their world views for cultural blind spots, so that they do not impose their own world view and cultural values on students (Sue, 1981).

School Policies

School handbooks, school board decisions, school rules, regulations, and guidelines—whatever regulatory structures guide the school operation and describe acceptable behavior and expected outcomes for students—must be imbued with equity considerations. If it is a system in which individual worth and dignity are nonnegotiable, the language used in the written policies of the school system will be nonsexist, nonracist, and inclusive of people from different microcultures.

Research Activity: Revisiting High School

This activity is intended for college students and preservice teachers.

Go to your high school principal and ask whether you may take a look at the written policies of the school regarding sex and race bias. Then get permission to visit several classrooms, the library, after-school activities, and so forth to see whether and how the school policies on equity are being practiced. Be prepared to share your findings in class.

Staff Development

The use of staff development to address sex and race discrimination in schools is a common practice. Yet research on the effect of such staff development indicates that it has little impact on enhancing teachers' delivery of an education that is multicultural (Sleeter, 1992).

Should we throw out staff development for race and sex equity because of these findings? Definitely not! We need to take staff development beyond individual awareness of prejudice and conflict (which is the focus of most staff development workshops) to the level of institutional discrimination. One reason we have not succeeded in making schools nonsexist and multicultural is that the focus of staff development has usually been on the *individual* rather than on the school as an organization. Sleeter (1992) says, "Because schools as organizations provide structural contexts that constrain what most teachers believe they can do with multicultural education, we need to focus as much on changing school structures as on educating individuals within schools" (p. 146).

Teachers in Sleeter's (1992) study assessed factors that prevented them from implementing more of what they had learned in staff development sessions, which included a broad range of multicultural topics such as ethnic learning styles, bilingual education, gender equity, and cooperative learning. Even though most of the teachers found the workshop sessions to be "enjoyable," "excellent," and "practical," they identified six existing school structures that they felt were barriers to changing their classroom practices:

1. *Time:* Twenty out of 30 teachers in Sleeter's (1992) study cited lack of time as a key factor that kept them from implementing more multicultural activities. Because of this, the teachers tended simply to add bits and pieces of multiculturalism to what was already happening in the classroom.

2. *Class size:* The teachers felt that they could not provide adequate instruction and individual attention to students in a class of 25 to 30 students, which was typical of the classrooms in the study. Sleeter (1992) notes that

when teachers are given that many children to teach, an underlying assumption (of school administrators and school board members) is that there is enough homogeneity among the children that the teacher can treat them all the same.

3. *Required curriculum:* Teachers felt that the prescribed content of the general education program, which they were required to cover for all students, could not be replaced by something like multicultural education. They felt tied to their textbooks and the standard curriculum because teachers at the next grade level would expect students already to know certain content, and because the districts used standardized testing to monitor students' progress through the curriculum.

4. *Structure of programs:* Differentiated programs (e.g., special education, remedial reading and math classes, bilingual education, English as a second language, and tracking at the secondary level) were a basic part of the structure in the districts, which led to the assignment of each teacher to a "slot" within the structure, such as "Chapter I teacher." The teachers thought of their students, then, in terms of their location in the academic structure, rather than according to their personal characteristics, interests, or strengths.

5. *Disjuncture between school and community:* Teachers who were structurally separated from the minority community (i.e., they did not live in the neighborhood in which they taught) associated pathologies, rather than strengths, with students from the low-income white, African-American, and Latino communities.

6. *Administrative and bureaucratic context:* Having little decision-making authority, little planning time, being told what to teach, and being isolated from one another, most teachers felt unable to change the system (Sleeter, 1992).

According to Nieto (1992), many of these same school structures are responsible for reproducing inequalities and discrimination in education.

Reflective Exercise: Overcoming Structural Barriers to Change

This exercise is intended for college students and for preservice and inservice teachers.

Reexamine the six structures that were identified as barriers to change in Sleeter's (1992) study. Consider them more specifically in relation to the reproduction of sex inequality and discrimination in schools. Reflect on how teachers can overcome the barriers that keep them from changing what they do in their classrooms relative to equity issues. For example, in response to the disjuncture between school and community, teachers could begin a home visit program so that they get to know the child's family, or invite the parents to the school to share something about their culture with the children (such as a family recipe, a craft, or a hobby). During these reciprocal visits, the teachers will begin to see that all the differences of children of color are not pathological and, hopefully, the parents will feel more involved in their children's education.

Evaluation of Total School Program for Equity

Another internal factor that could effect change for sex equity is systematic evaluation of the total school program by those people most closely involved in day-to-day school life and in making school policy: teachers, administrators, counselors, school psychologists, librarians, coaches, supervisors, curriculum coordinators, and school board members. As indicated in the previous section, it is necessary to go beyond educating individuals in school systems about sexism and racism in order to bring about change in schools. The school as an organization, and its various programs, must be evaluated for systemic infusion of nonsexist, culturally inclusive education. In some states, external agencies, such as the state department of education, conduct reviews, evaluations, or "equity audits" of schools for meeting equity standards, but I am proposing that people within the school district who are responsible for making policy, administering programs, and delivering instruction and services to students take responsibility for equity evaluation.

Figure 5.1 portrays the total education program as a system of identifiable structures (e.g., formal curriculum, assessment, and counseling). In the ideal school, all these structures would reflect sex and race equity.

Evaluation of the formal curriculum involves criteria related to curriculum structure, curriculum content, instructional strategies, and instructional materials. Then, there is the informal, hidden curriculum to evaluate. The equity climate of the school and the methodologies used in delivery of content are crucial factors in determining how well students gain nonsexist, culturally inclusive attitudes, knowledge, and skills. All of these elements of curriculum evaluation are considered below.

Evaluation of curriculum structure. Questions are asked that will help teachers, support staff, and administrators assess institutional strengths and weaknesses and make improvements in the educational program. Some criteria to guide your evaluation of structural aspects of the curriculum are as follows:

1. Practices are used that aim to eliminate sex-typed enrollments (80% or more of one sex), racial isolation, or isolation of special education students.

FIGURE 5.1. Program evaluation for nonsexist culturally inclusive education programs

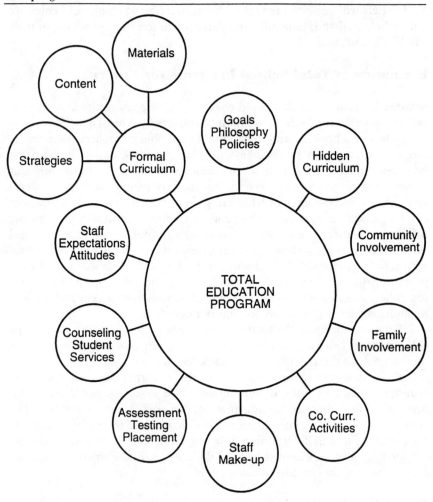

2. Course and program titles and descriptions are accurate, inclusive, up-to-date, and written in sex-fair and culturally sensitive language.
3. School district policies and educational goals consistently affirm non-sexist, culturally sensitive education.
4. Administrators visibly incorporate educational equity criteria into staff and program evaluation procedures.
5. In-service training on integrating nonsexist, multicultural education

concepts and strategies into all curriculum areas is provided for all staff members.

Evaluation of curriculum content. Some criteria for evaluating curriculum content for sex equity are as follows:

1. Nonsexist concepts are visibly integrated into the goals, philosophies, objectives, content, strategies, and evaluation components of course outlines and instructional resource guides in all curriculum areas, K–12.
2. There is content in the curriculum that is intended to cause students to explore the origins and effects of sexism, racism, elitism, and ableism in U.S. society.
3. There is content that helps students recognize gender, culture, disabled, age, and socioeconomic biases in educational and popular media.
4. There is content that helps students explore the ways that bias in language may convey stereotypes about groups based on gender, race, age, culture, ability, and economic status.
5. There is curriculum content that makes students aware of the valuable and unique contributions and perspectives of diverse racial/cultural groups, women, men, and ability groups.

Evaluation of the hidden curriculum. The hidden curriculum is the unwritten and unstated assumptions, values, and norms that drive social relations in the school. Some critics of education observe the hidden curriculum at work in schools that teach students the norms and values that are needed to fit into the work world (e.g., conformity and punctuality) and to become "good" workers (H. A. Giroux, 1988; Spring, 1972).

Evaluating the hidden curriculum (see Figure 5.1) is not as straightforward as, for example, evaluating teaching materials for sexist language. Teachers and other educators who are responsible for evaluating the hidden curriculum need to include qualitative methods of gathering data (e.g., case studies, interviews, and analyses of documents [policies, handbooks] and enrollment and grade reports) in order to reveal the nebulous dimensions of the hidden curriculum. I am sure that you can think of many pertinent examples, but here are some for your consideration:

1. Institutional norms (such as more money going into boys' sports programs than into girls' sports)
2. Role modeling (e.g., white males in most leadership and authority roles)
3. Ability grouping and tracking—practices that tend to reinforce existing gender, racial, and social-class patterns

4. Counseling based on social-class stereotypes and expectations (e.g., counseling most girls from working-class families to take secretarial courses)
5. Schedule patterns of course offerings (e.g., always offering computer classes at the same time as home economics classes—which are still popular with female students in rural schools—may prevent young women from gaining computer skills).

Evaluation of instructional strategies. Some evaluation criteria for sex equity in instructional strategies include the following:

1. Teachers include nonsexist, multicultural components in each course they teach.
2. All staff avoid using oral, written, or nonverbal communication patterns that may be sexist, racist, elitist, or ethnocentric.
3. Teachers monitor the quantity and quality of their interactions with male and female students; students of color and Anglo students; poor and nonpoor students; physically able and physically challenged students.
4. All staff use a variety of groupings and approaches to accommodate the learning and interaction styles of all students, regardless of ability, sex, culture, or race.
5. Classroom management strategies and student role assignments that reinforce nonsexist, culturally sensitive behavior are used.

Guidelines for nonsexist teaching. Self-assessment by individual teachers goes hand in hand with the evaluation of the curriculum and the total school program. Because of teachers' perceived lack of empowerment to effect change in the whole school organization (Sleeter, 1992), they usually feel that the only place they can initiate change is in their own classroom. In spite of the six barriers to implementing change outlined above, they do have some autonomy in their own classrooms. For example, nonsexist teachers would welcome the opportunity to engage in self-assessment of their programs for evidence of sex bias, whereas teachers who discount or deny that sexism is still a problem in schools would probably resist assessment of their classroom for sex bias.

Sadker and Sadker (1982) provide the classroom teacher with eight guidelines that can be used for individual assessment of nonsexist instruction. Nonsexist teaching should:

1. Be continuous and integral to daily instruction
2. Direct attention to the stereotypes and problems that affect boys as well as girls

3. Be concerned with discrimination on the basis of race, ethnicity, religion, class, age, and disability
4. Be a partnership between the teacher and parents and community members
5. Involve the total classroom environment, which includes:
   a. Its physical arrangement and organization
   b. Verbal and nonverbal language and interaction
   c. Selection and use of print and nonprint materials
   d. Development of lessons, units, and learning centers
6. Exemplify good teaching that is characterized by creativity, enthusiasm, humor, patience, flexibility, careful planning, and respect for diverse student opinions
7. Include the affective as well as the cognitive learning domain; that is, help students to reflect on and examine their feelings and attitudes as well as their ideas and knowledge
8. Be active and affirmative and intentionally incorporated into the classroom every day through examples, materials, references, lesson plans, learning stations, discussions, and assignments (pp. 134–137).

Evaluation of instructional materials. Evaluation of materials is another domain where the teacher does have some autonomy in deciding which supplementary materials to select and how a required item, such as a textbook, is used and presented to students. In addition to textbooks and supplementary materials, the following materials also should be scrutinized for bias: Audiovisual resources, posters and brochures, counseling materials, bulletin boards, student reference material, library materials, and computer software.

Evaluation of instructional materials for sex and race bias received a lot of attention in the 1960s and 1970s. For example, Arlow and Froschl (1976) evaluated 14 social studies textbooks in use at the time, then correlated their findings with those from other studies. The result of their research was the creation of a portrait of the treatment of women in high school history that is full of gaps, omissions, male-biased language and characterizations, and trivialization of women's contributions. To avoid the omissions and other weaknesses that Arlow and Froschl found, use the following criteria in evaluating curriculum and instruction materials:

1. Materials avoid reinforcing stereotypes about women and men, cultural/racial groups, the elderly, the poor, and the disabled.
2. The contributions and perspectives of both men and women, diverse racial/cultural groups, and the disabled are included in educational materials.

3. Materials deal openly and accurately with the effect of sexism, racism, elitism, ageism, and ableism in the workplace and in society.
4. Women and men, diverse racial/cultural groups, and the disabled are shown in both active leadership and passive roles in materials.
5. Materials emphasize the home and family responsibilities of both females and males and avoid linking these responsibilities solely to females.

Evaluation of computer software. While textbooks are the most commonly used instructional materials in the classroom, it is also important for educators to remember to critique other materials, such as computer software, for bias. For example, in a critique of 40 software programs designed for use in K–12 social studies, McCormick and Boney (1990) analyzed the programs for elements of invisibility, stereotyping, selectivity and imbalance, unreality, linguistic bias, and fragmentation and isolation—six forms of bias identified by McCune & Matthews (1978, cited in Gollnick, Sadker, & Sadker, 1982, pp. 72–73). Thirty-two of the programs were in a format with little potential for inclusion of nonsexist, multicultural elements: They were of the problem-solving variety in which the user manipulates numbers, decides which crop to plant, or names the capital city of a state. There were five programs that had the potential for equity inclusion because of the format or the program topic, but the writer simply failed to do so. Omissions and stereotyping were the two most serious problems found in the software programs that violated multicultural, nonsexist principles. For example, in "Choice or Chance? Electronic Program," women were effectively omitted from 362 years of U.S. history. The only direct reference to women was to Queen Elizabeth I as the funder and supporter of Sir Walter Raleigh's explorations (McCormick & Boney, 1990).

Student evaluation. Many types of assessment strategies are necessary to evaluate students' achievement and progress in a nonsexist, culturally inclusive manner. Paper-and-pencil tests are among those strategies, but they must be supplemented with other means, such as surveys, student portfolios, teacher observation of student performance in simulated or real-life situations as well as students' self-reports, sociograms, journals, and diaries. Sole reliance on only one form of assessment is inequitable because of learning style differences as well as the gender and cultural differences of students. A multifaceted approach is the key to equitable assessment of female students and students of color.

Overreliance on age-standardized achievement tests and on use of standardized IQ tests in schools for assessment, promotion, and/or placement are prime ways that schools play a role in reproducing inequality. Inequitable testing has resulted in a disproportionate placement of poor students and students of color in remedial and lower-track classes (Oakes, 1985). Mercer (1989) provides an excellent overview of the historical context of public education and testing, how educators became so enamoured with the IQ paradigm, and the negative effects of Anglo-dominant testing on students of color. She indicates that there is a decline in the use of intelligence testing in public schools and that alternative assessment paradigms are being developed that are more culturally sensitive. Four alternative assessment paradigms are:

1. The modified IQ paradigm with sociocultural norms (e.g., the System of Multicultural Pluralistic Assessment)
2. A cross-cultural achievement testing paradigm (multiple normative frameworks are used to provide varied information about the student's relative performance on a particular scale)
3. The competency approach to assessment (total reliance on curricular-based competency testing that is criterion-referenced for students of different ages in terms of levels of performance)
4. Assessment of learning process paradigm (it focuses on teaching the student to use efficient learning strategies [Mercer, 1989]).

Herman, Aschbacher, and Winters (1992) also provide educators with useful guidance on how to create and use alternative measures of student achievement.

EXTERNAL INFLUENCES THAT AFFECT EQUITY IN SCHOOLS

A quick review of articles in "a special section on children at risk" in the September 1992 *Phi Delta Kappan* poignantly paints a picture of some external realities of students' lives that have a negative impact on optimal learning in an equitable manner. These article titles illustrate and develop the theme of children at risk quite well: "Children with HIV-Related Developmental Difficulties," "Children Who Are Homeless: Educational Strategies for School Personnel," "The Educational Needs of Children Living with Violence," and "Beyond Parents: Family, Community, and School Involvement." These conditions affect the quality of life and school achievement of all children, regardless of their sex, race, disability, or socioeconomic status. As Stevens and Price (1992) write, "There is clear evidence that children from all socioeconomic levels are affected by these conditions. Nor will race determine which children will be affected" (p. 19).

Homelessness

In spite of the caveat just given, children living in poverty are more likely to experience *some* of these conditions, such as homelessness. The pauperization of children of all races and cultures goes hand in hand with that of their mothers, who increasingly find themselves homeless or living in poverty. (See Chapter 2 for more on the feminization of poverty.) Twenty-five years ago, working mothers with young children were an oddity; now, they are the norm. With the divorce rate over 50%, there are more single-parent families that are headed by females—about half of all poor families have a female head in the United States (U.S. Department of Commerce, Bureau of the Census, 1987). The cold fact is that increasingly schools are faced with children who have no home. In 1990, families made up 34% of the homeless population, and most of these families are headed by a single parent, usually a woman (Linehan, 1992).

When women get divorced their standard of living immediately declines by 73%, while that of men increases by 42% (Wolf, 1991b). These disparities are due to the economic and social realities that set women's lives apart from men's: Typically, women have fewer years of experience in the work force, less job training, and less education than men. Their employment is still clustered in 20 low-status, low-paying job categories, and they earn about 68 cents for every dollar earned by a man (Wolf, 1991b). Furthermore, following divorce most women still have the responsibility for child care, but their income for child support is not adequate, due to the factors mentioned above and the high number of men who default on child support. Reid (1992) reports:

> Of the 10 million women eligible for child support, a third live below the poverty line. . . .
> Only six out of ten eligible women even have child support orders. Of those who have orders, only half receive the full amount to which they are entitled. A quarter receive nothing. (p. 86)

Traditional women's work (the unpaid labor of child care, housework, elder care, and food production) is undervalued by society and not monetarily rewarded. Thus single mothers of all races and socioeconomic statuses who are still primarily responsible for the care of children, do not have adequate support in the private domain or in the workplace, where there is inadequate daycare, paid leave for childbirth, and flexibility to accommodate family crises. The Family and Medical Leave Act—which guarantees 12 weeks of unpaid leave and health benefits for a family or medical emergency and was signed into law by President Clinton on August 5, 1993—is a beginning step in the right direction to address some of the problems discussed above. Although it is clear that the economic problems faced by single mothers are so deep and pervasive that teachers are likely to see increasing numbers of poor and home-less children in their classrooms, it may not be so clear how this phenom-enon contributes to inequitable treatment in school. Most directly relevant to this concern is my earlier discussion (see Chapter 3) of the phenomenon of self-fulfilling prophecy wherein students live up (or down) to the teacher's expectations of them. Gollnick and Chinn (1994) contend:

> Too often, . . . teachers do classify their students by class and assign certain expec-tations to students based on perceived class status. Students at the lower ranges of socioeconomic status often are expected to be academically inferior and to exhibit disruptive behavior. Many of these students are hampered academically by such expectations. (p. 68)

Rist's (1970) study of an inner-city school confirmed that the kindergar-ten teacher's division of the children into three math and reading ability groups was based on nonacademic factors: Children in the high-ability group wore clean clothes, used standard English, and behaved well; whereas the children in the lower two groups wore dirty clothes, spoke black dialect, and came from less stable families than those in the high-ability group. Further, Rist found that the teacher interacted less with the children in the lower two groups.

Students in the lowest-ability groups—usually from low-income fami-lies—receive less quality instruction and more administrative and disciplin-ary attention from teachers than students in the highest-ability groups. A capstone stigma is the fact that the number of low-income students who are classified as mentally retarded is disproportionately high (Gollnick & Chinn, 1994).

Violence Against Women and Children

Battery is the number-one health problem of women according to the U.S. Surgeon General. It is the single major cause of injury to women, even ahead of car accidents and muggings (Assault Care Center Extending Shelter and Support, 1992); yet there is no public outcry or federal effort to bring atten-tion to this disgrace, much less to stop it. There is no "Just say 'no' to battery of women" campaign being touted in the media by well-known people. Every 18 seconds a woman is beaten in the United States, according to the National Coalition Against Domestic Violence. By conservative estimates, more than a million wives are battered each year and a rape occurs every minute, usually by someone the woman knows (Rovner, 1987). Many of these women are mothers of children who come to school traumatized by the violence at home. Approximately 14% of children between the ages of 3 and 17 have the burden of family violence to deal with (Craig, 1992). This violence is done to the children themselves. Rovner (1987) writes:

> Researchers are recognizing a pattern in domestic violence. The linchpin, it appears, the hidden generator of much of this trauma in the American family, is child abuse, especially child sexual abuse. Many experts believe child abuse may be at the root of a significant proportion of street violence as well. (p. 9E)

Focusing specifically on female children, MacKinnon (1987) states:

> One of two hundred of us [females], conservatively estimated, is sexually molested as a child by her father. When brothers, stepfathers, uncles, and friends of the family are included, some estimate that the rates rise to two out of five. (p. 23)

In *Secret Survivors*, Blume (1990) says that "35 percent of all reported child sex abuse cases in 1988 were of girls under 6" (cited in Bear, Schenk, & Buckner, 1992/1993, p. 44).

Educators are generating ways—beyond the legal obligation to report suspected child abuse—to meet the needs of children who have been abused or are living with violence. "Teachers have an opportunity afforded few adults to identify abused children and to start a process that will restore safety in the child's world" (Bear et al., 1992/1993, p. 42). Teachers can educate themselves about child abuse and provide a safe learning environment for the child in which trust and confidentiality are the foundations. Critical to creating a safe classroom environment are the teacher's caring, accepting attitude and the belief that the child is not to blame, according to Bear and colleagues, (1992/1993).

My rationale for including the discussion of violence against women and children in this examination of external factors that affect sex equity is as follows: Violence is seen by increasing numbers of today's young people as a way to solve problems; apparently, violence is becoming normalized. It is not surprising, then, that the problems of violence in the home and streets have spilled over into the classroom. Violence against women and children is one of many manifestations of sexism—as illustrated by the continuum of sexism (shown in Figure 5.2). The school, being a microcosm of the larger society, reflects sexist attitudes and practices, and increasingly, the violence in society against women and children is surfacing in schools. For example, sexual misconduct by heterosexual male teachers toward female students (Shakeshaft, 1990) has received considerable attention in recent years and has been the focus of many school districts' new or revised policies (Lawton, 1993). However, sexual misconduct exclusively involving students—which is predominantly male against female—is more prevalent and recently has come to be recognized as a form of violence (Henneberger & Marriott, 1993) that in the past has been brushed aside as a "boys will be boys" phenomenon. Accompanying this tendency to excuse boys' behavior is the tendency to blame the girl (e.g., for the seductive way she dresses) and to expect her somehow to control the boy's behavior (National Organization of Women, 1993). In 1993 the Wellesley Center for Research on Women and the National Organization of Women's Legal Defense and Education Fund released the results of a survey of over 4000 girls and young women from 9 to 19 years old concerning sex harassment. This report (Stein, Marshall, & Tropp, 1993) confirms that even though 39% of the girls and young women reported being harassed on a daily basis, nothing happened to the harasser in 45% of the incidents that were reported to a teacher or administrator. Blaming the victim was reported time and again, as this respondent's story (National Organization of Women, 1993) illustrates:

> I was wearing a silk black tank top and baggy jeans. Three guys cornered me and said, "You know if we raped you right now we could get away with it because you're dressed like a slut." . . . When I yelled out to my teacher she said, "You know you asked for it—you get what you deserve," and she wouldn't help me. (p. 1)

Sexism in Media and Advertisements

Teaching students to critically analyze media and advertisement for sexism provides them with the skills and mental "armor" to resist, to question, and to challenge the messages bombarding them daily. Brick (1991) writes:

> While researchers continue to investigate the impact of the media, including pornography, there is no doubt about the pervasiveness of the sexual scripts that invade children's consciousness from the earliest ages: violent, sexist cartoons; Barbie and Teen-Age Mutant Ninja Turtles; soaps and MTV. (p. 53)

Sexual exploitation reaches its nadir in today's television commercials, television music videos (MTV), and magazine advertisements. Everyone—from music producers to car companies to clothing and makeup manufacturers—uses sex to sell products, portraying women as objects or "mindless bimbos." It is an an eye-opener to take time to critique MTV for sexual exploitation. In several hours of MTV "research" comparing rock and country videos, I found that both types of music entertainment exploit women, not just the rock videos. The women in the videos by Van Halen (rock), Robert Palmer (rock), ZZ Top (country), and Great Plaines (country) all took on similar characteristics of style and movement. What did they all have in common? Wonderful, melodious voices and superb dancing skills? No, the things they all had in common were short skirts, tight clothes, large breasts, voluptuous lips, big gorgeous hair, and a look suggestive of making love to the screen.

Pornography. These portrayals as well as advertisements by Guess and Calvin Klein (and many others) use women's bodies to sell their products. U.S. advertisers are blatant pornographers when they show models in sexual positions to sell clothes—and other things as far-fetched as snow blowers or lawn mowers—and portray women in compromising, degrading, and weak positions that reduce them to mindless objects whose only purpose is to sexually entice and satisfy men. Such pervasive sexual images affect children's and teens' lives and sensibilities daily.

These messages and images, some overt and some subliminal, help maintain a sexist culture in which 50% of women report that they experience sexual harassment in their jobs ("Sex, Power, and the Workplace," 1993) and in which thousands of school girls, as discussed earlier, experience sexual harassment on a daily basis (Stein, 1992). Pervasive sexual images also nurture a culture in which youngsters are confused about the meaning of rape and sexuality. Seventeen hundred middle school children were interviewed by the Rhode Island Rape Crisis Center concerning their attitudes and knowledge about different sexual situations. Here are some of their responses: Most of the students (males and females) believed that sexual assault crimes are committed by strangers; most held the victim responsible for the assault; more than half thought that if the female walks alone at night or dresses sexily, she's asking to be raped; 61% thought it was acceptable for the male to force the female to have sex if they had had sex previously; 70% indicated that the male did not need the female's consent if they had marriage plans (Ellerbee, 1991). These and other disturbing responses to the interview questions (which were administered individually and anonymously) reflect, among other things, the devaluation and objectification of women and embedded beliefs about males' supremacy and right of access to women's bodies.

The harmfulness of pornography has been documented in numerous empirical studies. MacKinnon (1987) writes:

> Recent studies have found that exposure to pornography . . . makes both women and men substantially less able to perceive accounts of rape as accounts of rape; makes normal men more closely resemble convicted rapists psychologically; increases attitudinal measures that are known to correlate with rape, such as hostility toward women, propensity to rape, condoning rape, and predictions

that one would rape or force sex on a woman if one knew one would not get caught; and produces other attitude changes in men, such as increasing the extent of their trivialization, dehumanization, and objectification of women. (pp. 264–265)

Pornography, prostitution, violence against women, rape, sexual abuse of girls by fathers and male relatives—all are part of the institution of gender inequality. As MacKinnon (1987) argues:

Along with the rape and prostitution in which it participates, pornography institutionalizes the sexuality of male supremacy, which fuses the erotization of dominance and submission with the social construction of male and female. (p. 148)

Knowledge is power: Young women need to know the interrelation between all the elements of male supremacy in order to defend themselves or to seek help. Young women need to realize the connection between all aspects of sexism, starting with so-called "innocent" jokes. As the continuum of sexism depicted in Figure 5.2 illustrates, there is a connection between behaviors and practices that support a male-supremacy model of society.

As long as women believe the myth that rapists are usually strangers, they are defenseless against the perpetrators, who in 80% of cases is someone they know, most likely a date or boyfriend. College women need to be aware that advertisements in the university newspaper requesting submission of photos for possible inclusion in *Playboy* or some similar magazine are not worth the money they offer. This is a part of the web that male supremacy weaves to lure young women into the institution of gender inequality.

Popular ideals of beauty. The sociocultural roots of current ideals of beauty or conceptions of the ideal body image for females need to be exposed and explained to students. In *The Mismeasure of Woman*, Carol Tavris (1992) discusses the "ideal female shape," which she says is based on alternating visions of being like the male body (thin) or opposite from the male body, but never accepting of the female body as it is. Tavris reveals how the taken-for-granted male norm for everything from behavior to body type affects

FIGURE 5.2. Continuum of sexism

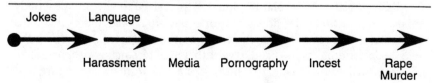

women's self-esteem, their achievement, and their problems. She says, "in the very era when educational and occupational opportunities for women have increased, the ideal body for women became thin, athletic, small-busted, and narrow-hipped" (p. 31). This describes our own era and the craze to make women shape themselves to the male norm in order to be successful and worthy of love (Faludi, 1991, Chapter 8; Wolf, 1991a, 1991b).

Thus we have women constantly on a diet (or worrying about being off one), trying to start again, not satisfied with their dress size or weight. Increasingly, girls are mirroring the same kind of behavior modeled by their mothers and teachers—bouncing from diet to diet and never being satisfied with their size, weight, or looks (Voss, 1991). Of great concern is the problem of girls and women with the eating disorders of bulimia and anorexia, both directly related to the internalized notion that "something is wrong with the way that I am" that is promoted by the beauty industry (Wolf, 1991b).

Teachers need to be role models in combating this sexist practice of equating the value and essence of women and girls with physical attractiveness. Teachers can integrate discussions of diversity and acceptance of differences with the topic of different body types—that it is normal, natural, and desirable that male and female body types are different and that within each sex, there are many acceptable attractive body types, not just one. Through a historical study of fashion and body image, students will see how the ideals of female beauty and body type have changed over time and how sociopolitical factors and commercialism have influenced women's conception of themselves (Faludi, 1991, Chapter 8; Wolf, 1991a).

A blurb from a recent advertisement for a "Happy to Be Me" doll (see Esteem International, Inc., in Appendix A) states:

> The medical community believes that the alarming increase in dieting, eating disorders, and low self-esteem resulting from a poor body image is due, in part, to the fact that the mental picture of a woman's body that many girls are forming has no basis in reality. (p. 1)

Creator of the "Happy to Be Me" doll and founder of Esteem International, Inc., Cathy Meredig describes female fashion dolls as providing poor role models for girls and portraying a negative image of women's bodies. She says, "Girls form a picture of an adult body that is considered lovable and acceptable by age six" (quoted in Palmer, 1992, p. 1). In her discussion, Meredig contrasted the regular fashion doll, perceived to have an ideal body, with her "Happy to Be Me" doll: The former has broader shoulders than hips, a waist that is half the size of its chest, and a stomach that is flat or indented, while the latter doll has hips and a waist that are "reasonably proportioned" and a rounded stomach—that is, more like a real woman (see Figure 5.3).

FIGURE 5.3. Logo for "Happy to Be Me" doll

HAPPY TO BE ME
DOLL   FASHION DOLLS

*A Unique Series of Real-life Story Books
and <u>Realistically Proportioned</u> Dolls
Designed to Nurture Healthy
Body Images and Self-acceptance.*

A Great Gift for all Special Little Girls!

Meredig tried to sell her dolls through three major toy manufacturers and was turned down repeatedly. The third company told her that the secretary to the president looks like a Barbie doll and "that he couldn't believe that American women would get it." This was a turning point for her, for she realized that she was "fighting an institutionalized way of looking at women and their place in the world" (quoted in Palmer, 1992, p. 3). Since then, she has successfully marketed the dolls primarily through direct-mail nationwide.

Her dolls are being used in some eating disorder clinics in the Twin Cities in Minnesota. When people in the clinic were asked which doll had an ideal body, they picked the fashion doll, but when they were asked which one had the most healthy body, the answer was the "Happy to Be Me" doll. However, the respondents were confused when they were asked which shape they would like their daughter to have. Meredig concludes, "We need to change the universal, mass thinking about the negative aspects of women's bodies" (quoted in Palmer, 1992, p. 3).

Many studies document that teachers' impressions of their students are frequently based on the student's physical attractiveness and that these impressions may influence their expectations about student behavior and achievement (Patzer, 1985; Ritts, Patterson, & Tubbs, 1992). As Patzer says:

> Those higher in physical attractiveness generally elicit more positive expectations and receive preferential treatment over those of lower physical attractiveness. . . . The effect of higher physical attractiveness on positive evaluations of children is well documented. (p. 47)

These findings clearly have serious implications for both male and female students; however, I argue that the greater inequity befalls female students, since they are still primarily valued for their physical beauty and attributes, not their brains or character. Teachers need to examine their own conceptions of ideal beauty and body type to avoid differential treatment and expectations of male and female students.

CONCLUSION: PARTNERSHIPS, POSSIBILITIES, NEW PARADIGMS

In the midst of transforming teacher education according to a nonsexist, culturally inclusive model, it is beneficial to be aware of similar efforts being made in other fields, such as in peace education, global education, environmental education, and ecofeminism. For example, ecofeminism evolved out of the convergence of the ecological and feminist movements in the late 1960s and early 1970s. Ecofeminism relates to the roles of women and how these roles are symbolically and culturally connected to nature. By the 1980s, ecofeminists had begun to make the connections between ecology, class, race, and the domination of women. They understood that racism, sexism, and anti-nature ideologies keep a male-dominated system alive and that if women are ever to be liberated universally, they will need to have a voice in determining the military, energy, economic, and ecological policies of the world (Heller, 1991).

In a discussion of feminism and ecology, theologian Rosemary Radford Ruether (1991) called for a total transformation of the model of relations between men and women, not simple equality between the sexes. This entails reshaping the patterns of patriarchal culture to embrace love and care for others and the earth; to recognize our interdependency with one another and with nature; and to think of human consciousness as our special gift that enables us to harmonize our needs with nature.

At the World Women's Congress for a Healthy Planet held in Miami, Florida, in November 1991, 1,500 women from around the world gathered, strategized, and prepared a 21-point agenda for delivery at the United Nations' "Earth Summit" the following June—all because they believe that the perspectives of women and indigenous peoples are critical to the survival of our planet. As the poorest of the poor, "They [women] and their children are frequently the first and most severely affected by environmental degradation" (Boddy, 1992, p. 1-C). Commenting on what she learned while participating in the Congress, Boddy (1992) writes:

> Since women and indigenous peoples have often been denied formal education, they have not typically been co-opted by technologies and systems bent on an industrialized view of progress-as-excessive-consumerism. They have a view of progress-as-sustaining-all-human-life. This view and their expert means for achieving that vision go unused and unrecognized.
>
> The hierarchical systems that place technology over nature, logic over intuition, male over female, white skin over black and rich over poor are the same systems that analyze environmental problems in isolation. . . . We cannot "save the planet" . . . without realizing how economics, industrialization, medicine, culture, population, militarism and custom are stirred together in a stew of environmental chaos. (p. 1-C)

The related themes of interdependency and connection that permeate the research literature and discussions of ecofeminists and feminist educators also are part of the dialogue of peace and global educators (Iowa Peace Institute, 1991; Reardon, 1985). To realize that people in widely divergent fields are working for similar ends is encouraging. Pritscher (1991) says:

> Chaos researchers have determined the existence of what they call the butterfly effect. This butterfly effect helps people to understand that a seemingly inconsequential act of a butterfly moving its wings today in Beijing, may several weeks hence, noticeably contribute to the cause of a storm in New York City. (p. 1)

Just as chaos researchers help us understand the intricacy of the interconnect-edness of all life systems, they also raise our awareness about the significance of sensitive dependence on initial conditions when studying a given scientific phenomenon. It is important for teachers to be sensitive and attentive to the "initial conditions" affecting their students' lives: Seemingly inconsequential things—such as whether the child has had breakfast before school or goes home to an empty house in the afternoon—matter. Paying attention to the "here and now" of students' lives helps build a caring school environment in which their growth and learning can be optimized.

In these times of social change and transformation in our schools and culture, the ability to accept ambiguity, an element of both chaos and change, is a mind-set that educators need for guiding the next generation forward into the twenty-first century. I think we can take courage from the multiple movements for change in different sectors of our culture and schools for a more equitable society and know that our initial efforts to transform education are worthy and just and have the potential to effect change for a better future.

Creating an Alternative Future

As we rapidly approach the beginning of a new millennium, we are leaving the industrial age behind for the communications age. To move ahead into the new age and embrace its opportunities, we have to leave the residues of the old age behind: Sexism, racism, elitism, and oppressive power, leadership, and organizational models. Some futurists "believe the world is experiencing a global paradigm shift that will result in a breakdown of elitism and a move away from hierarchical forms of organization" (Martin, J., 1990, p. 8).

New conceptions of leadership and power. Changes in social-class structure and in organizational paradigms require a drastically different type of leadership and a reconceptualization of power in human affairs. The fact of global interdependence has prompted futurists to project that leadership for the twenty-first century must stress cooperation and global understand-ing in order to ward off conflict and possible annihilation. Emerging from the last three decades of social change, a reevaluation of traditional female and male leadership styles has produced a modicum of acceptance of differ-ent (nontraditional) models of leadership and human relations. In Chapter 2, I discussed Eisler's (1987) work, in which she proposes to replace the old, dominator model with a collaborative, partnership model of human relations. Similarly, Nickles and Ashcraft (1981) contrast the "alpha" leadership style of males with the "beta" style of females: The alpha style is characterized as being focused on individualistic power, short-term goals, and hierarchical relationships, while the beta style is integrative, people-oriented, and focused on long-range goals. Although only the alpha style of leadership has been valued and nurtured in white, androcentric institutions, Nickles and Ashcraft (1981) argue that the beta perspective "involves a sensitivity to those who are not in power and fosters a more fertile environment for growth and learning" (p. 175). Infusion of the beta style of leadership into our androcentric global system—where aggression and dominance are equated with masculinity, and where "warfare is held to be the ultimate initiation into true manhood"— could not only help women to fulfill our leadership potential, but also could be the golden key to our global survival (Capra, 1988, p. 41).

During the last 30 years, we in the United States have undergone a some-times painful self-examination of our basic institutions and values. This period of social change has afforded us an opportunity to reexamine our attitudes about rigid sex roles and to consider a realignment of power between the sexes. It has also prompted dialogue about various delineations of institutional power—from the old, vertical system of authority, with a hierarchical, top-down flow of command to a facilitative, circular model of power. Dunlap and Goldman (1991) explicate the latter model as follows:

> Power as a "system of facilitation" is characterized by mutuality and synergy within the structured organizational context of public schools. Facilitative power replaces neither hierarchy nor authority. Instead, we suggest a shift in perspec-tive. Thinking of power as facilitative rather than hierarchical may better enable us to identify and predict what sorts of leadership activities actually occur in schools. In our view, power may primarily be an act of relationship between equals where acts of domination are the least desired alternatives. (p. 7)

Reflective Exercise: Creating an Alternative View of Power

This exercise is intended for college students and for preservice and in-service teachers.

Fast-forward your time machine to about 50 years in the future. In that year, there is equity for all people, and power is equally shared by men and women. The system of power that they have developed and use is based on a partnership, facilitative model.

Imagine that you are a teacher in a staff meeting in which a varied group of educators are discussing curriculum revisions for the new school term. Brainstorm with a small group of class members on questions such as these: What are you and the other educators doing? How are you seated in the room (in rows, around a table)? Who is doing what work? How is the work on curriculum revision being organized? What is your environment like? What do you see in the room?

Do not evaluate or judge the partnership society or the staff meeting that you envision.

Make a list of images that reflect the shared power between males and females in your partnership society, such as portrayals of the sexes in media and advertising; illustrations in children's books; videos about teachers, children, and administrators; children in cartoons; teacher–student interactions; murals on walls of city buildings; parent–child interactions; or artwork in museums.

With a partner, select one of your listed images of shared power to explore more fully. Then, reflect on some ways to get from the present to the partnership society you envisioned for the future. What things could be done to move toward a shared power model in the area that you chose to focus on? What changes need to be made? What benefits or losses would accrue to each sex? How you could adapt and use this activity with your class?

Throughout this book, I have discussed "the way things are"—sexist, racist *status quo* models of human relations and education—and I have proposed ways to replace these worn-out, debilitating models with a liberating paradigm that is nonsexist and culturally inclusive. The explication of the contemporary women's movement and its roots in previous movements for women's equality provided a historical and theoretical backdrop for examining the old problems of sexism and racism in light of current issues and developments. I hope that both the theoretical framework and the practical applications of sex and race equity in curriculum and instruction lay a foundation for cultural and curricular transformation and renewal that will help pass the torch for a more equitable society to the next generation.

Discussing the qualities of tomorrow's leaders, Patterson (1993) believes that they will approach the future in a radically different way: "They will relentlessly create a *preferred future* by imagining what could be and letting the pull of the imagined future lead the organization through uncharted waters to get there" (p. 38). I believe that teachers face a tremendous challenge and opportunity to help create a "preferred future" by providing leadership for nonsexist, culturally inclusive education. Their leadership is critical in helping to close the gap between our democratic ideals of equality and justice for all and the social practices of sexism and racism that oppress the majority of citizens. It is crucial for each educator to be proactive for sex and race equity right now, rather than waiting for the future or for someone else to do it. I believe in the wisdom of Sonia Johnson's (1989) statement that "what we are doing in the present is *creating* the future, *is* the future. . . . Just as there is no way to have peace but to be peaceful right now, there is no way to have joy, fearlessness, and freedom except to feel them right now" (pp. 39, 47).

SUMMARY

Chapter 5 has examined some internal and external factors that have an impact on equity in schools. Internal factors to assess for equity include personal and career counseling, school policies, staff development, the evaluation plan for the total school program, evaluation of curriculum and instruction materials, and methods of assessing student progress. All should be structured so as to empower students to reach their full potential.

There are numerous external factors that have an impact on equity in schools. This chapter discussed issues of poverty and the increase of homelessness among school children, violence against women and children, sexist media advertising and programming, sexual harassment, and pop culture's images of ideal beauty. The chapter concludes with a discussion of partnerships that exist between different groups that are working for a more equitable society, alternative models of leadership and power, some futurist considerations, and an injunction to educators to be proactive for education that is nonsexist and culturally inclusive *now*, not in an imagined future.

Review Questions

1. Write an imaginary dialogue between Catharine MacKinnon and Phyllis Schlafly on the topics of pornography and patriarchy.
2. Monitor MTV for one week and note the style and characterization of females and different racial groups. Assess the music videos for sexist and racist elements.
3. Collect magazine advertisements that illustrate the "objectification" of the female body. Write a "think piece" on objectification and current violence against and abuse of women and children.
4. Visit a homeless shelter or a sexual assault care center and volunteer your services for several weeks. Help serve meals and eat with the homeless or the women and their children. Keep a log of your activities and thoughts during this field experience.
5. Research the issue of equity and teacher assessment, that is, competency testing for teacher licensing. See Hawkins (1993), Smith (1986) in References, and McCormick (1986) in Appendix B.

Resources,
Readings,
References

Resources

Adolescent Pregnancy Prevention Clearinghouse
Children's Defense Fund
Education Improvement and Adolescent Pregnancy Prevention
25 E Street, NW
Washington, DC 20001
(202)628-8787
The Adolescent Pregnancy Clearinghouse handles requests for information about the connection between teenage pregnancy and broader life questions for youth. The Clearinghouse plays a role in advocating the Children's Defense Fund's contention that teenage pregnancy prevention strategies must be broader than sex education and family planning services.

Alpha Kappa Alpha Sorority (AKA)
5656 S. Stony Island Avenue
Chicago, IL 60637
(312)684-1282
Alpha Kappa Alpha is the world's oldest college-based sorority founded by black women. Sorority members conduct workshops on subjects of general interest, such as problems of black women in the job market. AKA also provides information about sex equity and minority-related topics.

American Association of School Administrators (AASA) Women's Caucus
Joan Kowal, Superintendent
Volusia County, FL 32721-2118
(904)734-7190
The AASA Women's Caucus is a professional organization of women in school administration that has been active since 1975.

American Association of University Professors (AAUP)
Committee W on the Status of Women in the Academic Professions
1012 14th Street, NW
Suite 500
Washington, DC 20005
(202)737-5900

The AAUP is a national organization concerned with issues affecting college and university staff. It was the first higher education association to develop a comprehensive policy on sexual harassment for use at the postsecondary level. Committee W on the Status of Women in the Academic Professions operates at the national, state, and local levels to provide support and assistance to individuals on campus and in the courts.

American Association of University Women (AAUW)
Anne L. Bryant, Executive Director
1111 Sixteenth St., NW
Washington, DC 20036-4873
(202)785-7700
Fax: (202)872-1425
The AAUW is the oldest and largest national organization for the betterment of women. It produces numerous publications on sex equity and Title IX. "The AAUW Report—How Schools Shortchange Girls" (1992) is a recent example.

American Civil Liberties Union (ACLU)
Women's Rights Project
132 W. 43rd Street
New York, NY 10036
(212)944-9800
The ACLU Women's Rights Project continues to advance the law toward the complete eradication of gender discrimination, attacks and exposes employment discrimination through selected cases and public education, and challenges (through legislative and legal action) government policies that disproportionately harm poor women and women of color. The Project is a part of the ACLU's overall efforts to defend and expand women's rights.

American Educational Research Association (AERA)
1230 17th Street, NW
Washington, DC 20036
(202)223-9485
Three groups collaborate within the AERA to promote equity issues related to women: the Committee on the Role and Status of Women in Educational Research and Development, Research on Women and Education, and Women Educators.

American Psychological Association (APA)
Women's Programs Office
750 1st Street, NE
Washington, DC 20002
(202)336-6044
The Women's Programs Office, located in the Public Interest Directorate of the APA, coordinates the organization's efforts to ensure equal opportunity for women psychologists as practitioners, educators, and scientists. Its goal is to eliminate gender bias in education and training, research, and diagnosis. The Office also monitors the welfare of women as consumers of psychological services, analyzes the impact of governmental initiatives on women, and promotes the development and application of psychological knowledge to address public policy issues affecting women.

Anti-Defamation League (ADL) of B'Nai B'rith
823 United Nations Plaza
New York, NY 10017
(212)490-2525
The ADL produces, and makes available through its catalog, materials to help eliminate all forms of bias and to improve intergroup and interpersonal relations.

Association for Women in Science (AWIS)
1522 K Street, NW
Suite 820
Washington, DC 20005
(202)408-0742
The AWIS promotes equal opportunities for women entering the sciences and attempts
to help them achieve their goals. It provides funding for predoctoral awards through
its educational foundation and testifies on sex discrimination matters before congressional committees.

Business and Professional Women's Foundation (BPW)
2012 Massachusetts Avenue, NW
Washington, DC 20036
(202)293-1100
The BPWF carries out an integrated program of research, information, dissemination,
and education to improve the quality of working life for women. It assists high
school–age women in assessing future occupational possibilities.

Center for Research on Women
Clement Hall, Room 339
Memphis State University
Memphis, TN 38152
(901)678-2770
The Center for Research on Women is an educational research facility with the mission to conduct research and disseminate information in the field of women's studies. Center information focuses on southern women and women of color in the United
States, with a particular emphasis on promoting the transformation of curriculum to
incorporate race and gender. The Center also maintains a computerized information
retrieval service that provides to educators, students, and researchers complete cita-
tions of social science and historical works.

Center for Women Policy Studies
2000P Street, NW
Suite 508
Washington, DC 20036
(202)872-1770
The Center for Women Policy Studies is a policy research and advocacy organization. It is concerned with educational equity, work and family issues, and discrimination against women and minorities. It publishes research dealing with gender equity
and has sponsored national conferences.

Coalition for the Advancement of Women of Color in Education
Contact: Charol Shakeshaft
Professor and Chair
Administration and Policy Studies
Hofstra University
Hempstead, NY 11550
(516)463-5758
The Coalition provides services and support for the advancement of women of color
in education.

Congressional Caucus for Women's Issues
2471 Rayburn House Office Building
Washington, DC 20515
(202)225-6740
The Congressional Caucus for Women's Issues is a legislative service organization
devoted to promoting legislation to ensure full legal and economic equity for
women.

Cooperative Urban Teacher Education Program (CUTE)
James Abbott, Executive Director
731 Minnesota Avenue
Kansas City, KS 66101
(913)621-2277
The CUTE Program collaborates with 15 or more colleges and universities in the Mid-
west to prepare teachers to work in multicultural, urban settings with diverse student
populations.

Council of Chief State School Officers (CCSSO)
Resource Center on Educational Equity
1 Massachusetts Avenue, NW
Suite 700
Washington, DC 20001-1431
(202)393-1228
The CCSSO represents the 57 public officials who head the departments of education
in the 50 states, five U.S. jurisdictions, the District of Columbia, and the U.S. Department of Defense Schools. Its Resource Center on Educational Equity provides services designed to achieve equity in education for female, disabled, limited English—
proficient, and low-income students, and students of color.

Council on Interracial Books for Children (CIBC)
Racism and Sexism Resource Center for Educators
1841 Broadway
New York, NY 10023
(212)757-5339
The CIBC produces and publishes multiethnic, nonsexist materials for elementary and
secondary schools and libraries. It also publishes *The Bulletin*, which includes reviews
of children's books and articles on sexism and other aspects of bias.

Curriculum Publications Clearinghouse
Western Illinois University
46 Horrabin Hall
Macomb, IL 61455
(309)298-1917
The Curriculm Publications Clearinghouse provides state-developed curriculum materials dealing with career education for disabled students at a minimum cost.

Educational Testing Service (ETS)
Test Collection
Princeton, NJ 08541
Among its many testing services, ETS prepares annotated bibliographies of tests. A particularly useful one is "Sex Roles and Attitudes Toward Women," February 1991, 34 pages. Write directly for ordering information.

EQUALS
Lawrence Hall of Science
University of California at Berkeley
Berkeley, CA 94720
(415)642-1823
EQUALS promotes the participation of females and people of color in math, science, and computer-assisted instruction. Through workshops and publications for students, parents, and educators, they teach and disseminate tested, successful equity strategies.

Funded by the U.S. Department of Education, the Educational Resources Information Centers (ERIC) play an important role in disseminating education information throughout the country. ERIC provides both printed materials and access to its resources through on-line computer searches. Below are some of the Clearinghouses that are most relevant to sex equity:

ERIC Clearinghouse on Counseling and Personnel Services
2108 School of Education Building
University of Michigan
610 E. University Street
Ann Arbor, MI 48109-1259
(313)764-9492

ERIC Clearinghouse on Elementary and Early Childhood Education
University of Illinois at Urbana–Champaign
805 W. Pennsylvania Avenue
Urbana, IL 61801-4897
(217)333-1386

ERIC Clearinghouse on Handicapped and Gifted Children
Council for Exceptional Children
1920 Association Drive
Reston, VA 22091-1589
(703)620-3660

ERIC **Clearinghouse on Languages and Linguistics**
Center for Applied Linguistics
1118 22nd Street, NW
Washington, DC 20037-0037
(202)429-9551

ERIC **Clearinghouse on Teacher Education**
American Association of Colleges for Teacher Education
One Dupont Circle, NW
Suite 610
Washington, DC 20036-1186
(202)293-2450

ERIC **Clearinghouse on Urban Education**
Teachers College, Columbia University
Main Hall, Room 303, Box 40
New York, NY 10027
(212)678-3433

Esteem International, Inc.
6563 City West Parkway
Eden Prairie, MN 55344
(612)828-6030
Fax: (612)828-9611
The founder of the toy company and creator of the "Happy to Be Me" doll is working to reverse the negative image of women's bodies that famous fashion dolls portray. The "Happy to Be Me" dolls are more like real women.

Feminist Press
City University of New York
311 E. 94th Street
New York, NY 10128
(212)360-5790
The Feminist Press is a nonprofit educational organization that publishes nonsexist books, curriculum materials, resource lists, anthologies, bibliographies, biographies, children's books, and reprints of important and neglected women's writings for every educational level.

Girls Incorporated
National Resource Center
441 W. Michigan Street
Indianapolis, IN 46202
(317)634-7546
Girls Incorporated is a clearinghouse of knowledge about girls' needs and concerns. The National Resource Center provides a link between theory and research and the practical application of such information. The organization serves as a repository of information on girls, as well as the research, training, and distribution arm of Girls Incorporated.

GrayMill Educational Consulting
Dolores Grayson
22821 Cove View
Canyon Lake, CA 92587
(909)244-5165
GrayMill Educational Consulting is an independent educational consulting agency that provides professional development services, seminars, conference speakers, and technical assistance to educators and community groups at the local, state, and national levels. Among its many services, GrayMill provides professional training through GESA (Gender/ Ethnic Expectations and Student Achievement) workshops for educators.

Global Village, Inc.
9537 Culver Boulevard
Culver City, CA 90232-2618
(310)204-4018
Global Village has been a distributor of educational materials concerned with multiculturalism, diversity, and tolerance to individuals, libraries, and schools since 1988.

Institute for Research on Women and Gender
763 Schermerhorn Extension
Columbia University
New York, NY 10027
(212)854-1556
The Institute for Research on Women and Gender is a research center funded by the Ford Foundation. Its purpose is to reform college curricula by integrating the new scholarship on race and gender into existing courses. The Institute's work at Columbia University includes undergraduate and post graduate courses of study.

Institute for Women's Policy Research
1400 20th Street, NW
Suite 104
Washington, DC 20036
(202)785-5100
The Institute for Women's Policy Research is a nonprofit research institute devoted to issues related to economic justice for women.

International Association of Physical Education and Sport for Girls and Women (IAPESGW)
50 Skyline Drive
Mankato, MN 56001
(507)345-3665
The IAPESGW was founded in 1949 to allow professional women to come together and exchange and discuss ideas and methods of physical education. It sponsors a congress every four years, as well as seminars to help bridge the gap between theory and practice in the field of sport science.

Jean Kilbourne
Lordly & Dame, Inc.
51 Church Street
Boston, MA 02116
(617)482-3593
A nationally known media analyst, lecturer, and writer, Kilbourne has researched the influence of advertising on societal attitudes and values. Her powerful presentations, a blend of fact, insight, humor, and commitment, help people see the hidden messages of advertisements that at first seem harmless but in fact are quite detrimental.

League of Women Voters of the United States
1730 M Street, NW
Washington, DC 20036
(202)429-1965
The League of Women Voters is a nonpartisan political action group that lobbies on national issues, coordinates strategies with other coalitions and organizations, and provides information to the public on civic issues. It disseminates objective information about elections and public issues, such as the Equal Rights Amendment.

Media Watch
Contact: Ann Simonton
1803 Mission Street
Suite 7
Santa Cruz, CA 95060
(408)423-6355
This is a nonprofit organization dedicated to improving the image of women in the media. Members work to educate people concerning the dire consequences of sexually objectifying women and children in the media and to help people become more critical consumers of all forms of mass media.

Mexican American Women's National Association
1201 16th Street, NW
Suite 230
Washington, DC 20036
(202)833-0060
The Mexican American Women's National Association is a nonprofit organization representing special interests and concerns of Mexican-American women. Its activities include meeting with local, state, and federal legislators in order to express the Association's viewpoint; coordinating educational and cultural events with a feminist perspective; and sponsoring leadership conferences. The Association publishes a quarterly newsletter. Membership information is available from local affiliates.

Mid-Atlantic Consortium
Contact: Jill Moss Greenberg
5454 Wisconsin Avenue
Suite 1500
Chevy Chase, MD 20815
(301)657-7741
Fax: (301)657-8782

This regional desegregation assistance center, federally funded under Title IV, provides assistance and resources to schools in Delaware, the District of Columbia, Maryland, Pennsylvania, Virginia, and West Virginia on gender equity issues.

Mid-Continental Regional Education Laboratory
Contact: Shirley McCune
2550 S. Parker Road
Suite 500
Aurora, CO 80014
(303)337-0990
The Mid-Continental Regional Education Laboratory, a regional desegregation center federally funded under Title IV, provides technical assistance and materials to school districts in Colorado, Iowa, Kansas, Missouri, Nebraska, North Dakota, South Dakota, and Wyoming on issues of sex, race and ethic equity; multicultural, nonsexist curricula; and intercultural relations.

National Association for Multicultural Education (NAME)
Carl A. Grant, President
College of Education
225 N. Mills Street
University of Wisconsin-Madison
(608)263-6386
Priscilla H. Walton, *NAME News* Editor
California Commission on Teacher Credentialing
1812 9th Street
Sacramento, CA 95814-7000
(916)324-2450
Fax: (916)327-3166
NAME, a national organization that brings together professionals from all academic disciplines and from multiple levels and types of educational institutions and occupations with an interest in multicultural education, was organized in 1991. It espouses the basic tenets of cultural pluralism and promotes equity for all regardless of culture, race, age, gender, language, ethnicity, or exceptionality. NAME sponsors an annual conference, a publication of the conference papers, and a newsletter.

National Association for Women Deans, Administrators, and Counselors (NAWDAC)
1325 18th Street, NW
Suite 210
Washington, DC 20036-6511
(202)659-9330
NAWDAC, founded in 1916, is dedicated to providing professional support for women educators through its programs, services, advocacy, and scholarly publications. It supports lifelong learning and actions that further learning, growth, and development for students and women professionals at all stages of development.

National Center for Fair and Open Testing (FAIRTEST)
342 Broadway
Cambridge, MA 02139
(617)864-4810

The National Center for Fair and Open Testing is an advisory organization. Its goal is to end abuses and misuses of standardized, multiple-choice tests and to make certain that the evaluation of students is fair, open, accountable, and educationally sound.

National Coalition Against Domestic Violence
P.O. Box 15127
Washington, DC 20003-0127
(202)293-8860
The Coalition provides educational services and information on domestic violence.

National Coalition for Sex Equity in Education (NCSEE)
Contact: Theodora Martin
One Redwood Drive
Clinton, NJ 08809
(908)735-5045
NCSEE is a group of advocates working to foster sex equity and parallel equity concerns of race, national origin, and disability in educational programs. Its stated goals are leadership and advocacy; research and development; professional development and renewal; collaboration and networking; and outreach. It trains specialists in sex equity in education and sponsors annual conferences that include informational workshops, research presentations, legislative updates, and resource sharing.

National Coalition for Women and Girls in Education
c/o American Association of University Women
1111 16th Street, NW
Washington, DC 20036
(202)785-7700
The National Coalition for Women and Girls in Education, part of the National Women's Law Center, is a group of more than 50 advocacy organizations devoted to achieving sex equity in education. Issues of interest include civil rights enforcement, testing, vocational education, and national educational goals.

The National Conference of Christians and Jews (NCCJ)
71 Fifth Avenue
New York, NY 10003
(212)206-0006
NCCJ is a comprehensive human relations organization made up of people from many racial, religious, and ethnic backgrounds who want a fair society in which differences are respected and prejudices overcome. Founded in 1927, it helps diverse groups discover their mutual self-interest within the common space of democracy. NCCJ publishes an annual list of "Books for Children and Young Adults" that support their philosophy of fairness and equity in society.

National Council of Jewish Women
53 W. 23rd Street
New York, NY 10021
(212)570-5001
The National Council of Jewish Women is dedicated to improving the quality of life

for individuals as well as strengthening Jewish communities. Activities include conferences on women's roles and on education for the disadvantaged.

National Council for Research on Women
Sara Delano Roosevelt Memorial House
47-49 E 65th Street
New York, NY 10021
(212)570-5001
The National Council for Research on Women is an independent association of U.S. research and policy organizations that provide instructional resources for research and policy issues and educational programs for women and girls. The National Network of Women's Caucuses, a project of the Council, brings together scholars and practitioners working to transform the disciplines and improve the status of women in the professions and on campuses.

National Diffusion Network
U.S. Department of Education
555 New Jersey Avenue, NW
Room 510
Washington, DC 20208-5645
(202)219-2134
The National Diffusion Network makes available to schools, colleges, and other institutions information about exemplary educational programs.

National Education Initiative
National Urban League
500 E. 62nd Street
New York, NY 10021
(213)310-9213
The National Education Initiative of the National Urban League disseminates information whose purpose is to eliminate racial segregation and discrimination in the U.S. and to achieve parity for African-Americans and other minorities in every phase of life. The organization works to eliminate institutional racism and to provide direct services to minorities in the areas of employment, housing, education, social welfare, health, family planning, mental retardation, law, consumer affairs, and youth/student concerns.

National Institute for Women of Color
1301 20th Street, NW
Washington, DC 20036
(202)296-2661
For specific information about available services, programs, and resource materials, contact the organization directly.

National Organization of Women (NOW) Action Center
1000 16th Street, NW
Suite 700
Washington, DC 20036
(202)331-0066

NOW is a political organization that works to bring about legal, political, social, and economic change for women so that they can exist in equal partnership with men, exercising their full rights and responsibilities. Formed in 1966, it has worked for passage of the Equal Rights Amendment, lesbian/gay rights, elimination of racism, older women's rights, and the elimination of education discrimination. NOW has chapters in all states and the District of Columbia.

NOW Legal Defense and Education Fund (LDEF)
Barbara Cox, President
99 Hudson Street
12th Floor
New York, NY 10013
(212)925-6635
NOW LDEF is a national, nonprofit women's advocacy organization. Among their many services and projects is collaboration with the Wellesley Center for Research on Women to investigate sexual harassment of young women in school and to identify preventive measures (results of the research were published in June 1993). A comprehensive list of articles, books, pamphlets, and resources on sexual harassment to assist teachers, parents, and administrators is available in the NOW LDEF "Sexual Harassment in the Schools Resource Kit," available by writing to the address above.

National Women's Hall of Fame
76 Fall Street
P.O. Box 335
Seneca Falls, NY 13148
(315)568-8060
The National Women's Hall of Fame is a nonprofit educational organization. The Hall of Fame celebrates and honors the achievements of women through its publication and its permanent exhibit hall. In addition to induction of women into the Hall of Fame, the organization sponsors traveling exhibits, an annual poster and essay contest, and other special observances.

National Women's History Project
7738 Bell Road
Windsor, CA 95492-8518
(707)838-6000
Fax: (707)838-0478
Organized in 1981, the National Women's History Project is a nonprofit, educational corporation whose purpose is to promote the study, celebration, and appreciation of multicultural women's history in every area (school, work, home, and community) and in kindergarten through university-level curricula and resources.

National Women's Law Center
1616 P Street, NW
Suite 100
Washington, DC 20036
(202)328-5160
For information about programs and publications, contact the organization directly.

National Women's Studies Association
University of Maryland
College Park, MD 20742-1325
(301)405-5573
The National Women's Studies Association describes itself as a professional educational organization and a national clearinghouse for information about women's studies research, curriculum program development, pedagogy, public policy, and feminist education in the community.

Native American Education Program
Resource Center
234 West 109th Street
Room 507
New York, NY 10025
(212)663-4040
The Program and Center provide services and resources for parents, students, and teachers Monday through Friday from 9:00 A.M. to 5:30 P.M.

New Frontiers Center for Educational Development
Heather Alberts, Program Director
620 North 7th Avenue
Tucson, AZ 85705
(602)791-3952
New Frontiers provides technical assistance through in-service training, media, and materials that support educational equity in Arizona and provides a support system for encouraging and sustaining greater exploration of nontraditional vocational education classes and choices for secondary school students.

Northwestern University Library
Judy Lowman, Assistant Curator
Special Collections Department
Evanston, IL 60208-2300
(708)491-3635
The Women's Collection of the Special Collections Department collects materials documenting the women's liberation movement internationally since the late 1960s. The collection has strong holdings in women's periodicals and ephemera and a growing collection of monographs. Call (708)491-2895 if you wish to donate materials, get information, or be placed on the mailing list.

Organization for the Study of Communication, Language, and Gender
Contact: Carol Ann Valentine
2607 S. Forest Avenue
Tempe, AZ 85282
(602)967-2817
This is a nonprofit professional group providing a forum for professional discussion, presentation of research, and the demonstration of creative projects in the areas of communication, language, and gender. The organization offers an interdisciplinary focus; its membership includes teachers, researchers, students, consultants, and practitioners.

Programs for Educational Opportunity
University of Michigan
1005 School of Education
Ann Arbor, MI 48109-1259
(313)763-9910
Programs for Educational Opportunity is a desegregation assistance center that helps school districts with their equity plans.

Project on Equal Education Rights (PEER)
NOW Legal Defense and Education Fund
99 Hudson Street
12th Floor
New York, NY 10013
(212)925-6635
PEER is a nonprofit information and public analysis organization. It functions as an advocate for quality equal education rights for women and girls. Originally founded to advocate for and monitor enforcement of Title IX of the Education Amendments of 1972, PEER analyzes public policy and works at the federal and state levels, organizes local advocacy, and conducts public information campaigns explaining the link between gender-role stereotyping and current issues in education (such as dropouts, early pregnancy and parenting, and occupational education).

Project on Women and Social Change
Smith College
138 Elm Street
Northampton, MA 02063
(413)585-3591
The Project on Women and Social Change is an interdisciplinary research and development group whose members have focused on women's contributions to social change and the ways in which women are affected by change.

Rush Publishing Company Inc.
P.O. Box 1
Rush, NY 14543
(716)634-4418
Rush Publishing Company disseminates feminist journals and publications dealing with feminist studies to academic and other communities. Among the publication distributed by Rush Publishing is *Women Studies Abstracts.*

Southwest Center for Educational Equity of the Southwest Regional Laboratory (SWRL)
Contacts: Harriet Doss-Willis, Jennie Spencer Green
4665 Lampson Avenue
Los Alamitos, CA 90720
(310)598-7661
Fax: (310)985-9635
The Center, as part of SWRL, a regional desegregation assistance center, is federally

funded under Title IV. It provides technical assistance and materials on equity issues to schools in California, Arizona, and Nevada.

Southwest Institute for Research on Women (sirow)
University of Arizona
Douglass Hall, Room 102
Tucson, AZ 85721
(602)621-7338
sirow serves as a center for information and referral within the southwest region and as a source of information on the region's research and activity for the rest of the country. It identifies, coordinates, and disseminates research on women in the Southwest and serves the states of Arizona, Colorado, New Mexico, and Utah.

U.S. Commission on Civil Rights
Office of Information and Publicity
Clearinghouse Division
1121 Vermont Avenue, NW
Room 709
Washington, DC 20245
(202)376-8177
The U.S. Commission on Civil Rights has administrative oversight responsibilities for all federal civil rights legislation, including legislation affecting sex equity. The Office of Information and Publicity makes available a guide providing detailed information about laws concerning sex discrimination in the U.S.

Wellesley College Center for Research on Women
Wellesley College
Wellesley, MA 02181-8259
(617)283-2500
The Center conducts and disseminates research on gender equity in schools. Collaborative projects with other agencies and schools are hallmarks of the Center's research.

Wider Opportunities for Women (wow)
1325 G Street, NW
Lower Level
Washington, DC 20005
(202)638-3143
wow is a multifaceted women's employment organization that works on a national level to achieve economic independence and equality of opportunity for women and girls. It is nationally recognized for its model skills training and job placement programs for women. In addition to leading a national network of 400-plus independent women's employment programs and advocates in more than 40 states, wow also coordinates the Educational Equity Options Project, whose purpose is to overcome barriers to women's and girls' participation in nontraditional vocational education programs.

Women in Development Resource Center
Agency for International Development Information Center
Room 105 SAAT
Washington, DC 20523-1801
(703)875-4830
The Women in Development Resource Center disseminates information on the integration of women into all agency-funded activities. It provides information to researchers, policy makers, university and college faculty, and the general public.

Women's Action Alliance
Contact: Jo Sanders
370 Lexington Avenue
Suite 603
New York, NY 10017
(212)532-8330
The Women's Action Alliance is a national feminist organization involved in projects dealing with education, employment, health, and other areas important to women. The Alliance's Sex Equity in Education Program conducts educational equity projects, including computer equity for girls via a Computer Equity Expert Project and nontraditional vocational preparation for young women. The Information Services Program provides information on women's issues and conducts networking projects. The Women's Centers Program provides technical assistance and is involved in a number of projects benefiting women's center's programs. The alliance also sponsors the Women's Action Alliance Library and a history archive.

Women's Educational Equity Act Publishing Center (WEEA)
Education Development Center
55 Chapel Street
Newton, MA 02160
(800)225-3088
The Women's Educational Equity Act Publishing Center is a nonprofit education and research and development organization. It disseminates materials developed and prepared as a result of support from the Women's Educational Equity Act program, a federal program whose goal is to eliminate inequality in education. Publications are designed for teachers, counselors, administrators, parents, businesses, and community members committed to equal educational opportunities.

Women's Opportunity Resource Development (WORD)
127 N. Higgins
3rd Floor
Missoula, MT 59802
(406)543-3550
WORD sponsors educational and employment-related programs for Montana women in such areas as increasing self-sufficiency and increasing accessibility to programs for all people of all backgrounds, ages, and incomes. WORD's Equity in Education Program works to raise awareness of gender-equity issues in the schools, such as the computer gender gap, stereotypical language in textbooks, and stereotypical career choices.

Women's Research and Education Institute
1700 18th Street, NW
Room 400
Washington, DC 20009
(202)328-7070
The Women's Research and Education Institute conducts research on women's economic issues. It is responsible for *The American Woman*, an annual status report.

Women's Sports Foundation (WSF)
342 Madison Avenue
Suite 728
New York, NY 10173
(212)972-9170
The WSF provides services, opportunities, advocacy, and recognition programs. The WSF's Leadership Development Fund and its Coaches Advisory Roundtable seek to enhance and encourage leadership qualities of women both in and out of sports.

The Women's Studies Program
George Washington University
217 Funger Hall
2201 G Street
Washington, DC 20052
(202)994-6942
The Women's Studies Program at George Washington University offers graduate coursework. Coursework focuses on the study of women's lives as they are affected by gender, sexuality, sexual preference, age, race, class, ethnicity, and religion; it also examines academic disciplines and public policies from a feminist perspective.

Recommended Readings

Ahlum, C., & Fralley, J. (1973). *Feminist resources for schools and colleges.* Old Westbury, NY: Feminist Press.

Aldous, J. (1972). Children's perceptions of adult role assignment: Father absence, class, race and sex influence. *Journal of Marriage and Family, 34*(1), 55–65.

Allen, P. (1992). *The sacred hoop—Recovering the feminine in American Indian traditions.* Boston: Beacon.

American Association of Retired Persons. (1985). *Growing together: An intergenerational sourcebook.* Washington, DC: Author.

Andrzejewski, J. (Ed.). (1994). *Oppression and social justice: Critical frameworks.* Needham Heights, MA: Ginn.

Atwood, M. (1985). *The handmaid's tale.* New York: Ballantine.

Bem, D., & Bem, S. (1970). *Training the woman to know her place: Beliefs, attitudes and human affairs.* Belmont, CA: Brooks/Cole.

Berman, L., & Miel, A. (1983). *Education for world cooperation.* West Lafayette, IN: Kappa Delta Pi.

Beyer, G. (1985). Critical thinking: What is it? *Social Education, 49*(4), 270–276.

Beyer, G. (1985). Teaching critical thinking: A direct approach. *Social Education, 49*(4), 297–303.

Bleich, D. (1989). Homophobia and sexism as popular values. *Feminist Teacher, 4*(2/3), 21–28.

Brock-Utne, B. (1985). *Educating for peace: A feminist perspective.* New York: Teachers College Press.

Canfield, J., & Wells, H. (1976). *100 ways to enhance self-concept in the classroom.* Englewood Cliffs, NJ: Prentice-Hall.

Cashdan, L. (1989). Anti-war feminism: New directions, new dualities—A Marxist-humanist perspective. *Women's Studies International Forum, 12*(1), 81–85.

Chesler, P. (1978). *About men.* San Diego, CA: Harcourt Brace Jovanovich.

Codianni, A., Cortes, C., & Tipple, B. (1981). Toward educational equity for all. Manhattan, KS: Midwest Race Desegregation Assistance Center.

Colangelo, N., Dustin, D., & Foxley, C. (1985). *Multicultural, nonsexist education—A human relations approach.* Dubuque, IA: Kendall Hunt.

Collier-Thomas, B. (1982). The impact of black women in education: An historical overview. *Journal of Negro Education, 51,* 173–180.

Collis, B. (1985). Sex-related differences in attitudes toward computers: Implications for counselors. *The School Counselor, 33*(2), 120–130.

Council of Chief State School Officers. (1977). *Implementing Title IX and attaining sex equity.* Washington, DC: National Foundation for the Improvement of Education.

Council on Interracial Books for Children. (1980). *Guidelines for selecting bias-free textbooks and storybooks.* New York: Racism and Sexism Resource Center for Educators.

Daly, M., & Caputi, J. (1987). *Webster's first new intergalactic wickedary of the English language.* Boston: Beacon.

Daly, M. (1973, 1985). *Beyond God the father—Toward a philosophy of women's liberation.* Boston: Beacon.

D'Andrea, M., Daniels, J., & Heck, R. (1991). Evaluating the impact of multicultural counseling training. *Journal of Counseling & Development, 70,* 143–150.

Darling-Hammond, L. (1993). Reframing the school reform agenda—Developing capacity for school transformation. *Phi Delta Kappan, 74*(10), 752–761.

DeClue, D. (1979). *Women shaping history.* Milwaukee: Raintree.

Diaz, C. (Ed.). (1992). *Multicultural education for the 21st century.* Washington, DC: National Education Association.

DuBois, E., & Ruiz, V. (Eds.). (1990). *Unequal sisters: A multicultural reader in U.S. women's history.* New York: Routledge.

Dunn, R., Beaudry, J., & Klavas, A. (1989). Survey of research on learning styles. *Educational Leadership, 46*(6), 50-58.

Edmondson, J. (1983). *Choices and challenges: A course in personal planning and self-awareness for teen-aged women and men.* Santa Barbara, CA: Advocacy Press.

Egan, K. (1992). *Imagination in teaching and learning—The middle school years.* Chicago: University of Chicago Press.

EQUALS Project. (1980). *Use EQUALS to promote the participation of women in mathematics.* Berkeley: University of California Press.

Estes, C. P. (1992). *Women who run with the wolves—Myths and stories of the wild woman archetype.* New York: Ballantine.

French, M. (1988). Text as context. *Women's Studies Quarterly, 16,* 11–17.

Gilligan, C., Lyons, N., & Hanmer, T. (Eds.). (1990). *Making connections—The relational worlds of adolescent girls at Emma Willard School.* Cambridge, MA: Harvard University Press

Gilman, C. P. (1979). *Herland—A lost feminist utopian novel.* New York: Pantheon. (Original work published 1915)

Greenberg, J. (1987, July/August). An interview with Jane Evans: It's still a man's world. *Careers,* pp. 32–36.

Griffin, P. (1983). *Fair play in the gym: Race and sex equity in physical education.* Amherst: University of Massachusetts Press.

Haber, L. (1979). *Women pioneers of science.* New York: Harcourt Brace Jovanovich.

Hamilton, C. (1989). Women in politics: Methods of resistance and change. *Women's Studies International Forum, 12*(1), 129–135.

Hansot, E., & Tyack, D. (1988). Gender in American public schools. *Signs: Journal of Women in Culture and Society, 13,* 741–760.

Harris, M. (1988). *Women and teaching: Themes for a spirituality of pedagogy.* New York, NY: Paulist Press.

Hewlett, S. (1986). *A lesser life: The myth of women's liberation in America.* New York: Morrow.

Hoffman, N. (1981). *Woman's true profession.* Old Westbury, NY: Feminist Press.

Hotelling, K., & Forrest, L. (1985). Gilligan's theory of sex-role development: A perspective for counseling. *Journal of Counseling and Development, 64,* 183–186.

Howe, F. (1973, May). Sexism, racism, and the education of women. *Today's Education,* pp. 47–48.

Howe, K. G. (1985). The psychological impact of a women's studies course. *Women's Studies Quarterly, 13*(1), 23–24.

Hurston, Z. (1990). *Their eyes were watching God.* New York: Harper & Row.

Hymowitz, C., & Weisman, M. (1978). *A history of women in America.* New York: Bantam.

Jardine, A., & Smith, P. (Eds.). (1987). *Men in feminism.* New York: Methuen.

Johnson, D. W. (1984). *Circles of learning: Cooperation in the classroom.* Alexandria, VA: Association for Supervision and Curriculum Development.

Kahn, K. (1989). Challenging authority: Civil disobedience in the feminist anti-militarist movement. *Women's Studies International Forum, 12*(1), 75–80.

Kingsolver, B. (1988). *The bean trees.* New York: Harper & Row.

Lee, P., & Gropper, N. (1974). Sex-role culture and educational practice. *Harvard Educational Review, 44*(3), 369–410.

Lerner, G. (Ed.). (1973). *Black women in white America: A documentary history.* New York: Random House.

Lorde, A. (1984). *Sister outsider.* Trumanburg, NY: Crossing Press.

Mairs, N. (1990). *Carnal acts—Essays.* New York: HarperCollins.

Mairs, N. (1986). *Plaintext—Deciphering a woman's life.* New York: Harper & Row.

Massialas, G. (1985). *Fair play: Developing self-concept and decision-making skills in the middle school.* Newton, MA: EDC/Women's Educational Equity Act Publishing Center.

McCarthy, C. (1986, November). Study war no more. *The Progressive,* pp. 26–28.

McClelland, A. (1992). *The education of women in the United States—A guide to theory, teaching, and research.* New York: Garland.

McCormick, T. (1986). Multicultural education and competency testing: Conflicts and consequences. *Urban Educator, 8*(1), 31–42.

National Advisory Council on Women's Educational Programs. (1977). *Sex discrimination in guidance and counseling* (Report Review and Action Recommendations). Washington, DC: U.S. Department of Health, Education, and Welfare.

Neuenschwander, J. (1976). *Oral history as a teaching approach.* Washington, DC: National Education Association.

Peterson, J. (1985). The counselor and change: Counseling for cultural transition. *Counseling and Values, 29*(2), 117–127.

Purdy, L. (1989). Feminist healing ethics. *Hypatia, 4*(2), 9–14.

Reardon, B. (1988). *Comprehensive peace education: Educating for global responsibility*. New York: Teachers College Press.

Riley, G. (1986). *Inventing the American women—A perspective on women's history 1607– 1877*. Arlington Heights, IL: Harlan Davidson.

Rodriguez, F. (1986). *Equity education: Imperatives, issues and implementation*. Washington, DC: University Press of America.

Rothbart, M., & Maccoby, E. (1966). Parents' differential reactions to sons and daughters. *Journal of Personal and Social Psychology, 4*, 237–243.

Ruether, R. (Ed.). (1973). *Religion and sexism: Images of women in the Jewish and Christian religious traditions*. New York: Simon & Schuster.

Saario, T., Tittle, C., & Jacklin, J. (1973). Sex-role stereotyping. *Harvard Educational Review, 43*(3), 386–416.

Sadker, M., & Sadker, D. (1980). Sexism in teacher education texts. *Harvard Educational Review, 50*(1), 36–46.

Sadker, M., Sadker, D., & Kaser, J. (1986). *The communications gender gap*. Washington, DC: The Mid-Atlantic Center for Sex Equity.

Sadker, M., Sadker, D., & Steindam, S. (1989). Gender equity and educational reform. *Educational Leadership, 46*(6), 44–47.

Sadker, M. Sadker, D., & Klein, S. (1991). The issue of gender in elementary and secondary education. In G. Grant (Ed.), *Review of Research in Education, 17* (pp. 269–334). Washington, DC: American Education Research Association.

Schubert, W., & Ayers, W. (Eds.). (1992). *Teacher lore: Learning from our own experience*. White Plains, NY: Longman.

Schuman, J. (1981). *Art from many hands—Multicultural art projects for home and school*. Englewood Cliffs, NJ: Prentice-Hall.

Shapiro, J., Kramer, S., & Hunerberg, C. (1981). *Equal their chances: Children's activities for nonsexist learning*. Englewood Cliffs, NJ: Prentice-Hall.

Simeone, A. (1987). *Academic women working towards equality*. South Hadley, MA: Bergin & Garvey.

Smith, N. (1988). The emergence of a nonracist approach to sex equity. *Educational Considerations, 15*(1), 8–9.

Sprung, B., Froschl, M., & Campbell, P. (1985). *What will happen if . . . Young children and the scientific method*. New York: Educational Equity Concepts.

Stensrud, R., & Stensrud, K. (1982, October). Transpersonal relations: Counseling for the "we" decade. *Counseling and Values*, pp. 27–35.

Stratham, A., Richardson, L., & Cook, J. (1991). *Gender and university teaching*. Albany: State University of New York Press.

Tafolla, C. (1992). *Sonnets to human beings and other selected works*. Santa Monica, CA: Lalo Press.

Tetreault, M. (1987). Rethinking women, gender and the social studies. *Social Education, 51*(3), 170–178.

Tiedt, P., & Tiedt, I. (1990). *Multicultural teaching: A handbook of activities, information and resources*. Boston: Allyn & Bacon.

Trecker, J. (1973). Teaching the role of women in American history. In J. Banks (Ed.),

Teaching ethnic studies (pp. 244–261). Washington, DC: National Council for the Social Studies.

Valett, R. E. (1991, Spring). Developing creative imagination. *Holistic Educational Review, 4*(1), 22–27.

Vaughan, F. (1982, February). Choosing wholeness: Transpersonal values in counseling for women. *Counseling and Values*, pp. 102–109.

Wallace, J. (1989, March). What the world needs now: More women in mathematics and science. *Educational Leadership, 46*(6), 46.

Wattenberg, E. (1986, January/February). The fate of baby boomers and their children. *Social Work*, pp. 20–28.

Weiler, K. (1988). *Women teaching for change—Gender, class, and power.* South Hadley, MA: Begin and Garvey.

Weinberg, C. (Ed.). (1972). *Humanistic foundations of education.* Englewood Cliffs, NJ: Prentice-Hall.

White, A. (1984, June). Where have all the women writers gone? *The Personnel and Guidance Journal*, 631–636.

Whyte, J. (1986). The development of sex stereotyped attitudes among boys and girls: Different models of their origins and their educational implications. In *Girls and women in education—A cross-national study of sex inequalities in upbringing and in schools and colleges* (pp. 57–70). Paris: Organisation for Economic Co-Operation and Development.

Women on Words and Images. (1972). *Dick and Jane as victims: Sex stereotyping in children's readers.* Princeton, NJ: Author.

References

Allport, G. (1954). *The nature of prejudice.* Cambridge, MA: Addison Wesley.

American Association of University Women. (1992). *The AAUW report: How schools shortchange girls.* Washington, DC: Author.

Arlow, P., & Froschl, M. (1976). Women in the high school curriculum: A review of U.S. history and English literature texts. In F. Howe (Ed.), *High school feminist studies* (pp. xi-xxxi). Old Westbury, NY: Feminist Press.

Assault Care Center Extending Shelter and Support. (1992). Test your violence IQ. Ames, IA: Author.

Balser, D. (1987). *Sisterhood and solidarity: Feminism and labor in modern times.* Boston: South End.

Bandura, A. (1982). Self-efficacy mechanisms in human agency. *American Psychologist, 37,* 122–147.

Banner, L. W. (1974). *Women in modern America—A brief history.* New York: Harcourt Brace Jovanovich.

Bear, T., Schenk, S., & Buckner, L. (1992/1993). Supporting victims of child abuse. *Educational Leadership, 50*(4), 42–47.

Belenky, M., Clinchy, B., Goldberger, N., & Tarule, J. (1986). *Women's ways of knowing.* New York: Basic Books.

Bell, L. (1988, March). Just as good as the males but without their competition: A pluralistic look at female achievement. Paper prepared for the Project on Equal Education Rights Research Seminar, "Equal Education for Girls is Poverty Prevention for Women."

Bem, S. L. (1981). Gender schema theory: A cognitive account of sex typing. *Psychological Review, 88,* 354–364.

Bem, S. L. (1983). Gender schema theory and its implications for child development: Raising gender-aschematic children in a gender-schematic society. *Signs, 8,* 598–616.

Bennett, C. (1990). *Comprehensive multicultural education—Theory and practice.* Boston: Allyn & Bacon.

Bigby, P. C. (1990). Study material for "Black History Showdown 1990"—A television game show. Sponsored by Martin Luther King Day, Inc., an Iowa-based nonprofit organization.

Bird, C. (1971). *Born female: The high cost of keeping women down.* New York: Simon & Schuster.

Blume, E. (1990). *Secret survivors.* New York: The Free Press.

Boddy, P. (1992, January 5). World women's congress for a healthy planet—Viewing life from the bottom up. *Des Moines Sunday Register,* p. 1–C.

Bodger, C. (1985, January). Sixth annual salary survey—Who does what and for how much. *Working Woman, 10*(1), 65–67.

Bornstein, R. (1982). Sexism in education. In M. Sadker & D. Sadker (Eds.), *Sex equity handbook for schools* (pp. 9–59). New York: Longman.

Borzak, L. (1971). *The women's liberation movement: A rhetorical study.* Unpublished paper. Northwestern University Library Special Collections, Women's Ephemera Folder No.1, Feminism/Women's Liberation, Evanston, IL.

Brick, P. (1991). Fostering positive sexuality. *Educational Leadership, 49*(1), 51/53.

Brophy, J., & Good, T. (1974). *Teacher-student relationships: Causes and consequences.* New York: Holt, Rinehart & Winston.

Bruner, J. (1977). *The process of education.* Cambridge, MA: Harvard University Press. (Original work published 1960)

Buek, A. P., & Orleans, J. H. (1973). Sex discrimination—A bar to a democratic education: Overview of Title IX of the Education Amendments of 1972. *Connecticut Law Review, 6*(1), 1–27.

Bush proposes changes to 1990 Civil Rights Act. (1990). *National NOW Times, 22*(6), 7.

Butler, J. E. (1993). Transforming the curriculum: Teaching about women of color. In J. Banks & C. Banks (Eds.), *Multicultural education—Issues and perspectives* (pp. 149–167). Boston: Allyn & Bacon.

Cade, T. (1970). *The Black woman: An anthology.* New York: New American Library.

Canadian women ahead. (1989, July). *The Feminist Majority Report, 2*(1), 2.

Capra, F. (1988). National insecurity. *New Age Journal, 5*(2), 41.

Carden, M. L. (1974). *The new feminist movement.* New York: Russell Sage Foundation.

Carnegie Forum on Education and the Economy. (1986). *A nation prepared: Teachers for the 21st century* (A Report of the Task Force on Teaching as a Profession.) New York: Author.

Chodorow, N. (1978). *The reproduction of mothering.* Berkeley: University of California Press.

Chodorow, N. (1989). *Feminism and psychoanalytic theory.* New Haven, CT: Yale University Press.

Cohen, R. (1968). The relation between socio-conceptual styles and orientation to school requirements. *Sociology of Education, 41*, 201–220.

Connor, J., Serbin, L., & Ender, R. (1978). Responses of boys and girls to aggressive, assertive, and passive behaviors of male and female characters. *Journal of Genetic Psychology, 133*, 59–69.

Conservatives kill domestic violence bill. (1980). *Congressional Quarterly Almanac, 36*, 443–445.

Corporate women and the mommy track. (1989). *The Feminist Majority Report, 2*(1), 4.

Council of Chief State School Officers. (1977). *Implementing Title IX and attaining sex equity—Application materials for instructional personnel.* Washington, DC: Author.

Craig, S. (1992). The educational needs of children living with violence. *Phi Delta Kappan, 74*(1), 67–71.

Daley, S. (1990, October 10). Inspirational black history draws academic fire. *New York Times,* pp. A-1, B-8.

Darling-Hammond, L. (1990, November). Restructuring education: Women's work. Keynote address at the 16th annual conference of Research on Women and Education (Special Interest Group of American Educational Research Association), Milwaukee.

de Beauvoir, S. (1953). *The second sex.* New York: Knopf.

Decker, B. (1983). Cultural diversity, another element to recognize in learning styles. *National Association of Secondary School Principals Bulletin, 67*(464), 43–48.

Digest of Education Statistics. (1988). Washington, DC: National Center for Education Statistics.

DuBois, E. (1978). *Feminism and suffrage—The emergence of an independent women's movement in America 1848–1869.* Ithaca, NY: Cornell University Press.

Dunlap, D., & Goldman, P. (1991). Rethinking power in schools. *Educational Administration Quarterly, 27*(1), 5–29.

Dunn, R., Beaudry, J., & Klavas, A. (1989). Survey of research on learning styles. *Educational Leadership, 46*(6), 50–58.

East, C. (1975). *Chronology of the Women's Movement in the U.S. 1961–1975.* Washington, DC: National Commission Observation of International Women's Year.

Ebbeck, M. (1984). Equity for boys and girls: Some important issues. *Early Child Development and Care, 18,* 119–131.

Edelman, M. (1988). 1995: Poverty, the underclass and the workplace, *The World, 2*(2), 6.

Edwards, B. (1989). *Drawing on the right side of the brain.* Los Angeles, CA: Jeremy P. Tarcher.

Egan, K. (1992). *Imagination in teaching and learning—The middle school years.* Chicago: University of Chicago Press.

Ehrenreich, B., & Stallard, K. (1982, July/August). The nouveau poor. *Ms.,* pp. 217–224.

Eisler, R. (1988). *The chalice and the blade.* San Francisco: Harper & Row.

Ellerbee, L. (1991, August 25). Rape: Teaching that no means no. *Des Moines Sunday Register* (Des Moines, IA), p. 2–C.

Etaugh, C., Levine, D., & Mannella, A. (1984). Development of sex biases in children: 40 years later. *Sex Roles, 10,* 911–922.

Evans, S. (1990, March 22). *Redefining public and private: The history of women in America.* Public lecture. Iowa State University, Ames, IA.

Faludi, S. (1991). *Backlash—The undeclared war against American women.* New York: Crown.

Feldstein, J., & Feldstein, S. (1982). Sex differences on television toy commercials. *Sex Roles, 8,* 581–587.

Firestone, S. (1970). *The dialectics of sex: A case for feminist revolution.* New York: Morrow.

Freeman, F. M. (1973, August 16). Women's rights in the 70s. Unpublished paper. Northwestern University Library Special Collections, Women's Ephemera Folder No. 1, Evanston, IL.

Freeman, J. (1975). *The politics of women's liberation.* New York: McKay.

Freud, S. (1924). The dissolution of the Oedipus complex. *Standard Edition of the complete psychological works* (vol. 19), pp. 172–179. London: Hogarth Press and Institute of Psychoanalysis.

Freud, S. (1965). *New introductory lectures on psychoanalysis.* New York: Norton. (Original work published 1933).

Friedan, B. (1963). *The feminine mystique.* New York: Norton.

Futrell, M. (1989, September). Mission not accomplished: Educational reform in retrospect. *Phi Delta Kappan, 71*(1), 8–14.

Gilligan, C. (1977). In a different voice: Women's conception of self and of morality. *Harvard Educational Review, 47*(4), 481–517.

Gilligan, C. (1982). *In a different voice—Psychological theory and women's development.* Cambridge, MA: Harvard University Press.

Gimbutas, M. (1980). *The early civilizations of Europe* (Monograph for Indo-European Studies 131). Los Angeles: University of California Press.

Gimbutas, M. (1982). *The goddesses and gods of Old Europe, 7000–3500 B.C.* Berkeley: University of California Press.

Gimbutas, M. (1987). T*he language of the goddess: Images and symbols of Old Europe.* New York: Van der Marck.

Ginsburg, M., & Clift, R. (1990). The hidden curriculum of preservice teacher education. In W. Houston (Ed.), *Handbook of research on teacher education* (pp. 450–465). New York: Macmillan.

Giroux, H. A. (1988). *Teachers as intellectuals.* Granby, MA: Bergin & Garvey.

Giroux, J. B. (1989). Feminist theory as pedagogical practice. *Contemporary Education, 61*(1), 6–10.

Gollnick, D., & Chinn, P. (1994). *Multicultural education in a pluralistic society* (4th ed.). Columbus, OH: Merrill.

Gollnick, D., Sadker, M., & Sadker, D. (1982). Beyond the Dick and Jane syndrome: Confronting sex bias in instructional materials. In M. Sadker & D. Sadker (Eds.). *Sex equity handbook for schools* (pp. 60–95). New York: Longman.

Gordon, A. D. (1988–89). Writing the lives of women. *NWSA Journal, 1*(2), 221–237.

Government's pay rates challenged. (1989). *National NOW Times, 22*(2), 8.

Gozemba, P., & Humphries, M. (1989). Women in the anti-Ku Klux Klan movement, 1865–1984. *Women's Studies International Forum, 12*(1), 35–40.

Grant, C. (1978). Education that is multicultural—Isn't that what we mean? *Journal of Teacher Education, 29*, 45–49.

Grant, C. (1990). Barriers and facilitators to equity in the Holmes Group. *Theory Into Practice, 29*(1), 50–54.

Grant, C., & Sleeter, C. (1986). *After the school bell rings.* Philadelphia, PA: Falmer.

Grant, C., & Sleeter, C. (1988). Race, class, and gender and abandoned dreams. *Teacher College Record, 90*(1), 19–40.

Grant, G. (1991). *Review of research in education 17.* Washington, DC: American Educational Research Association.

Grayson, D. (1987). Gender/ethnic expectations and student expectations. A summary of the areas of disparity. Unpublished manuscript. Earlham, IA: GrayMill Foundation.

Greenberg, J. (1987, July/August). An interview with Jane Evans: It's still a man's world. *Careers*, pp. 32–36.

Greer, G. (1971). *The female eunuch.* New York: McGraw-Hill.

Grund, N. (1989a). Facts in brief—Women are earning more doctorates. *Higher Education and National Affairs, 38*(9), 3.

Grund, N. (1989b). Full-time faculty in higher education by race/ethnicity—Minority faculty initiatives cited. *Higher Education & National Affairs, 38*(5), 1, 4.

Guild, P., & Garger, S. (1985). *Marching to different drummers.* Alexandria, VA: Association for Supervision and Curriculum Development.

Haaken, J. (1988). Field dependence research: A historical analysis of a psychological construct. *Signs, 13*(2), 311–330.

Haberman, M. (1987). *Recruiting and selecting teachers for urban schools* (ERIC/CUE Urban Diversity Series, No. 95). Milwaukee: University of Wisconsin Press.

Hall, R. (1982). *The classroom climate: A chilly one for women?* Washington, DC: Association of American Colleges, Project on the Status and Education of Women.

Haroutunian-Gordon, S. (1988). Mind over machine: A plea for the intuitive conception of mind. *Educational Researcher, 17*(3), 50–52.

Harrison, C. (1988). *On account of sex.* Berkeley: University of California Press.

Harvey, G. (1986). Finding reality among the myths: Why what you thought about sex equity in education isn't so. *Phi Delta Kappan, 67*(7), 509–512.

Hawkins, D. (1993). New teacher exams unveiled after three-year wait—Test billed as culturally sensitive alternative to NTE. *Black Issues in Higher Education, 9*(25), 7, 9–10.

Heller, C. (1991, April 21). *Ecofeminist movement attacks racist, sexist, anti-nature beliefs.* Lecture, Iowa State University, Ames, IA: Iowa State University.

Henneberger, M., & Marriott, M. (1993, July 11). For some, youthful courting has become a game of abuse. *New York Times*, pp. 1, 14.

Herman, J., Aschbacher, P., & Winters, L. (1992). *A practical guide to alternative assessment.* Alexandria, VA: Association for Supervision and Curriculum Development.

Hodgkinson, H. L. (1989). *The same client: The demographics of education and service delivery systems.* Washington, DC: Institute for Educational Leadership.

Hodgkinson, H. L. (1990, June 4). *From minority to majority: Essential responses to a future that is already here.* Keynote address presented at the 3rd annual national conference on Race and Ethnic Relations in American Higher Education, Santa Fe, NM.

Hoffman, L. (1972). Early childhood experience and women's achievement motives. *The Journal of Social Issue, 28*, 129–156.

Hole, J., & Levine, E. (1971). *Rebirth of feminism.* New York: Quadrangle Books.

Houston, B. (1985). Gender freedom and the subtleties of sexist education. *Educational Theory, 35*(4), 359–370.

Hoyenga, K., & Hoyenga, K. (1993). *Gender-related differences—Origins and outcomes.* Boston: Allyn & Bacon.

Illich, I. (1982). *Gender.* New York: Pantheon.

Ingersoll, F. S. (1983). Former congresswomen look back. In I. Tinker (Ed.), *Women in Washington* (pp. 191–207). Beverly Hills, CA: Sage.

Into the Dark Ages—Head on against abortion. (1991, June 23). *Des Moines Sunday Register* (Des Moines, IA), p. 2-C.

Iowa Peace Institute. (1991, October 25). Healthy Planet—Peace, Environment, and Population Conference. Iowa Peace Institute, Grinnell, IA.

Irving, K. (1989). (Still) hesitating on the threshold: Feminist theory and the question of the subject. *NWSA Journal, 1*(4), 630–643.

Jackman, J. (1987). It's time to face reality. *National Now Times, 20*(4), 4–5.

Jackson, G., & Cosca, C. (1974). The inequality of educational opportunity in the Southwest: An observational study of ethnically mixed classrooms. *American Educational Research Journal, 11*, 219–229.

Jenkins, M. (1988). She issued the call—Josephine St. Pierre Ruffin, 1842–1924. *Sage, 5*, 74–76.

Johnson, D. W. (1982). Cooperative learning. Letter to editor. In E. Wynne (Ed.), *Character policy: An emerging issue* (pp. 147–148). Washington, DC: University Press of America.

Johnson, D. W. (1986, April). *Learning together—Effective use of cooperative groups and orientations.* Workshop presentation at the Mid-West Human Relations Association Conference, Minneapolis, MN.

Johnson, D. W. & Johnson, R. T. (1981). Effects of cooperative and individualistic learning experiences on interethnic interaction. *Journal of Educational Psychology, 73*, 444–449.

Johnson, R. T., & Johnson, D. W. (1989/1990). Social skills for successful group work. *Educational Leadership, 47*(4), 29–33.

Johnson, S. (1986, October 15). Male dominance dates back. *Iowa State University Daily* (Ames, IA), p. 15.

Johnson, S. (1989). *Wildfire: Igniting the she/volution.* Albuquerque, NM: Wildfire.

Jones, K. (1989). Le mal des fleurs: A feminist response to *The closing of the American mind. Women and Politics, 9*(4), 1–22.

Kagan, J., Moss, H., & Sigel, I. (1963). Psychological significance of styles of conceptualization. In J. Wright & J. Kagan (Eds.), *Basic cognitive processes in children* (pp. 73– 112). Monographs of the Society for Research in Child Development, 28(2), Serial No. 86.

Keefe, J., & Languis, M. (1983). (no title). *Learning stages network newsletter, 4*(2), 1.

Klein, S. (Ed.). (1985). *Handbook for achieving sex equity through education.* Baltimore: Johns Hopkins University Press.

Klein, S. (1987). The role of public policy in the education of girls and women. *Educational Evaluation and Policy Analysis, 9*(3), 219–230.

Kohlberg, L. (1966). A cognitive-developmental analysis of children's sex-role concepts and attitudes. In E. Maccoby (Ed.), *The development of sex differences* (pp. 82–173). Stanford, CA: Stanford University Press.

Laird, S. (1988). Reforming "woman's true profession": A case for "feminist pedagogy" in teacher education? *Harvard Educational Review, 58*(4), 449–463.

Lakoff, R. (1976). Languages and women's place. New York: Harper Colophon.

Lawton, M. (1993). Sexual harassment of students target of district policies. *Education Week, 12*, pp. 1, 15–16.

Lee, V., & Bryk, A. (1986). Effects of single-sex secondary schools on student achievement and attitudes. *Journal of Educational Psychology, 78*, 381–395.

Levitin, T., & Chananie, J. (1972). Responses of female primary school teachers to sex-typed behaviors in male and female children. *Child Development, 43*, 1309–1316.

Lewis, M. (1989, October). *Desire, threat, and resistance in the feminist classroom: The possibility of feminist pedagogy.* Paper presented at the American Educational Studies Association Annual Conference, Chicago.

Linehan, M. (1992). Children who are homeless: Educational strategies for school personnel. *Phi Delta Kappan, 74*(1), 61–66.

Little Soldier, L. (1989, October). Cooperative learning and the Native American Indian student. *Phi Delta Kappan, 71*(2), 161–163.

Lockheed, M., & Harris, A. (1984). Cross-sex collaborative learning in elementary classrooms. *Educational Researcher, 21*, 275–294.

Lockheed, M., & Klein, S. (1985). Sex equity in classroom organization and climate. In S. Klein (Ed.), *Handbook for achieving sex equity through education* (pp. 189–217). Baltimore, MD: Johns Hopkins University Press.

Longstreet, W. (1978). *Aspects of ethnicity—Understanding differences in pluralistic classrooms.* New York: Teachers College Press.

Maccoby, E. & Jacklin, C. (1974). *The psychology of sex differences.* Stanford, CA: Stanford University Press.

MacKinnon, C. A. (1987). *Feminism unmodified—Discourses on life and law.* Cambridge, MA: Harvard University Press.

Marilley, S. (1989). Towards a new strategy for the ERA—Some lessons from the American Woman Suffrage Movement. *Women and Politics, 9*(4), 23–42.

Marten, L., & Matlin, M. (1976). Does sexism in elementary readers still exist? *The Reading Teacher, 29*, 764–767.

Martin, J. R. (1982). Excluding women from the educational realm. *Harvard Educational Review, 52*(2), 133–148.

Martin, J. R. (1984). Bring women into educational thought. *Educational Theory, 34*, 341–354.

Martin, J. R. (1985). *Reclaiming a conversation: The ideal of the educated woman.* New Haven: Yale University Press.

Martin, J. (Ed.). (1990, Spring). Developing leaders for tomorrow. *The Stanley Foundation Courier*, (4), 8–9.

Matlin, M. W. (1987). *The psychology of women.* Fort Worth, TX: Holt, Rinehart and Winston.

McArthur, L., & Eisen, S. (1976). Achievements of male and female storybook characters as determinants of achievement behavior by boys and girls. *Journal of Personality and Social Psychology, 33*, 467–473.

McCain, N. (1985, July 14). Things you wanted to know about women but (maybe) were afraid to ask. *Des Moines Sunday Register* (Des Moines, IA), p. E-7.

McCormick, T. (1990, January). Counselor-teacher interface: Promoting nonsexist education and career development. *Journal of Multicultural Counseling and Development, 18*(1), 2–10.

McCormick, T., & Boney, S. (1990). Computer-assisted instruction and multicultural nonsexist education: A caveat for those who select and design software. *Computers in the Schools, 7*(4), 105–124.

McCormick, T., & McKay, J. (1989). Our story: The Japanese American Internment (video tape and teachers' guide). Ames, IA: Iowa State University Foundation.

McCormick, T., & Noriega, T. (1986). Low versus high expectations effects on minority students. *Journal of Educational Equity and Leadership, 6*(3), 224–234.

McCune, S., & Matthews, M. (Eds.). (1978). *Implementing Title IX and attaining sex-equity: A workshop package for postsecondary educators.* Washington, DC: U.S. Government Printing Office.

Mead, M. (1949). *Male and female.* New York: Morrow.

Melnick, S. (1977). Sexism and language: Two dimensions. In C. Grant (Ed.), *Multicultural education: Commitments, issues, and applications* (pp. 60–71). Washington, DC: Association for Supervision and Curriculum Development.

Mercer, J. (1989). Alternative paradigms for assessment in a pluralistic society. In J. Banks & C. McGee Banks (Eds.), *Multicultural education—Issues and perspectives* (pp. 289–304). Boston: Allyn & Bacon.

Metha, A. (1983, Fall). A decade since Title IX: Some implications for teacher education. *Action in Teacher Education, 5*(3), 24.

Miller, J. (1976). *Toward a new psychology of women.* Boston: Beacon.

Millett, K. (1969). *Sexual politics.* New York: Ballantine.

Millsap, M. (1983). Sex equity in education. In I. Tinker (Ed.), *Women in Washington* (pp. 116–119). Beverly Hills, CA: Sage.

Mischel, W. (1970). *Sex-typing and socialization.* In P. H. Mussen (Ed.), *Carmichael's manual of child psychology* (3rd ed.) (pp. 3–72). New York: Wiley.

Morgan, R. (Ed.). (1970). *Sisterhood is powerful.* New York: Vintage.

Myrdal, G. (1944). *An American dilemma.* New York: Harper & Row.

National Advisory Council on Women's Educational Programs. (1977, August). *Sex discrimination in guidance and counseling.* (*Report Review and Action Recommendations*). Washington, DC: U.S. Department of Health, Education, and Welfare.

National Commission on Excellence in Education. (1983). *A nation at risk.* Washington, DC: U.S. Government Printing Office.

National Organization of Women. (1972). *Report on sex bias in the public schools* (rev. ed.). New York: Education Committee, NOW.

National Organization of Women. (1990, Summer). NOW organizes freedom summer for students. *National NOW Times, 22*(6), 14.

National Organization of Women. Legal Defense and Education Fund. (1993, Spring). No more boys will be boys. *LDEF In Brief,* pp. 1, 5.

Nickles, E., & Ashcraft, L. (1981). *The coming matriarchy: How women will gain the balance of power.* New York: Berkley.

Nieto, S. (1992). *Affirming diversity: The sociopolitical context of multicultural education.* New York: Longman.

Noddings, N. (1984). *Caring: A feminine approach to ethics and moral education.* Berkeley: University of California Press.

Noddings, N. (1986, November). Fidelity in teaching, teacher education, and research for teaching. *Harvard Educational Review, 56*(4), 496–510.

Noddings, N. (1989, May). Theoretical and practical concerns about small groups in mathematics. *The Elementary School Journal, 89*(5), 607–623.

Noddings, N. (1990). Feminist critiques in the professions. In C. Cazden (Ed.), *Review of Research in Education, 16* (pp. 393–424). Washington, DC: American Educational Research Association.

Noddings, N. (1992). *The challenge to care in schools: An alternative approach to education.* New York: Teachers College Press.

Noddings, N., & Shore, P. (1984). *Awakening the inner eye—Intuition in education.* New York: Teachers College Press.

Noun, L. (1969). *Strong-minded women—The emergence of the woman-suffrage movement in Iowa.* Ames, IA: Iowa State University Press.

Noun, L. (1993, July 7). Carrie Chapman Catt, a bigot? It's a conclusion that's hard to avoid. *Des Moines Sunday Register* (Des Moines, IA), p. 1-C.

Oakes, J. (1985). *Keeping track: How schools structure inequality.* New Haven, CT: Yale University Press.

Organisation for Economic Co-Operation and Development. (1986). *Girls and women in education—A cross-national study of sex inequalities in upbringing and in schools and colleges.* Paris: Author.

Orlich, D. (1989). Education reforms: Mistakes, misconceptions, miscues. *Phi Delta Kappan, 70*(7), 512–517.

Pai, Y. (1990). *Cultural foundations of education.* Columbus, OH: Merrill.

Palmer, J. (1992, April 24). Anti-Barbie doll is quite popular. *Iowa State University Daily* (Ames, IA) pp. 1, 3.

Patterson, J. L. (1993). Creating a preferred future. *Leadership for tomorrow's schools.* Alexandria, VA: Association of Supervision and Curriculum Development.

Patzer, G. (1985). *The physical attractiveness phenomena.* New York: Plenum.

Perry, D. G., & Bussey, K. (1979). The social learning theory of sex differences: Imitation is alive and well. *Journal of Personality and Social Psychology, 37,* 1699–1712.

Pitcher, E., & Schultz, L. (1983). *Boys and girls at play—The development of sex roles.* South Hadley, MA: Bergin & Garvey.

Planned Parenthood Federation of America. (1991, May 23). Letter. New York: Author.

Pollard, D. (1992). Toward a pluralist perspective on equity. *Women's Educational Equity Act Publishing Center Digest.* Newton, MA: WEEA Publishing Center.

Prescott, S. (1989/1990, Winter). Teachers' perceptions of factors that affect successful implementation of cooperative learning. *Action in Teacher Education, 11*(4), 30–34.

Pritscher, C. (1991). Chaos research and demarginalizing the marginalized. Unpublished manuscript, Bowling Green State University, Bowling Green, OH.

Ramirez, M., & Castaneda, A. (1974). *Cultural democracy, bicognitive development and education.* New York: Academic Press.

Rawalt, M. (1983). The Equal Rights Amendment. In I. Tinker (Ed.), *Women in Washington* (pp. 49–78). Beverly Hills, CA: Sage.

Reardon, B. (1985). *Sexism and the war system.* New York: Teachers College Press.

Reid, J. (1992). Making delinquent dad pay his child support. *Ms, 3*(1), 86–88.

Rist, R. C. (1970). Student social class and teacher expectations: The self-fulfilling prophecy in ghetto education. *Harvard Educational Review, 40*(3), 411–451.

Ritts, V., Patterson, M., & Tubbs, M. (1992). Expectations, impressions, and judgments of physically attractive students: A review. *Review of Educational Research, 62*(4), 413–426.

Rosenthal, R. (1987). Pygmalion effects: Existence, magnitude, and social importance. *Educational Researcher, 16*(9), 37–41.

Rosenthal, R., & Jacobson, L. (1968). *Pygmalion in the classroom: Teacher expectations and pupil's intellectual development.* New York: Holt, Rinehart and Winston.

Rossi, A. (1964). Equality between the sexes: An immodest proposal. In R. J. Lifton (Ed.), *The woman in America* (pp. 98–143). Boston: Beacon.

Rovner, S. (1987, September 17). Child abuse called linchpin of domestic abuse, rape. *Des Moines Sunday Register* (Des Moines, IA), p. 9-E.

Ruether, R. (1991, February 3). Religion and Eco-Feminism: Symbolism and social connections between the oppression of women and the domination of nature. Public lecture, Iowa State University, Ames, IA.

Saario, T., Jacklin, C., & Tittle, C. (1973). Sex role stereotyping in the public schools. *Harvard Educational Review, 43,* 386–416.

Sadker, M., & Sadker, D. (1982). *Sex equity handbook for schools.* New York: Longman.

Sadker, M., & Sadker, D. (1985a, January). Is the O.K. classroom O.K.? *Phi Delta Kappan, 66,* 358–361.

Sadker, M., & Sadker, D. (1985b, March). Sexism in the schoolroom of the '80s. *Psychology Today,* pp. 54–47.

Sadker, M., & Sadker, D. (1985c). *Effectiveness and equity in college teaching: Final Report.* Washington, DC: Fund for the Improvement of Postsecondary Education.

Sadker, M., & Sadker, D. (1986). Sexism in the classroom: From grade school to graduate school. *Phi Delta Kappan, 67*(7), 512–515.

Sadker, M., & Sadker, D. (1987). *The intellectual exchange—Excellence and equity in college teaching.* Kansas City, MO: The Mid-Continent Regional Educational Laboratory.

Sadker, M., Sadker, D., & Long, L. (1993). Gender and educational equity. In J. Banks & C. Banks (Eds.), *Multicultural education—Issues and perspectives* (pp. 108–128). Boston: Allyn & Bacon.

Sagan, E. (1988). *Freud, women, and morality—The psychology of good and evil.* New York: Basic Books.

Sanders, A. (1989). Chipping away at civil rights. *Time, 133*(26), 63, 66.

Sapon-Shevin, M. (1991, Summer). Cooperative learning: Liberatory praxis or hamburger helper. *Educational Foundations, 5*(3), 5–17.

Schau, C., & Tittle, C. (1985). Educational equity and sex role development. In S. Klein (Ed.), *Handbook for achieving sex equity through education* (pp. 78–90). Baltimore: Johns Hopkins University Press.

Schneir, M. (Ed.). (1972). *Feminism: The essential historical writings.* New York: Vintage.

Schreiber, L. (1993, January 24). What kind of abortions do we want? *Des Moines Sunday Register* (Des Moines, IA), p. 2-C.

Schubert, W. H. (1993). Curriculum reform. In G. Cawelti (Ed.), *Challenges and achievements of American education* (pp. 80–115). Alexandria, VA: Association for Supervision and Curriculum Development.

Scott, K. (1985). Social interaction skills: Perspectives on teaching cross-sex communication. *Social Education, 47,* 610–615.

Seifer, N. (1976, February). *Where feminism and ethnicity intersect: The impact of parallel movements* (Working Paper, Series No. 16, Institute on Pluralism and Group Identity). Northwestern University Library Special Collections, Women's Ephemera Folder No. 7, Feminism/Women's Liberation Movement Papers and Articles, Evanston, IL.

Sex, Power and the Workplace. (1993, January 14). Public Television Program, Iowa Public Television.

Shakeshaft, C. (1986). A gender at risk. *Phi Delta Kappan, 67*(7), 499–503.

Shakeshaft, C. (1990, April). In *loco parentis: Sexual abuse in public schools.* Paper presented at the American Educational Research Association meeting, Boston.

Slavin, R. (1989, March). *Cooperative learning: Kids helping kids, teachers helping teachers.* Introductory address, Symposium at the American Association of Colleges for Teacher Education Conference, San Diego, CA.

Slavin, R. (1991). Synthesis of research on cooperative learning (pp. 71–82); Group rewards make groupwork work (pp. 89–91). *Educational Leadership, 48*(5).

Sleeter, C. (1992). Restructuring schools for multicultural education. *Journal of Teacher Education, 43*(2), 141–148.

Sleeter, C., & Grant, C. (1988). *Making choices for multicultural education—Five approaches to race, class, and gender.* Columbus, OH: Merrill.

Smith, P. (Ed.). (1986). Equity and excellence in teacher assessment. *Urban Educator, 8*(1), 1–149.

Sperry, R. W. (1973). Lateral specialization of cerebral function in the surgically separated hemispheres. In F. McGuigan & R. Schoonover (Eds.), *The psychophysiology of thinking* (pp. 209–229). New York: Academic Press.

Spring, J. (1972). *Education and the rise of the corporate state.* Boston: Beacon.

St. Peter, S. (1979). Jack went up the hill . . . but where was Jill? *Psychology of Women Quarterly, 4,* 256–260.

States can limit abortions. (1989, July 3). *Daily Tribune* (Ames, IA), pp. A-1–A-2.

Stein, N. (1992, November 4). School harassment—An update. *Education Week,* p. 37.

Stein, N., Marshall, N., & Tropp, L. (1993). *Secrets in public: Sexual harassment in our schools.* Wellesley, MA: Center for Research on Women, Wellesley College.

Stengel, B. S. (1986, November). *Men coaching women: Fact of life or cause for concern?* Paper presented at American Educational Studies Association Conference, Pittsburgh, PA.

Stevens, L., & Price, M. (Eds.). (1992). A special section on children at risk. *Phi Delta Kappan, 74*(1), 15–40.

Sue, D. (1981). *Counseling the culturally different—Theory and practice.* New York: Wiley.

Supreme Court delivers another blow to minorities. (1989, June 16). *Des Moines Register* (Des Moines, IA), pp. A-1, A-12.

Tavris, C. (1992). *The mismeasure of woman—Why women are not the better sex, the inferior sex, or the opposite sex.* New York: Simon & Schuster.

Tavris, C., & Offir, C. (1977). *The longest war—Sex differences in perspective.* New York: Harcourt Brace Jovanovich.

Taylor, V. (1989). Social movement continuity: The women's movement in abeyance. *American Sociological Review, 54*(5), 761–776.

Tetreault, M. (1989). Integrating content about women and gender into the curriculum. In J. Banks & C. McGee Banks (Eds.), *Multicultural education—Issues and perspectives* (pp. 124–144). Boston: Allyn & Bacon.

Tetreault, M. (1993). Classrooms for diversity: Rethinking curriculum and pedagogy. In J. Banks & C. McGee Banks (Eds.), *Multicultural education—Issues and perspectives* (pp. 129–148). Boston: Allyn and Bacon.

Tetreault, M., & Schmuck, P. (1985). Equity, educational reform and gender. *Issues in Education, 3*(1), 45–65.

Thorne, B., & Luria, Z. (1986). Sexuality and gender in children's daily worlds. *Social Problems, 33,* 176–190.

300,000 rally for abortion rights. (1989). *National NOW Times, 22*(4), 1.

Title IX complaints pick up after passage of CRRA. (1988). *National NOW Times, 21*(4), 13.

Toufexis, A. (1989). Now for a woman's point of view—Feminist scholars challenge male bias in the U.S. legal system. *Time, 133*(16), 51–52.

Truely, W. (1991). The needs of African American girls. *National NOW Times, 23*(4), 4.

Tucker, S. (1989). Sex-stereotyping and bias in reading schemes. *Primary Teaching Studies, 4*(3), 192–195.

U.S. Commission on Civil Rights. (1973). *Teachers and students: Differences in teacher interaction with Mexican American and Anglo students. Report V: Mexican American Study.* Washington, DC: U.S. Government Printing Office.

U.S. Department of Commerce, Bureau of the Census. (1987). *Statistical Abstracts of the United States* (107th ed.). Washington, DC: U.S. Government Printing Office.

Vann, R. (1990, October 18). *Sexist language: Innocent or injurious.* YWCA Presentation, Ames, IA.

Viverito, P. (1985, September 25). Women said to hold fewer coaching positions and administrative jobs than in the early 1970's. *The Chronicle of Higher Education,* p. 35.

Voss, M. (1991, June 9). Even thin kids worry about fat. *Des Moines Sunday Register* (Des Moines, IA), pp. 1-E, 5-E.

Warren, K. (1989, Fall). Rewriting the future—The feminist challenge to the malestream curriculum. *Feminist Teacher, 4,* 46–52.

Whyte, J. (1984). Observing sex stereotypes and interactions in the school lab and workshop. *Educational Review, 36*(1), 75–86.

Wilbur, G. (1989, March). *Empowerment as a means to an equity culture and equitable outcomes.* Paper presented at the American Educational Research Association Annual Meeting, San Francisco.

Witkin, H., & Asch, S. (1948). Studies in space orientation, part III: Perception of the upright in the absence of a visual field. *Journal of Experimental Psychology, 38*, 603–614.

Witkin, H., Moore, C., Goodenough, D., & Cox, P. (1977). Field-dependent and field-independent cognitive styles and their educational implications. *Review of Educational Research, 47*, 1–64.

Wolf, N. (1991a). *The beauty myth.* New York: Morrow.

Wolf, N. (1991b). Faith healers & holy oil—Inside the cosmetic industry. *Ms, 1*(6), 64–67.

Women crack political glass ceiling. (1992). *Feminist Majority Report, 4*(4), 1.

Women's Center, Iowa State University. (1989, Spring). Quote of the month. *Womenews,* p. 1. (Original in *NOW News,* February 1981).

Women's Educational Equity Act. (1976). *First annual report.* Washington, DC: U.S. Department of Health, Education and Welfare.

Zeitlin, J. (1983). Domestic violence: Perspectives from Washington. In I. Tinker (Ed.), *Women in Washington* (pp. 263–275). Beverly Hills, CA: Sage.

INDEX

About the Author

Theresa Mickey McCormick is a Professor of Curriculum and Instruction at Iowa State University and specializes in multicultural nonsexist teacher education. She has written, edited, and designed curriculum materials for classroom use, has written numerous journal articles, contributed chapters to books, and made national conference presentations on multicultural nonsexist education topics throughout the country.

She received an Ed.D. in Curriculum and Instruction from West Virginia University in 1982. Dr. McCormick taught in the West Virginia public schools for eleven years in art and multicultural education. In addition to teaching, researching, and writing, Dr. McCormick is a diversity facilitator at her campus and provides multicultural nonsexist education workshops for other groups outside the university.

Throughout her career, Dr. McCormick has kept alive some form of artistic activity, including painting and fabric collage. She is a mother of two children and has one grandchild.